The Semantics of Evaluativity

OXFORD STUDIES IN THEORETICAL LINGUISTICS

GENERAL EDITORS

David Adger and Hagit Borer, Queen Mary, University of London

ADVISORY EDITORS

Stephen Anderson, Yale University; Daniel Büring, University of California, Los Angeles; Nomi Erteschik-Shir, Ben-Gurion University; Donka Farkas, University of California, Santa Cruz; Angelika Kratzer, University of Massachusetts, Amherst; Andrew Nevins, University College London; Christopher Potts, Stanford University; Barry Schein, University of Southern California; Peter Svenonius, University of Tromsø; Moira Yip, University College London.

For a complete list of titles published and in preparation for the series, see pp. 203–4.

The Semantics
of Evaluativity

JESSICA RETT

Great Clarendon Street, Oxford, OX2 6DP,
United Kingdom

Oxford University Press is a department of the University of Oxford.
It furthers the University's objective of excellence in research, scholarship,
and education by publishing worldwide. Oxford is a registered trade mark of
Oxford University Press in the UK and in certain other countries

First Edition published in 2015
Impression: 1

Published in the United States of America by Oxford University Press
198 Madison Avenue, New York, NY 10016, United States of America

British Library Cataloguing in Publication Data
Data available

Library of Congress Control Number: 2014937965

ISBN 978-0-19-960247-6 (hbk.)
      978-0-19-960248-3 (pbk.)

Printed and bound by
CPI Group (UK) Ltd, Croydon, CR0 4YY

Links to third party websites are provided by Oxford in good faith and
for information only. Oxford disclaims any responsibility for the materials
contained in any third party website referenced in this work.

Contents

General preface

The theoretical focus of this series is on the interfaces between subcomponents of the human grammatical system and the closely related area of the interfaces between the different subdisciplines of linguistics. The notion of "interface" has become central in grammatical theory (for instance, in Chomsky's Minimalist Program) and in linguistic practice: work on the interfaces between syntax and semantics, syntax and morphology, phonology and phonetics, etc. has led to a deeper understanding of particular linguistic phenomena and of the architecture of the linguistic component of the mind/brain.

The series covers interfaces between core components of grammar, including syntax/morphology, syntax/semantics, syntax/phonology, syntax/pragmatics, morphology/phonology, phonology/phonetics, phonetics/speech processing, semantics/pragmatics, and intonation/discourse structure, as well as issues in the way that the systems of grammar involving these interface areas are acquired and deployed in use (including language acquisition, language dysfunction, and language processing). It demonstrates, we hope, that proper understandings of particular linguistic phenomena, languages, language groups, or inter-language variations all require reference to interfaces.

The series is open to work by linguists of all theoretical persuasions and schools of thought. A main requirement is that authors should write so as to be understood by colleagues in related subfields of linguistics and by scholars in cognate disciplines.

The standard view of the semantics of adjectival constructions like *John is (2 meters) tall* is that it involves null morphemes; these either add in information to the structure, or modify information already present in the lexical items. This makes the relationship between the presumed syntax and its semantics straightforward, but the relationship between syntax and the overt morphology becomes less transparent. In the present volume, Jessica Rett argues that this approach is a mistake, and proposes instead that the relevant information is part of pragmatic calculations made by interlocutors, so the core phenomena lie at the syntax–pragmatics, rather than the syntax–semantics interface. This approach is not only able to capture some unnoticed subtleties in the behavior of adjectives, it also allows a quite dramatic simplification of their semantics, and raises provocative questions about the use of null morphemes elsewhere.

David Adger
Hagit Borer

Acknowledgments

This project is the result of several years of research that began at Rutgers and extended through several years at UCLA. My original work on evaluativity was presented in several places, including Rutgers, UCLA, SALT 17, USC, Princeton, and the University of Massachusetts, Amherst. For advice on that original work, I am indebted to Chris Barker, Daniel Büring, Veneeta Dayal, Hans Kamp, Slavica Kochovska, Pam Munro, Roumyana Pancheva, Russ Schuh, Bernard Schwarz, Roger Schwarzschild, and Ed Stabler for their help. I am certain this is only a partial list.

The work on evaluativity that forms the bulk of the present book has relied on funding from the UCLA COR faculty grants, and the research help those grants have afforded. This help includes, but is not limited to, some of the world's most clever and patient research assistants: Natasha Abner, Kaeli Ward, and Lauren Winans, as well as Robin Rett, who compiled the index. I'm extremely grateful to the UCLA community at large for all its support, including Sam Cumming, Gabriel Greenberg, Ed Keenan, Yael Sharvit, Ed Stabler, and participants of the Language Workshop and the Syntax/Semantics Seminar. Outside of UCLA, I've benefitted significantly from discussion with Adrian Brasoveanu, Ivano Caponigro, Benjamin George, Michael Glanzberg, Larry Horn, Chris Kennedy, Jeff King, Nathan Klinedinst, Ernie Lepore, Sarah Murray, Rick Nouwen, Adam Sennet, Will Starr, Matthew Stone, and David Wolfsdorf; and audiences at the University of Michigan and Cornell University.

There are several people who have played even more significant supporting roles more generally. I have two brothers, Doug and Adam, whose extreme heights have contributed immensely to the data in this book. They are the two weirdest, kindest, and tallest brothers a girl could ask for (TPO). My parents have gone to nearly ridiculous lengths to support my intellectual curiosity throughout my life, driving me around to dozens of extracurricular classes and, once I could drive myself, leaving work to rescue me on the frequent occasions I'd lock myself out of the car. They remain, thankfully, nearly ridiculously supportive despite the fact that my intellectual curiosity has led me away from home, in search of elusive linguistic truths.

Roger Schwarzschild has served as guru, muse, and language, life, and dance coach; it would be extremely hard to imagine what this book would be without his influence and friendship. Finally, Sam Cumming has helped in every way imaginable: with the data in this book, the theory, and the edits; with support, both emotional and pizza; and by being the one who is always turning up the music in my life.

List of abbreviations

3	third-personal agreement
AA	absolute adjective
AA	absolute aspect
CA	comparative aspect
COD	comparison of deviation
COP	copula
DEG	a null degree operator (proposed in Piñón 2005)
DP	determiner phrase
EVAL	a null degree operator (proposed in Rett 2007, 2008)
GCI	generalized conversational implicature (proposed in Grice 1975)
GEN	genitive
FEM	feminine
INSTR	instrumental
MEAS	a null measurement operator
M-Op	a null measurement operator
MP	measure phrase
MPE	measure phrase equative
NEG	negative
NOM	nominative
O	object agreement
OBL	oblique
OT	Optimality Theory
PA	partial adjective
PCI	particularized conversational implicature (proposed in Grice 1975)
PERF	perfect aspect
POS	a null degree operator (proposed in Bartsch and Vennemann 1972)
PRES	present tense
QUD	question under discussion
RA	relative adjective
S	subject agreement
SG	singular
SSM	a null adjectival modifier (proposed in Breakstone 2012)
TA	total adjective
TOP	topic
VP	verb phrase

1

Introduction

> "I'm not considered tall."
> "And yet you are extremely tall."
> "Yes."
>
> Jonathan Franzen, *Freedom*

The field of degree semantics has at its core the contrast between the sentences in (1) (Bartsch and Vennemann 1972; Cresswell 1976).

(1) a. Adam is tall.
     b. Adam is 6ft tall.

Sentences like (1a), which involve an unmodified or unbound gradable adjective, are called "positive constructions." Sentences like (1b) are called "measure phrase constructions" because they contain a measure phrase ("MP"), composed of a numeral and an optional measure noun.

The sentences in (1) contrast in a very interesting way. In both sentences, the adjective *tall* relates the subject (*Adam*) to a degree of tallness. But in (1a) it seems to additionally require that Adam's degree of tallness exceed some relevant standard of tallness. I'll refer to this semantic property as "evaluativity."[1] A adjectival construction is evaluative iff it makes reference to a degree which exceeds a contextually valued standard.

This semantic difference goes against our usual expectations of compositional systems, wherein the addition of meaning generally requires the addition of a morpheme. It raises questions about the meaning of adjectives like *tall*: if *tall* means something like "counts as tall in the context," what makes this meaning disappear in (1b)? Or if *tall* means something less than that, where does the evaluativity in (1a) come from?

---

[1] The term "evaluativity" comes, as far as I can tell, from Neeleman et al. (2004). Seuren (1984) refers to the same semantic property as "orientedness," Bierwisch (1989) as "norm-relatedness," Murphy (2006) as "committedness," and Doetjes (2012) as "non-neutrality." Although I view it as slightly more intuitive than the others, the term "evaluativity" is potentially confusing given that adverbs which are derived from predicates like *surprise* have traditionally been called "evaluative" (Katz 1972, among others).

MP constructions like (1b) have had a substantial influence on degree-semantic treatments of gradable adjectives. A simplified version of this argument is as follows: gradable adjectives like *tall* and non-gradable adjectives like *freckled* contrast in their ability to be modified by MPs, in a way that seems parallel to the contrasting ability of transitive and intransitive verbs to select for an object.

(2)   a. Adam is 6ft tall.
      b. Adam is (*100-spot) freckled.

(3)   a. Adam likes his sister.
      b. Adam ran (*his sister).

The result is a semantics of gradable adjectives in which they denote relations between individuals and degrees, as in (4) (Cresswell 1976). In this framework, the difference between gradable and non-gradable adjectives is one of valency.

(4) $[\![\text{tall}]\!] = \lambda x \lambda d.\text{tall}(x, d)$

$\text{tall}(x, d)$ should be read as "x is tall to at least degree d." In this approach an adjective like *tall* denotes a relation between individuals and degrees on tallness. *Tall* associates each individual with several degrees of tallness, rather than one degree of maximum tallness (or height). The difference between an individual's height and her tallness is significant on this view, and I will use the terms carefully.

This simple and intuitive treatment of gradable adjectives falls short of predicting the truth conditions of positive constructions like (1a): first, it incorrectly predicts that the sentence denotes a degree property instead of a proposition ("the extra argument problem"). And second, it fails to predict that the sentence is evaluative ("the evaluativity problem").

Let me quickly say a little bit more about what it means to be evaluative. Intuitively, for positive constructions like (1a) to be true, it is not sufficient that Adam have some degree d of tallness; this would make any statement of the form in (1a)—when the subject denotes a three-dimensional object—trivially true. Instead, for (1a) to be true, Adam needs to be tall to a degree that exceeds a contextually sensitive standard of tallness. As I will discuss in Chapter 2, the standards invoked by evaluative constructions vary from context to context, depending on the relevant comparison class.

Within traditional degree semantics, the tension between a relational analysis of gradable adjectives (as in (4)) and the proper semantic treatment of positive constructions has been been resolved with a null morpheme called "POS" (Bartsch and Vennemann 1972; Cresswell 1976; Kennedy 1999). I'll provide a general-purpose definition of POS here; Chapter 2 will present it in much more detail.[2]

(5) $[\![\text{POS}]\!] = \lambda \mathcal{G}_{\langle e, \langle d, t \rangle \rangle} \lambda x \exists d [\mathcal{G}(x, d) \wedge d > s]$, for some contextually valued standard s

---

[2] Whether or not null morphemes like POS are in the domain of the interpretation function $[\![\cdot]\!]$ is open to debate, but I follow convention in using the interpretation function to define the meaning of null morphemes regardless.

POS denotes a function from gradable adjective meanings (type $\langle e, \langle d, t \rangle \rangle$, like *tall* in (4)) to individual properties, type $\langle e, t \rangle$ (the same type as non-gradable adjectives like *freckled*) by restricting ($d > s$) and binding ($\exists d$) the gradable adjective's degree argument.

As it is formulated in (5), POS solves both the extra argument and the evaluativity problems at once: evaluativity is introduced by relating the degree argument of the gradable adjective to a contextual standard s, and the extra argument problem is eliminated by the quantifier, which existentially binds the degree argument, resulting in a proposition. Consequentially, a constituent [POS $\mathcal{A}$] for a gradable adjective $\mathcal{A}$ has the semantic type of a non-gradable adjective, and its meaning is evaluative. (6) gives the meaning of (1a) in this theory.

(6) $[\![$Adam is tall$]\!] = \exists d[\text{tall}(\text{adam}, d) \wedge d > s_{\text{tall}}]$

In my previous work on evaluativity (Rett 2007, 2008), I argued that it is a mistake to conflate the evaluativity problem with the extra argument problem. The POS approach incorrectly predicts that evaluativity is restricted to adjectival constructions in which the degree argument is not overtly bound or valued, like positive constructions. (I will call an argument "manipulated" if it is either bound by a quantifier or valued by another element.)

But in fact, evaluativity is a property of some adjectival constructions with overtly manipulated gradable adjectives (Lyons 1977; Bierwisch 1989).

(7)   a. How short is Adam?
      b. Adam is as short as Doug.

(7a) is a question with a *wh*-phrase *how* ranging over the degree argument of *short*. (7b) is an equative with the morpheme *as*—generally characterized as a degree quantifier—ranging over the degree argument.

The question in (7a)—as opposed to *How tall is Adam?*—presupposes that Adam is short. And the equative in (7b)—again opposed to the equative *Adam is as tall as Doug*—seems to presuppose that Adam and Doug are short. This is evaluativity, broadly construed: in addition to the standard truth-conditional content of degree questions and equatives, these constructions require that the degree in question exceed (in this case, on the "short" scale) the relevant contextual standard.

Because POS serves a dual function—it binds the degree argument of the gradable adjective and contributes evaluativity—it cannot account for the evaluativity of constructions like those in (7), in which the gradable adjective is modified or bound by a degree quantifier (depending on your analysis of *how* and *as*; more in Chapter 2). It also cannot address the absence of evaluativity in comparative constructions (8a) or in equative constructions with positive antonyms (8b).

(8)   a. Adam is shorter than Doug.
      b. Adam is as tall as Doug.

The comparative in (8a) doesn't presuppose that Adam or Doug is short, and the equative in (8b) doesn't presuppose that either are tall.

To account for this relatively wide distribution of evaluativity, I proposed in Rett (2007, 2008) a modifier version of POS, called EVAL. EVAL can contribute evaluativity to an adjectival construction without manipulating a degree argument. Its domain is a degree property—applied after the individual argument of a gradable adjective is saturated—and its range is an evaluative degree property.

(9) $[\![\text{EVAL}]\!] = \lambda D_{\langle d,t \rangle} \lambda d.D(d) \wedge d > s$, for some contextual standard s.

This approach allows for a separate treatment of the type difference between (1a) and (1b) and the difference in evaluativity. I proposed that the unsaturated, unbound degree argument in a positive construction is resolved by existential closure (Heim 1987), while the distribution of evaluativity—given that the distribution of EVAL, as a degree modifier, is in principle unrestricted—is determined based on a semantic markedness competition. In particular, I argued that for equatives (but not for comparatives), a sentence with an unmarked, positive antonym is semantically equivalent to its counterpart with a marked, negative antonym; given a *ceteris paribus* prohibition against markedness, the result is that the negative-antonym sentence is acceptable only if it includes an EVAL. I'll review this proposal in more detail in Chapter 2.

These null morpheme approaches to the evaluativity problem—the differences between the sentences in (1), now coupled with the difference in evaluativity between, e.g., (7b) and (8b)—leave a lot to be desired. For many, beginning with Klein (1980, 1982), the idea that the interpretation of positive constructions like (1a) requires a null morpheme (while more complicated constructions like comparatives do not) places too much of a strain on compositionality. Klein used this complaint to motivate an alternative theory to degree semantics. Others, especially those concerned with the semantics of vagueness, have followed, resulting in very diverse semantic theories and logics for prima facie simple sentences like *Adam is tall* (for an overview, see Burnett 2012).

Even for those committed degree semanticists who are comfortable with null morphemes and contextual variables, POS or EVAL raise somewhat uncomfortable questions. The phenomenon of evaluativity seems cross-linguistically robust. Why would natural language systematically incorporate this particular meaning? If evaluativity is so widespread and common, why does no language have an overt counterpart of POS or EVAL? (Some have argued that there are overt counterparts of POS or EVAL; I'll address these claims in Chapter 2.) And why does evaluativity seem to be restricted to the degree domain? For instance, why don't sentences like *I forgot to turn off the stove*—used by Partee (1973) to argue that tense is pronominal—mean "There was a past time t such that I forgot to turn off the stove at t and t was significantly long ago"?

The goal of this book is to apply Grice's theory of conversational implicature (and modern adaptations of it) to the work in Rett (2007, 2008) which framed evaluativity in terms of markedness and semantic competition. I will argue that evaluativity in equative constructions like (7b) is a natural consequence of the markedness contrast between positive and negative antonyms (like *tall* versus *short*) given the maxim of Manner (Grice 1975; McCawley 1978; Horn 1984, 1989; Levinson 2000), which compels speakers to use marked expressions only in describing marked situations. And I will argue that evaluativity in positive constructions like (1a) is the product of a particular type of Quantity implicature that arises in cases of uninformativity.

This characterization of evaluativity doesn't involve a null morpheme and doesn't treat evaluativity as exceptional: it is part of a larger phenomenon of conversational implicatures, and arises from the structure of the degree domain (Bolinger 1972). I will show that current theories of conversational implicature, coupled with recent characterizations of not-at-issue content, accounts for the different status of evaluativity in positive constructions (where it seems asserted) and, e.g., equative constructions (where it seems presupposed). And I will show that this implicature-based approach accounts for the wide variety of data discussed in Rett (2008) as well as some new observations related to adjectival constructions and manner implicatures generally.

This characterization of evaluativity has profound consequences on the semantics of positive constructions, gradable adjectives, and on degree semantics in general. It allows for a semantic treatment of adjectives and adjectival constructions that is truly compositional. It is consistent with Bobaljik's (2012) observation that comparatives and superlatives are marked relative to positive constructions across languages, and satisfies Klein's (1980) wish that the positive construction consequently be treated as the primary use of adjectives relative to their use in comparatives. It supplements standard degree-semantic accounts of adjectives and adjectival constructions, but because the proposal here is cast in terms of implicature, it can be adapted into any semantic theory of adjectives with a robust characterization of the semantics/pragmatics interface. And it provides a framework for analyzing other arguably related phenomena in which the speaker's positive evaluation is reflected in a way not tied to vocabulary or syntax, as in *not unhappy*, *quite a dog*, or *a number of shoes* (Bolinger 1972; Atlas and Levinson 1981; Horn 1991a).

I'll begin by presenting in more detail the problem of evaluativity and the standard degree-semantic treatments of it. This will require a brief tutorial in degree semantics, and will end with a review of various applications of POS outside of evaluative constructions. In Chapter 3 I present the approach to evaluativity defended in Rett (2007, 2008). It too treats evaluativity with a null morpheme, EVAL, but one whose distribution across adjectival constructions is made obligatory only by considerations of markedness. Chapter 4 takes up the discussion of markedness by examining its role in competition-based accounts of other phenomena. Chapter 5 presents the core of the main hypothesis, namely that a neo-Gricean analysis of manner implicatures can account for the interaction between evaluativity and markedness. Chapter 6 discusses extensions of this account, and Chapter 7 concludes.

2

The null morpheme POS

> As far as I can tell, there is no independent justification for introducing POS; it is merely a device for fixing up the semantics.
>
> Klein (1980: 3)

> The operator "positively," call it POS, is invisible, which made E. Klein think that it doesn't exist.
>
> Von Stechow (1984: 59)

This chapter presents a brief history of the null morpheme POS, first proposed in Bartsch and Vennemann (1972), and how it has shaped recent theories of gradable adjectives, adjectival constructions, and event semantics. I begin with a brief tutorial in degree semantics to provide a lingua franca (for a more extensive review, see Morzycki forthcoming). Section 2.2 presents iterations of POS throughout time and their relationship to evaluativity. Section 2.3 discusses recent applications of POS outside of adjectival constructions.

2.1 A background in degree semantics

2.1.1 Degrees as semantic primitives

The introduction of degrees as distinct entities in formal semantics originally comes from Cresswell (1976). However, the proposal to introduce non-standard objects into the logical form to deal with, for instance, comparatives began with Bartsch and Vennemann (1972) (see also Sapir 1944; Fillmore 1965; Seuren 1973). Bartsch and Vennemann argued that a syntactic and semantic analysis of a number of constructions— positive constructions, comparatives, equatives and superlatives, exemplified in (1), which I refer to as "adjectival constructions"—require the introduction of new semantic objects into logical form.

(1) a. Doug is tall. *positive construction*
    b. Doug is taller than Adam. *comparative*
    c. Doug is as tall as Adam. *equative*
    d. Doug is the tallest in his class. *superlative*

In their semantic account of these constructions, Bartsch and Vennemann propose a null measure function f^M that maps its arguments—an individual x and a linearly ordered dimension of measurement D—onto equivalence classes: sets of individuals that share a common value (e.g., 5ft) for a particular dimension of measurement (e.g., height). The adjectives *tall* and *wide* differ in dimensions (height versus width), while the antonyms *tall* and *short* share a dimension but differ in their ordering. *Tall* is dubbed the unmarked adjective, associated with the ordering $>$, while *short*, the marked member of the pair, is defined in terms of the reverse ordering $<$.

The idea, expanded and further formalized in Klein (1980, 1982), is to introduce total orderings and reverse total orderings into the semantic theory using sets of individuals as a proxy for degrees. A clause like *Doug is tall*, an assumed constituent of the comparative (1b), effectively denotes Doug's equivalence class in the "tall" domain: the set of individuals that are his exact height, putting aside issues of granularity.

Cresswell (1976) introduces degrees into his formalism to do the work of Bartsch and Vennemann's equivalence classes. He says (p. 41):

When we make comparisons we have in mind points on a scale. The scale can be represented by a relation, and the points on the scale by the field of that relation. (A relation in set theory is a set of ordered pairs; the field of a relation is the set of all things that are related in one direction or another to something else.) Where $>$ is a relation we denote its field by $\mathcal{F}(>)$:

[(2)]   A DEGREE (of comparison) is a pair $\langle u, > \rangle$, where $>$ is a relation and $u \in \mathcal{F}(>)$.

Following the syntactic account of comparatives proposed in Bresnan (1973), wherein each clausal argument of a clausal comparative is formed from a *wh*-operator ranging over degrees (see also Chomsky 1965), Cresswell proposes that instead of a comparison class, the adjectival constructions in (1) have as a semantic component the set of degrees $\{d : \text{John is } d\text{-tall}\}$. (I'll present more details in §2.1.5; see also von Stechow 1984.)

Cresswell's approach takes for granted that degrees, like individuals, are semantic primitives. The question of what types of entities should be treated as primitives in the semantic ontology is, from my point of view, a matter of personal preference. On the one hand, Klein (1980, 1982) considered it important to eliminate degrees from the ontology if they could be otherwise replicated. On the other hand, the ontology in Champollion (2010) includes both degrees and numbers as primitives. It will become clear in what follows that a typed semantic framework with primitive degrees is very useful for treating the adjectival phenomena discussed in the book. This is sufficient, in my mind, to justify the conclusion of degrees into the ontology; however, as noted above, I take the implicature-based theory of evaluativity in Chapter 5 to be consistent with degree-free semantic approaches as well.

I'll briefly mention one empirical consideration for treating degrees as semantic primitives: there are demonstratives that reference degrees, and there are *wh*-phrases that are restricted to degrees (just as in the individual domain).

(3) a. [gestures] Doug is yea tall.
    b. How tall is Doug?
    c. How many siblings does Doug have?

The demonstrative *yea* in (3a) picks out a particular degree in context. Depending on one's theories of the semantics of *wh*-phrases, *how* and *how many* in (3b) and (3c) denote either degree predicates (type $\langle d, t \rangle$) or degree quantifiers (type $\langle \langle d, t \rangle, \langle \langle d, t \rangle, t \rangle \rangle$); see George 2011, for a review of semantic theories of *wh*-phrases). Following Cresswell's (1976) assumption that the degree domain has parallels to other domains, von Stechow (1984) defines and motivates a degree definite modelled on Russell's (1905) definition of *the*.

See Kennedy (1999) for a comprehensive defense of a degree-based semantic theory. Among other things, treating degrees as ontological primitives will allow for a characterization of the difference between gradable and non-gradable adjectives in terms of valency. This is the subject of the next section.

2.1.2 *The semantics of adjectives*

Gradable adjectives (also referred to as scalar adjectives) contrast with non-gradable or non-scalar adjectives in their ability to be modified by an intensifier ((4) and (6)); and occur in a comparative ((5) and (7)) while maintaining their primary meaning.

(4) a. Doug is very/really tall.   *gradable*
    b. Doug is very/really smart.

(5) a. Doug is taller than Adam.   *gradable*
    b. Doug is smarter than Adam.

(6) a. #Skye is very/really Australian.   *non-gradable*
    b. #Skye is very/really pregnant.

(7) a. #Skye is more Australian than Leah.   *non-gradable*
    b. #Skye is more pregnant than Leah.

Non-gradable adjectives can receive an interpretation in these environments but only, in contrast to the interpretations of gradable adjectives, if their meaning is coerced in some way. Skye's pregnancy is coerced into having a temporal meaning in (6b) and (7b); instead of requiring that Skye be pregnant to a greater degree than Leah, (7b) requires that Skye have been pregnant for a longer period of time than Leah. The predicate *Australian* in (6a) and (7a) invokes some notion of prototypicality, requiring an examination of Skye's and Leah's prototypically Australian traits, not just their nationality.

Cresswell's idea is that the contrasting distribution of these adjectives (and a similar distinction for adverbs) can and should be cast in terms of the valency of the functions they denote (although see Kamp 1975 for a Montogovian semantics of adjectives in a non-degree semantics). Non-gradable adjectives, like verbs and other predicates, denote properties of individuals (as in (8a)), while gradable adjectives denote relations between individuals and degrees (as in (8b)).[1]

(8) a. $[\![$Australian$]\!] = \lambda x.$australian(x)
     b. $[\![$tall$]\!] = \lambda x \lambda d.$tall$(x, d)$

tall(x, d) should be read as "x is tall to at least degree d."

The explanation for the contrast between the acceptable and the unacceptable sentences above can thus be cast in terms of type mismatch: intensifiers like *very* are degree modifiers, and non-gradable adjectives don't have degree arguments; therefore intensifiers can't modify non-gradable adjectives. Similarly, we can (and will) assume that the comparative morpheme is a degree quantifier, which is why it can't bind the arguments of non-gradable adjectives. Coerced interpretations of non-gradable adjectives, when possible, involve a homomorphism from some available scale (like the temporal scale) to a degree scale (see Krifka 1989).

Many individual properties carry selectional restrictions that resemble presuppositions about the individuals they are predicated of; *green*, for instance, can only be predicated of individuals that are extended in space (i.e., not ideas). Similarly, gradable properties carry selectional restrictions about the relationship between the individual and degree they are predicated of. A sentence of the form "*x is Adj*" presupposes that *x* instantiates the gradable predicate denoted by *Adj* to some degree. This assumption correctly predicts that, e.g., an adjective like *fat* can't be predicated of two-dimensional objects and that *curvy* can't be predicated of a liquid (9).

(9) a. #This piece of paper is fat.
     b. #This sauce is curvy.

Gradable adjectives can thus be thought of as denoting partial functions from individuals to sets of degrees, undefined for those individuals that do not exhibit the property to any degree (Kennedy 1999). I'll refer to this as the **positive extension presupposition** of gradable adjectives, but will leave the restriction implicit in the presentation of adjectives here.

The characterization of gradable adjectives represented in (8b) is widely adopted in current theory (Hellan 1981; Hoeksema 1983; von Stechow 1984; Heim 1985, 2000; Gawron 1995; Rullmann 1995; Izvorski 1995; Schwarzschild 2008). I will refer to it as the **relational account** of gradable adjectives.

One prominent alternative, originating with Bartsch and Vennemann (1972), characterizes gradable adjectives as denoting functions from individuals to degrees (type $\langle e, d \rangle$). I'll refer to this as the **measure function account** of gradable adjectives.

---

[1] I use a sans serif font to denote predicates in the metalanguage; I will refer to predicate extensions instead of intensions wherever possible to simplify discussion.

(10) $[\![tall]\!] = \lambda x.\mathsf{tall}(x)$ *measure function approach*

Importantly, the output of (10) is the degree(s) to which the individual argument is tall, not a proposition. To denote a proposition, the output of a measure function in this account itself serves as the input for degree operators like POS or the comparative morpheme (for details, see Kennedy 1999, 2001).

Following many (e.g., Heim 2000), I will view these accounts as notational variants of one another, but the formal differences between the two will be relevant for comparing different formulations of POS.

Other alternative approaches to the semantics of gradable adjectives build instead on Bartsch and Vennemann's equivalence classes, notably Klein (1980, 1982), Neeleman et al. (2004), van Rooij (2011), and Doetjes et al. (2011), but more recently work in trivalent, supervaluationist, or other alternative logics (e.g., Moltmann 2009; Cobreros et al. 2012; Burnett 2012). Recently, Kennedy (2009), Beck et al. (2009), and Bochnak (forthcoming) have argued that languages differ in whether their adjectives denote "transitive" (type $\langle e, \langle d, t \rangle \rangle$) or 'intransitive' (type $\langle e, t \rangle$) functions. I will not consider these approaches here, but I do not intend to suggest that they're not worth considering. The use of equivalence classes in trivalent logics seems especially promising for the treatment of vagueness, a problem I will do my best to sidestep in what follows.

2.1.3 *Semantic properties of scales*

I assume, following Bartsch and Vennemann (1972), a degree *d* of type $\langle d \rangle$ is shorthand for a triple consisting of a point *p* on a dimension $\mathcal{D}$ with a strict ordering $>_+$ or $>_-$ (see also the notion of "thick degrees" used in Grosu and Landman 1998). Examples of dimensions are height and weight; the antonyms *tall* and *short* encode the difference between the two orderings along the "height" dimension.

The result of this assumption is that any degree *d* identifies not just a point but a point on a scale (i.e., an ordered dimension). I assume that the scale a degree is associated with is contextually determined although heavily constrained, when relevant, by linguistic considerations (Schwarzschild 2006b; Rett 2014b). For instance, in the sentence *The container is 6 inches* could, depending on context, involve a dimension of length, width, depth, or diameter. But in the sentence *The container is 6 inches wide*, the degrees associated with the container are degrees of wideness (on a positive-ordered scale of width). Similarly, the sentence *The painting is big enough for that room* could be about the painting's width or height, while the sentence *The painting is wide enough for that room* is unambiguously about its width.

There are two alternatives to this approach, both of which I take to be notational variants, at least for the task at hand. Schwarzschild and Wilkinson (2002) propose that adjectival constructions (comparatives, in particular) are best treated in a formal semantics in which intervals—continuous, strictly ordered sets of degrees—are ontological primitives, instead of degrees. These intervals reflect a dimension and order of measurement more transparently than does a degree-based approach.

In recent work, Schwarzschild (2012) adapts this interval-based approach to explicitly represent the dimension and order of measurement, as in (11) (for "directed scale segments" σ, ranging over triples $\langle s, e, <_\sigma \rangle$ with a starting point s, and endpoint e, and a dimension $<_\sigma$).

(11) $[\![\text{tall}]\!] = \lambda\sigma\lambda x.\text{END}(\sigma) = x \wedge <_\sigma = \text{height}$ *directed scale segment approach*

Intervals will be useful in the present approach, as well. Recall that all degrees are defined in terms of a dimension of measurement and a strict ordering on that dimension of measurement (a version of Bartsch and Vennemann's linearly ordered measure functions). This means that, in a context in which the dimension of measurement is fully determined, an individual's set of degrees along that measurement will be strictly ordered with respect to each other.

As discussed in Beck and Rullmann (1999), this set of degrees could in principle correspond to a non-monotonic, non-dense set, one in which the inclusion of degree d in the set entails neither the inclusion of $d - 1$ nor $d + 1$. Their examples are sets of degrees corresponding to quantities of processors Windows NT can support (1, 2, and 4) or of people who can play a particular game (between 4 and 6). These non-monotonic instances are relatively rare, and predicates, as far as I can tell, always require a special context to make them non-monotonic. I will therefore treat gradable predicates as intrinsically either downward- or upward-monotonic and will assume that context can reduce the extension of a predicate so that it is effectively non-monotonic. A set of degrees, then, will typically be an interval: a continuous, possibly dense set of points along a strictly ordered dimension.

As an example, consider the dimension of quantity/cardinality. The number of children John has can be represented as a set of continuous degrees along a dimension (quantity) with a particular ordering (positive), i.e., an interval. In a situation in which John has three children, Amy, Bill, and Cindy, then the set of degrees corresponding to the quantity of children John has is as in (12).[2]

(12) $\{d: \text{John has } d \text{ children}\} = \{1,2,3\}$

This is a downward-monotonic interval (and therefore quantity is a downward-monotonic dimension of measurement): for any $d' \in \{d : \text{John has } d \text{ children}\}$, we

---

[2] I will assume that the relevant predicate or dimension of measurement coupled with the context determines how fine-grained the difference in degrees is. In the case of height, degrees could range over millimeters (in a context in which scientists are monitoring plant growth) or stories (in a discussion of skyscrapers). In the case of quantities, whether the degrees range over whole numbers or positive reals depends in part on whether the entity measured is a plural or mass (see for instance Chierchia 1998, 2010; Schwarzschild 2011).

can infer that the quantity $d' - 1$, for any $d' > 0$, is also in that set. The definition in (13) is from Heim (2000) (see also Kennedy 1999).

(13)   A function f of type $\langle e, \langle d, t \rangle \rangle$ is **downward-monotonic** iff
$$\forall x, d, d'[f(x)(d) \wedge d' < d \rightarrow f(x)(d')]$$

It is often assumed within degree semantics that predicates like *be d tall* (in contrast to *have a height of d*) are also downward-monotonic. In particular, if it's true that John is tall to a degree d, then it's also true that he is tall to degree $d - 1$. This assumption, among other things, helps to account for the "weak" interpretations of equatives like *John is as tall as Mary* in contexts in which John is in fact taller than Mary, as I'll show in §2.1.5.

Following Bartsch and Vennemann and others, *tall* and *short* are antonyms, which means that they invoke the same dimension but reverse orderings. Among other things, this can account for the entailment pattern in (14).

(14)   Doug is taller than Adam. $\leftrightarrow$ Adam is shorter than Doug.

If *be tall* is a downward-monotonic predicate, then *be short* is an upward-monotonic predicate: we can infer from the inclusion of a degree d in a set to the inclusion of a degree $d + 1$ in that set. This means that if Doug is 6ft tall, then the set of degrees to which he is tall can be described as in (16a), and the set of degrees to which he is short can be described as in (16b).[3]

(16)   a. $\{d : \text{Doug is } d\text{-tall}\} = \{\text{1ft, 2ft, 3ft, 4ft, 5ft, 6ft}\} = (0,6\text{ft}]$
         b. $\{d : \text{Doug is } d\text{-short}\} = \{\text{6ft, 7ft, 8ft, 9ft, } \ldots, \infty\} = [6\text{ft}, \infty)$

The intervals in (16) each share an endpoint—their maximal degree, 6ft—but they differ in their ordering and consequently the points they contain.

Recent work by Rotstein and Winter (2004) and Kennedy and McNally (2005) suggests that adjectives differ not only in their dimension of measurement and ordering or polarity but in their scale structure as well. One major distinction is between relative (or dimensional) adjectives like *tall* and *short*, on the one hand, and absolute adjectives like *open* and *closed*. Relative and absolute adjectives differ in whether they are associated with scales with natural endpoints, like upper or lower bounds. The claim is that relative adjectives are associated with boundless scales; there is no inherent upper or lower bound on height, modulo the positive extension

---

[3] Intervals can be defined in terms of their lower and upper bounds. In this notation, the round brackets signify open bounds (bounds which are not included in the interval) and the square brackets signify closed bounds (bounds which are included in the interval).

(i)   a. $(a, b) = \{x : a > x > b\}$ c. $[a, b) = \{x : a \geq x > b\}$
       b. $(a, b] = \{x : a > x \geq b\}$ d. $[a, b] = \{x : a \geq x \geq b\}$

I will assume that infinity imposes an open bound, but there is as far as I know no consensus on the issue.

presupposition. In contrast, absolute adjectives are associated with bounded scales; there is, arguably, an upper bound on purity.

This theory can be used to explain, among other things, the distribution of some degree modifiers across the relative and absolute adjective classes.

(17) Relative adjectives
      a. ??Adam is completely tall/short.
      b. ??The pond is 100% deep/shallow.
      c. ??Max is fully eager/uneager to help.

(18) Absolute adjectives
      a. The figure was completely visible/invisible.
      b. The room was 100% full/empty.
      c. The flower was fully open/closed.

Following work by Yoon (1996), Kennedy and McNally (2005) also examine the contrast between total and partial adjectives, antonym pairs in which the antonyms appear to lexicalize either lower or upper bounds, as demonstrated (in part) by their distribution with these same degree modifiers:

(19) Lower-bound (partial) adjectives
      a. The pipe is completely ??famous/unknown.
      b. The room became 100% ??loud/quiet.
      c. The pipe is fully ??bent/straight.

(20) Upper-bound (total) adjectives
      a. The treatment is completely safe/??dangerous.
      b. This product is 100% pure/??impure.
      c. We are fully certain/??uncertain about the results.

There are other, arguably related, differences between relative and absolute adjectives. For instance, the two types behave differently in definite descriptions (Kennedy 2007; Syrett et al. 2009).

(21) a. Pass me the tall one.
      b. Pass me the empty one.

In a context in which there are several glasses of differing heights, (21a), formed with a real adjective, will pick out the individual that instantiates the gradable predicate to the highest degree (i.e., the tallest one), regardless of whether or not that glass counts as tall in the context. In contrast, in a context in which there are several identical glasses containing differing amounts of liquid, (21b), formed with an absolute adjective, will fail to pick out the glass with the least amount of liquid in it, unless that glass is empty.

In other words, the DP formed with the absolute adjective will only have a referent in a context in which exactly one individual counts as empty.

This difference seems related in some sense to evaluativity; while the discussion of evaluativity in this book will focus on constructions containing relative adjectives, I will return to discuss the semantics and evaluativity of absolute and total/partial adjectives in §5.4.

2.1.4 *Numerals and measure phrases*

Some gradable adjectives can occur with measure phrases (MPs) like *4ft*, as in (22).

(22)   a. Adam is 4ft tall.
       b. Doug is 10 years old.

I follow Kennedy and Svenonius (2006) in referring to these adjectives as **measure adjectives** (see also Klooster 1972).

The assumption that gradable adjectives lexicalize a degree argument allows for a straightforward treatment of Measure Phrase (MP) constructions like those in (22) by analyzing MPs as naming or denoting degrees along a particular dimension. The result is a compositional semantics for MP constructions that looks like (23) (Cresswell 1976; von Stechow 1984, among others), which I will revise shortly.

(23)   Adam is 6ft tall.
       a. $[\![\text{tall}]\!] = \lambda x \lambda d.\text{tall}(x, d)$ from (8b)
       b. $[\![\text{tall}]\!]([\![\text{Adam}]\!]) = \lambda d.\text{tall}(\text{adam}, d)$
       c. $[\![\text{6ft}]\!] = 6\text{ft}$ type $\langle d \rangle$
       d. $[\![\text{tall}]\!]([\![\text{Adam}]\!])([\![\text{6ft}]\!]) = \text{tall}(\text{adam}, 6\text{ft})$

However, further investigation into the distribution of MPs across gradable adjectives has led many to suggest that this perspective is too simplistic. If MPs saturate the degree variables of gradable adjectives, why are they ungrammatical with some positive-polar antonyms (24)? And why are they generally prohibited with negative-polar antonyms (25)?

(24)   a. *The car drove 60 mph fast.
       b. *The box is 40 lb heavy.

(25)   a. *Adam is 4ft short.
       b. *The board is 4in narrow.

The first question—regarding which positive-polar gradable adjectives are measure adjectives and why—is an extremely tricky one, given that languages differ in, for instance, whether or not (24b) is grammatical. In English, the class of measure adjectives is relatively small, and is a strict subset of those adjectives whose dimensions of measurement have widely recognized units of measurement.[4] See Schwarzschild (2005); Murphy (2006); Kennedy and Svenonius (2006) for discussion.

The second question—regarding why negative-polar antonyms are incompatible with MPs—seems more tractable because this generalization is fairly cross-linguistically robust (although see Doetjes 2012 and the discussion in Chapter 6 for evidence that it is not exceptionless). I'll briefly present the solution in Schwarzschild (2005) (see also Morzycki 2008), but must note that there are at least two compelling alternatives proposed by Sassoon (Sassoon 2010a,b) and Winter (Winter 2005, 2009; Doetjes 2012).

Schwarzschild (2005, 2006a, 2012) proposes that MPs measure sets of degrees (are "predicates of gaps"), based in part on their ability to function as comparative differentials, as in (26a), and to modify PPs, as in (26b) (although see Winter 2006 for an alternative vector-based treatment of these data).

(26)   a. Adam is 2in taller than Doug.
       b. Doug drove 20 mph over the speed limit.

In this account, MPs denote semantic objects of type $\langle\langle d,t\rangle, t\rangle$, as in (27). I've changed Schwarzschild's formalism slightly so that it is more consistent with the framework above. (28) presents a compositional semantics for the positive construction.

(27) $[\![6\text{ft}]\!] = \lambda D \in D_{\langle d,t\rangle}.6\text{ft}(D)$

(28)   Doug is 6ft tall.
       a. $[\![\text{tall}]\!] = \lambda x \lambda d.\text{tall}(x, d)$
       b. $[\![\text{tall(Doug)}]\!] = \lambda d.\text{tall}(\text{doug}, d)$
       c. $[\![6\text{ft(tall(Doug))}]\!] = 6\text{ft}(\lambda d.\text{tall}(\text{doug}, d))$

The truth conditions in (28c) should be read as "the set of degrees to which Doug is tall measures 6ft." Another way of describing these truth conditions is "the space between Doug's highest point and his lowest point measures 6ft."

Schwarzschild argues that this characterization of MPs—in which they measure the size of a set of degrees—correctly predicts the incompatibility of MPs and negative antonyms. Recall (from (16), repeated in (29)) that an individual's measure along a positive dimension is fully bounded, with a lower bound of zero and an upper bound determined by its maximum value. In contrast, an individual's measure along a negative dimension is only partially bounded by its maximum value (which, in this case, is 6ft, the highest degree on the "short" scale).

---

[4] Lehrer (1985), citing Jackendoff (1977), gives a complete list of measure adjectives in English: *deep, tall, thick, old, high, long, late/early, wide/broad*, listing *full/empty* and *strong* as "peripheral" (in the case of *full* and *empty* because they are modifiable by fractions but not MPs like *2 liters*).

(29) a. $\{d : \text{Doug is } d\text{-tall}\} = \{1\text{ft}, 2\text{ft}, 3\text{ft}, 4\text{ft}, 5\text{ft}, 6\text{ft}\} = (0, 6\text{ft}]$
      b. $\{d : \text{Doug is } d\text{-short}\} = \{6\text{ft}, 7\text{ft}, 8\text{ft}, 9\text{ft}, \ldots, \infty\} = [6\text{ft}, \infty)$

Schwarzschild proposes that we can explain the incompatibility of MPs with negative antonyms this way: the definition in (27) predicts that *Adam is 6ft short* would be true iff the set of degrees corresponding to Adam's shortness measures 6ft. This is false but, worse, it's trivially false for any combination of negative adjective and MP. Schwarzschild claims that this fundamental uninformativity is responsible for the ungrammaticality of all combinations of MPs and negative antonyms. Thus, we can account for the unacceptability of MPs and negative antonyms, as well as the ability of MPs to behave as comparative differentials, if we adopt a view of MPs as measuring sets of degrees, rather than naming a degree.

I will end this section by discussing the relationship between numerals like *five* and MPs like *5ft*. I will assume that numerals are just MPs with null measure operators whose dimension of measurement is quantity. This is the intuition behind the formalese "5-many pizzas" for the English *5 pizzas*.

The positing of a null morpheme to semantically compose numerals and nouns dates back to Bartsch and Vennemann (1972) and Cresswell (1976), and it has been steadily adapted throughout the degree semantic literature, by e.g. Higginbotham (1993), Nerbonne (1995), Schwarzschild (2002, 2006b), Villalba (2003), Kennedy and Svenonius (2006), Nakanishi (2007a,b), and Champollion (2010). See Rett (2014b) for an overview. Effectively, these proposals are concerned with reconciling a degree-semantic perspective on the meaning of numerals like *5* with the traditional picture of nouns like *pizza* as denoting individual properties. They postulate a null measure operator—often a null *many* or *much*—to function as a combinator for DPs like *5 pizzas*.

Some degree-semantic characterizations of this null *many* involve an individual existential quantifier, as in (30) from Hackl (2000) (see also its precursors in Heycock 1995; Romero 1998):

(30) $[\![\text{many}]\!] = \lambda d \lambda P \lambda Q \exists x [P(x) \wedge Q(x) \wedge |x| = d]$

This definition treats the null *many* as a scopable quantifier with an additional degree argument corresponding to the cardinality ($|\cdot|$) of the bound individual.

I will instead follow accounts of this null *many* that characterize it on par with gradable adjectives, along the lines of (31) where μ is a constant measure function.[5]

(31) $[\![\text{many}]\!] = \lambda x \lambda d.\mu(x, d)$

---

[5] I use μ here (instead of $|\cdot|$, as in (30)) to represent the dimension of measurement associated with *many* so that this definition can be more easily extended to the mass quantity adjectives, *much* and *less*, which measure quantities that aren't cardinalities. I intend μ to be a contextually valued variable ranging over dimensions of measurement.

There are many motivations for this non-quantificational treatment of *many* (and *much, few, less*) as an adjective encoding the dimension of quantity, beginning with morphological work in Bresnan (1973), syntactic work in Jackendoff (1977) and Corver (1997), and semantic work in Hoeksema (1983) and Grosu and Landman (1998). Recent arguments for and adaptations of this **quantity adjective** treatment of *many, much, few* and *less* (and their null counterparts) can be found in Rett (2006, 2008, 2014b) and Solt (2009, 2010).

According to this treatment of quantity adjectives, they too have evaluative positive constructions; cf. *The guests were many.* (To my knowledge, von Stechow 1984: 66 was the first to treat constructions with unmodified quantity adjectives as positive constructions.)

Since they are defined similarly to (other) gradable adjectives, the evaluativity of positive constructions formed from quantity adjectives poses the same problem as other positive constructions, e.g., *John is tall.* That is, standard degree-semantic approaches predict either that these sentences denote sets of (non-evaluative) degrees, as in (32b), or, assuming an application of existential closure, that they denote very weak existential truth conditions (TCs), as in (32c).[6] This proposition is weak because it asserts what it presupposes, given the positive extension presupposition from §2.1.2: namely, that there is some quantity of guests in the context. As with other positive constructions, the truth conditions are better modeled as in (32d).

(32) The guests were many.
     a. $[\![many]\!] = \lambda x \lambda d.\mu(x, d)$
     b. $[\![\text{The guests were many}]\!] = \lambda d.\mu(\iota x[\text{guests}(x)], d)$ *predicted TCs*
     c. $[\![\text{The guests were many}]\!] = \exists d[\mu(\iota x[\text{guests}(x)], d)]$ *predicted TCs, ∃-closure*
     d. $[\![\text{The guests were many}]\!] = \exists d[\mu(\iota x[\text{guests}(x)], d) \wedge d > s]$ *desired TCs*

As I'll discuss in Chapter 3, there are additional parallels between gradable adjectives and quantity adjectives that make the analysis in (31) tempting.

I'll close with a note about numerals and scalar implicature. Readers will likely be familiar with the claim that numerals are scalar items, interpretable in some contexts as "at least *n*" and in others as "exactly *n*" (and possibly, in some contexts, as "at most *n*"; Breheny 2008). It's not clear whether the same thing is true for MPs with explicit measure nouns, which seem to receive an "exactly" interpretation, at least in some constructions, as demonstrated in (33b) (from Koenig 1991: 144).

(33) a.   Mary has three children, in fact four.
     b. ??This book will cost you $3, in fact $4.

A degree-semantic account of MPs and numerals as denoting degrees (type $\langle d \rangle$, as in (23)) is consistent with an "at least" treatment of these elements, while the

---

[6] I will present this problem more carefully in §2.2.2.

gap-predicate treatment in (28) predicts that MPs and numerals can only measure downward-monotonic sets and can only receive an "exactly" interpretation. I suspect that an accurate account will need to be more flexible than either of these approaches. But because numerals and MPs do not play a big role in the discussion here, I will remain agnostic on the issue. Interested readers should consult Koenig (1991), Geurts (2011), Kennedy (2013), and Spector (2013) for good discussion of the relevant issues.

2.1.5 Degree quantifiers

In a cross-linguistic survey of comparison constructions, Stassen (1985) notes that languages employ a number of different comparison strategies. (34) lists several for English (for details see Kennedy 2009; Sawada 2009; Kubota and Matsui 2010).

(34) a. Doug is taller than Adam.   *explicit comparative*
      b. Compared/Relative to Adam, Doug is tall.   *implicit comparative*
      c. Doug is tall and Adam is not tall.   *conjoined comparative*

Haspelmath and Buchholz (1998) shows that across languages there are different strategies for equating individuals in comparison constructions. (35) lists several for English. I'll label these strategies in a way that parallels the comparative data.

(35) a. Doug is as tall as Adam.   *explicit equative*
      b. Doug and Adam are equally tall.   *conjoined equative*
      c. Doug and Adam have the same height.   *possessive equative*

Only explicit comparatives and equatives have been argued to involve degree quantifiers; I focus on them here and return to other strategies of comparison in §6.1.1.

There is a strong syntactic and semantic tradition of analyzing the comparative morpheme (*-er* in English) as denoting a degree quantifier of type $\langle\langle d, t\rangle, \langle\langle d, t\rangle, t\rangle\rangle$ (Ross 1967; Bresnan 1973; Seuren 1973; McConnell-Ginet 1973; Kamp 1975; Cresswell 1976; Hellan 1981; Hoeksema 1983; von Stechow 1984). These accounts generally assume that comparatives like the one in (36a) have an underlying structure more like (36b), possibly achieved by elision (Bresnan 1973).

(36) a. Doug is taller than Adam (is ~~tall~~).
      b. *-er*([OP$_{d'}$ Adam ~~is d'-tall~~])([OP$_d$ Doug is d-tall])

The assumption in (36b) is that the comparative morpheme takes two syntactic objects: an internal argument corresponding to the *than* clause and an external argument composed of the overt subject and adjectival predicate. Both clauses involve movement of a *wh*-operator that is base-generated in the degree argument position of the adjective and raises to abstract over this position (Chomsky 1977). This operator is null in matrix clauses but is overt in some languages and in some dialects of English (e.g., *John is taller than what you are*). See Lechner (2001) and Pancheva (2006) for a discussion of how this account of comparatives extends to phrasal comparatives like

John is not taller than himself (*is). As a result, the comparative is defined in terms of two sets of degrees (type $\langle d, t \rangle$), the degree version of individual quantifiers like *every* and *some*.

There are a number of competing semantic characterizations of the comparative (for overviews, see von Stechow 1984; Schwarzschild 2008), with different advantages and disadvantages. I have chosen the definition in (37) mainly because it is transparently relatable to the equative construction. In (37), the comparative morpheme denotes a relation between sets of degrees D and D'. It predicts a comparative is true iff the maximum degree in the set denoted by the matrix clause exceeds the maximum degree in the set denoted by the *than* clause.

(37) $[\![\text{-er}]\!] = \lambda D' \lambda D.\text{Max}(D) > \text{Max}(D')$,
   where $\text{Max}(D) = \iota d[d \in D \wedge \forall d' \in D[d' \neq d \rightarrow d' < d]]$

The definition of maximality here is based on the one in Rullmann (1995) and is crucially sensitive to the direction of the scale associated with the degrees d. So, if $d > d'$ on the 'tall' scale, then $d' > d$ on the 'short' scale, and so forth for other antonym pairs.

The result is the compositional semantics demonstrated in (38).

(38) Doug is taller than Adam.
   a. $[\![\text{OP}_d \text{ Doug is } d\text{-tall}]\!] = \lambda d.\text{tall}(\text{doug}, d)$
   b. $[\![\text{OP}_{d'} \text{ Adam is } d'\text{-tall}]\!] = \lambda d'.\text{tall}(\text{adam}, d')$
   c. $[\![\text{-er}([\text{OP}_{d'} \text{ Adam is } d'\text{-tall}])([\text{OP}_d \text{ Doug is } d\text{-tall}])]\!]$
      $= \text{Max}(\lambda d.\text{tall}(\text{doug}, d)) > \text{Max}(\lambda d'.\text{tall}(\text{adam}, d'))$

The truth conditions in (38c) can be read as, "The maximum degree to which Doug is tall is higher on the 'tall' scale than the maximum degree to which Adam is tall," or more succinctly, "Doug's height exceeds Adam's height."

This represents an idealized analysis of the comparative: as it stands, (37) cannot accurately predict the behavior of quantifiers in *than* clauses (Larson 1988; Heim 2000; Schwarzschild 2008) or the ability of comparatives to be modified as they are by differentials in, e.g., *Doug is 2 inches taller than Adam* (von Stechow 1984; Hellan 1981; Schwarzschild 2006a). But it will suffice for present purposes.

Important for the discussion here is the relationship between the comparative and equative constructions. While the comparative has received more attention in the semantics literature than the equative, the interpretations of the two constructions are quite closely related. I follow Horn (1972), Klein (1980), von Stechow (1984), Bierwisch (1989), and many others in assuming that the comparative and equative are syntactically and semantically similar, differing only in the strictness of their ordering (for recent discussion, see Rett 2010, 2013, 2014a).

(39) $[\![\text{as}]\!] = \lambda D' \lambda D.\text{Max}(D) \geq \text{Max}(D')$

The result is the compositional semantics demonstrated in (40). The truth conditions in (40c) can be read as, "Doug's height is at least as tall as Adam's height."

(40) Doug is as tall as Adam.
  a. $[\![\mathrm{OP}_d \text{ Doug is } d\text{-tall}]\!] = \lambda d.\mathsf{tall}(\mathsf{doug}, d)$
  b. $[\![\mathrm{OP}_{d'} \text{ Adam is } d'\text{-tall}]\!] = \lambda d'.\mathsf{tall}(\mathsf{adam}, d')$
  c. $[\![as([\mathrm{OP}_{d'} \text{ Adam is } d'\text{-tall}])([\mathrm{OP}_d \text{ Doug is } d\text{-tall}])]\!]$
      $= \mathrm{MAX}(\lambda d.\mathsf{tall}(\mathsf{doug}, d)) \geq \mathrm{MAX}(\lambda d'.\mathsf{tall}(\mathsf{adam}, d'))$

It's been claimed that equatives can receive an "at least" or an "exactly" interpretation, depending on context. These two interpretations are illustrated in (41).

(41) Doug is as tall as Adam is . . .
  a. . . . so you were wrong to say he is taller.   *"exactly"*
  b. . . . in fact, he's taller.   *"at least"*

In (41a), the continuation is a felicitous contradiction of an "at least" interpretation of the equative, showing that the equative is compatible with an "exactly" interpretation. In (41b), the continuation affirms that the equative is compatible with an "at least" interpretation.

In this respect, equatives resemble numerals, as illustrated in (42).

(42) John has three children . . .
  a. . . . so you were wrong to say he has four.   *"exactly"*
  b. . . . in fact, he has four.   *"at least"*

Accordingly, both phenomena have been treated as involving scalar implicatures (Horn 1972, among others).[7] In such accounts, the weak, "at least" interpretation is assumed to be lexically encoded by the numeral or equative, with the strong, "exactly" interpretation arising when possible as a result of pragmatic strengthening. See Geurts (2011) for a discussion of quantity implicatures; I will return to a more in-depth discussion of implicature in Chapter 4.

And, in fact, the definitions in (37) and (39) correctly predict that the comparative asymmetrically entails the equative, as shown in (43).

(43) a. Doug is taller than Adam. $\rightarrow$ Doug is as tall as Adam.
      b. Doug is as tall as Adam. $\nrightarrow$ Doug is taller than Adam.

In an intensional version of the account above, the comparative construction would be characterized as denoting a subset of the worlds denoted by its equative counterpart.

---

[7] There are, to my knowledge, two accounts of equatives that do not conform to this generalization. The proposals in Cresswell (1976), Seuren (1984), von Stechow (1984), and Schwarzschild and Wilkinson (2002) analyze the two interpretations of the equative as a lexical ambiguity. And the syntactic proposal in Bhatt and Pancheva (2004) analyzes the two readings as a scope ambiguity.

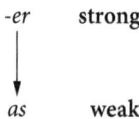

FIGURE 2.1. A Horn scale for comparatives and equatives

This difference makes the comparative and equative constructions likely candidates for being members of the same Horn scale, as illustrated in Figure 2.1.[8]

If the comparative and equative constructions are in fact members of the same Horn scale, a (neo-)Gricean approach to conversational implicature predicts that the weak, "at least" interpretation assigned to the equative can be strengthened in certain contexts. Informally, the reasoning goes as follows. The hearer assumes that the speaker is obeying Grice's (1975) Maxims of Quantity ("Make your contribution as informative as required") and Manner ("Avoid obscurity of expression"), and so would utter the more informative comparative in a situation in which Doug is in fact taller than Adam. From this assumption, the hearer thus reasons that the speaker, uttering the equative, believes that Doug isn't taller than Adam (Soames 1982; Russell 2006). As a result, the weak, "at least" semantic interpretation of the equative is pragmatically strengthened with the implicatum: "and Doug is not taller than Adam."

To sum up: explicit comparatives and equatives are syntactically similar but differ semantically in the strictness of their ordering. While the comparative strictly orders individuals with respect to a particular dimension of measurement, the equative imposes a non-strict, "at least" ordering. We can account for its "exactly" interpretation using scalar implicature: in most contexts, the hearer assumes that the comparative doesn't hold, and the meaning of the equative is pragmatically strengthened. This analysis seems to fit the data, as demonstrated in (41), although see Rett (2010, 2014a) for more extensive discussion. The relationship between the comparative and equative morphemes will be important for the discussion of the distribution of evaluativity in Chapters 3–5.

The next section presents a discussion of the evaluativity of positive constructions in the context of this degree-semantic framework.

2.2 Evaluativity and POS

The importance of evaluativity to the semantics of adjectives (and correspondingly, as we've seen, degree semantics in general) is best illustrated by the contrast in (44).

---

[8] Of course, this isn't sufficient to predict that the comparative and equative are members of the same Horn scale (Fox 2006). Such a theory must be supplemented with assumptions about what can count as a scalemate with what. For instance, the overtly modified equative *Doug is at least as tall as Adam* participates in the same entailment relations with the comparative, but doesn't behave like a scalemate. See Rett (2014a) and Chapter 5 for more extensive discussion.

(44) a. Doug is tall.
      b. Doug is 6ft tall.

The Principle of Compositionality (often attributed to Frege 1884) assumes that the meaning of a sentence depends on the meaning of its morphemes and the syntax used to combine them. This equation suggests a direct correlation between the number of morphemes in a sentence and the number of semantic restrictions placed on that sentence's truth conditions. Yet the pair in (44) appears to be a counterexample to such a generalization. The absence of an MP in (44a) corresponds to the addition of a semantic property—evaluativity, the requirement that John's height exceed a contextual standard—and that the presence of the MP *6ft* in (44b) corresponds to the absence of evaluativity. How can this be?

This question has been at the forefront of degree-semantic treatments of gradable adjectives. These accounts have tended to base their semantic characterization of gradable adjectives on their behavior in comparatives or MP constructions and have transferred this characterization to adjectives in the positive construction only secondarily (Bartsch and Vennemann 1972; Cresswell 1976; von Stechow 1984; Kennedy 1999).

The comparative also contrasts with positive constructions in regards to evaluativity: neither sentence in (45) requires that Adam or Doug be tall or short, respectively. (45a) could be truthfully and felicitously uttered in a context in which Adam and Doug are clearly short, and (45b) could be truthfully and felicitously uttered in a context in which they are clearly tall.

(45) a. Adam is taller than Doug.
      b. Adam is shorter than Doug.

Assuming that the comparative form *taller* is composed of the bare adjective *tall*, the contrast in evaluativity between (44a) and (45a) poses roughly the same problem as does the pair in (44). As Klein (1980) puts it (p. 2):

(46) **Klein's Principle**
      If *A* is a positive adjective, then the meaning of [$_{AP}$ *A-er than X*] is a function of the meaning of *A*.

Klein calls this principle "merely a special case of Frege's principle of compositionality, applied to a class of English surface structures. For example, [$_{AP}$ *taller than Jude is*] is a complex expression, and *taller* is derived by a regular morphological process from [$_A$ *tall*]. If Frege's principle is accepted at all, then [(46)] seems to follow automatically. It is difficult to escape the conclusion that the meaning of the positive adjective is a basic component of the comparative." (See also Kamp 1975.)

And, in fact, recent work by Bobaljik (2012) (with roots in Bartsch and Vennemann 1972) shows a very strong trend across languages for the comparative to be formed from positive adjectives, but not vice versa. This tension posed by evaluativity—the

addition of meaning in the absence of added morphology—caused degree semanticists like Cresswell to propose the null morpheme POS and others, like Klein, to
eschew degrees for a logic in which these constructions modify or restrict comparison
classes.[9]

The rest of this chapter presents the null morpheme POS and an explanation of its
use in the positive construction and elsewhere. But before I present the details of the
account, I will say a little more about the nature of the contextual standard invoked by
evaluativity.

2.2.1 *The nature of the standard*

A positive construction like *Adam is tall* is evaluative, which means that its truth conditions contain the requirement that the relevant degree be significantly high. I have
used the term "contextual standard" in describing evaluativity because, empirically,
what counts as significantly high varies from context to context. In this section, I
will briefly discuss some interesting observations about the nature and value of the
standard invoked by evaluative constructions.

Von Stechow (1984) references Aristotle (1963) in his discussion of this point (p. 60):

(47) a. This corn is big.
  b. This mountain is small.
  c. In the summer, there are only few people in Athens, but there are a lot of people in the
     village.

According to Aristotle, [(47a)] means that this corn is big with respect to other corns, [(47b)]
means that this mountain is small with respect to other mountains, and [(47c)] means that the
number of people dwelling in Athens in summer time is small with respect to the number of
people who stay in Athens during the winter, but the other way round for the village.

In other words, positive constructions seem to be interpreted as though they had
an implicit *for*-phrase, covert versions of the *for*-phrases in (48), which seem to make
explicit which comparison class is relevant for the computation of the evaluative
standard.

(48) a. This corn is big for corn.
  b. This mountain is small for a mountain.

Overt *for*-phrases can introduce a variety of comparison classes, e.g., *This corn is big
for organic corn* or *This corn is big for vegetables grown in a drought* (Ludlow 1989).

---

[9] Degree semanticists have argued that Klein's (1980, 1982) analysis is empirically inadequate, incapable
of properly treating MPs, equative modifiers like *twice*, and comparisons of deviation like *The meal was
more expensive than it was tasty* (von Stechow 1984; Kennedy 1999). However, recent research is trying to
address these shortcomings (Larson 1988; Neeleman et al. 2004; Doetjes et al. 2011; van Rooij 2012), and
Klein's logic is not the only alternative to degree semantics on the market (Moltmann 2009; Cobreros et al.
2012; Burnett 2012).

The ability of these *for*-phrases to paraphrase the variable interpretations of positive constructions from context to context has led many to conclude that evaluativity is calculated with respect to a comparison class (by taking an average, perhaps) which is either implicit or explicitly introduced by a *for*-phrase.

However, Kennedy (2007: 8) argued that the comparison classes invoked by positive constructions need not correspond to the meaning of overt *for*-phrases. He observed that the sentences in (49) are not contradictory, suggesting that the positive construction in the second conjuncts are not interpreted as 'small for an elephant' (cf. Ludlow 1989; Bogal-Allbritten 2011; Fleisher 2011).

(49)   a. Jumbo is small for an elephant, but he is not small.
       b. Jumbo is a small elephant, but he is not small.

However, it remains true that a *for DP* presupposes that the subject is a member of the class associated with the DP, as (50) (from Kennedy 2007: 13) shows.

(50)   ??That mouse is (obviously) not small for an elephant.

From this, Kennedy (2007) concludes, following Rusiecki (1985), that a *for*-PP "does not provide a comparison class argument for the positive form, but rather restricts the domain of the measure function denoted by the adjective to just those objects that are members of the set defined by the nominal complement of *for*" (p. 13).[10] In other words, the evaluative standard is calculated relative to a comparison class, and this comparison class is restricted but not necessarily fully determined by overt *for*-phrases.

The same sort of argument can be made for modified nominals in attributive positive constructions, as demonstrated in (49b). That is, when a gradable adjective modifies a noun, as in *Doug is a tall man*, the noun generally restricts the comparison class affiliated with the evaluative standard for that adjective. But it doesn't fully determine the comparison class, which can be further restricted by other linguistic material or otherwise valued by context, as the examples in (51) show (Partee 1994).

(51)   a. My two-year-old son built a really tall snowman yesterday.
       b. The D.U. fraternity brothers built a really tall snowman last weekend.

Despite the fact that the attributive adjective (*tall*) is modifying the same nominal (*snowman*) in both sentences, the subject of the sentence affects the relevant comparison class (and consequently the relevant standard). (51a) is most naturally interpreted as meaning "tall for a snowman built by a two-year-old," and (51b) "tall for a snowman built by fraternity brothers."

However, Kennedy (2007) argues that while attributive positive constructions require that the relevant individual be in the extension of the modified nominal,

---

[10] See Sassoon (2010a) and Fults (2011) for more discussion.

the comparison class invoked in these constructions can in principle be independent from the noun's extension. An example is in (52): the modified nominal, *BMW*, is interpreted as a restriction on Kyle's car, but it does not seem to be restricting the comparison class according to which Kyle's car is judged to be expensive. In (52), the relevant comparison class seems to be "for a car," significantly weaker than it would be if it were restricted by the modified numeral.

(52)   Kyle's car is an expensive BMW, though it's not expensive for a BMW. In fact, it's the least expensive model they make.

Bogusławski (1975) and Kennedy (2007) additionally caution against the view that the standard of comparison is calculated as an average of values of the relevant comparison class; Bogusławski argues that if this were the case, (53) would be a contradiction.

(53)   Nadia's height is greater than the average height of a gymnast, but she is still not tall for a gymnast.

The acceptability of (53) (and those sentences in (49)) might however be the result of a contextual change in granularity; it is notoriously hard to fix contextual variables across clauses. The examples in (54) demonstrate that contextual variables or parameters for a single item can change across conjuncts of the same sentence, albeit with the help of focal stress.

(54)   a. Adam is tall, but he's not TALL.
       b. Doug drank all the beer, but he didn't drink ALL the beer.

So while it seems possible to make some generalizations about how the evaluative standard is valued and restricted, the context sensitivity of the standard makes it hard to say with absolute assuredness what the value of a particular comparison class or standard is for out-of-the-blue sentences.

In sum, the value of the standard invoked by an evaluative construction depends on which comparison class the individual in question is being evaluated relative to, although the nature of this dependency can't be reduced to an average. Toledo and Sassoon (2011) argue that the comparison class is determined by the individual the adjective is predicated of, and that the calculation tends to be made in one of two ways: extensionally (in terms of other members of an extensional set) or intensionally (in terms of that individual's possible-world counterparts). They additionally offer evidence that how the comparison class is calculated differs across adjective classes; see §5.4 for more discussion on the interaction of evaluativity and adjective class.

The relevant comparison class is often, but not always, valued by nominals in attributive sentences (cf. (52)). It is often, but not always, supplied by overt *for*-phrases (cf. (49)). However, these *for*-phrases always restrict the comparison class, as (50) shows.[11]

Based on parallel data from the phenomenon of quantifier domain restriction (Stanley 2002), Kennedy (2007) has argued that there is empirical evidence that the comparison class, despite being supplied by context, is syntactically encoded in positive constructions. The relevant data are reproduced below, with (55) from Stanley (2002) and (56) from Kennedy (2007).

(55)   a. In most of his classes, John fails three students.
      b. paraphrase: in most of John's classes x, John fails three students in x

(56)   a. Everyone in my family is tall.
      b. paraphrase: for every x in my family, x has a height that exceeds the standard for a comparison class based on x

Pinkal (1979), in contrast, argues that the comparison class is a discourse-salient property with no syntactic realization. The account proposed in Chapter 5 will most closely resemble Pinkal's proposal. This suggests the need for an independent explanation of the binding facts observed in (56). There are a number of alternative proposals inspired by the quantifier domain restriction data in (55); see Sennet (2011, 2012) for an overview.

A number of semanticists and philosophers have viewed evaluativity (and its context sensitivity) to be intrinsically tied to vagueness (see, for instance, Klein 1980). However, there is reason to treat vagueness and context sensitivity as separate phenomena. Graff (2000) argues that even explicitly restricted positive constructions like *A rent of $725 is expensive for an apartment on this street*—a sentence in which the *for*-phrase does seem to completely determine the value of the standard—are subject to the Sorites Paradox and borderline cases (see also Pinkal 1995; Rusiecki 1985). While this is by no means the last word on the topic, it is enough to allow me to set aside considerations of vagueness in what follows. Those interested should refer to Cobreros et al. (2012) and Burnett (2012) for a recent semantics of adjectival constructions in which the role of vagueness is much more central.

2.2.2 *The semantics of POS*

The problem posed by the positive construction is this: a characterization of gradable adjectives as denoting relations between individuals and degrees, based as we saw on their behavior in comparative and MP constructions, predicts the following compositional meaning for positive constructions:

---

[11] A similar argument can be made for "attributive-with-infinitive" constructions like *a long book to assign*. Fleisher (2011) analyzes these infinitival clauses as degree relatives, restricting the domain of POS for the purposes of evaluativity.

(57) ⟦Adam is tall⟧ = λ*d*.tall(adam, *d*)

There are two distinct problems with this prediction. First, it gets the type wrong (the **extra argument problem**): it predicts positive constructions denote sets of degrees or degree properties instead of propositions.

Let's assume for now a process of existential closure (or, if preferred, a covert type-shifting operator; Grano 2012; Bogal-Allbritten 2013) that can bind free variables at the end of utterances or clauses (Kamp 1981; Heim 1982; Diesing 1992). This fixes the first problem, resulting in (58).

(58) ⟦Adam is tall⟧ = ∃*d*[tall(adam, *d*)]

This brings us to the second problem, the **evaluativity problem**. As it stands, our semantics of the positive construction—even if we help ourselves to existential closure—incorrectly predicts that all positive constructions are trivially true (and uninformative). Recall from §2.1.2 the **positive extension presupposition** of gradable adjectives: the assumption, based on data like (9), that gradable adjectives can only be felicitously predicated of individuals who instantiate the denoted property to some degree *d*. The positive extension proposition carried by a sentence like *Adam is tall* corresponds exactly to the truth conditions attributed to the positive construction in (58), and they are too weak: in actuality, the sentence requires not just that Adam have some degree of tallness, but that he be tall to a significant degree.

Proposals of POS, beginning in Bartsch and Vennemann (1972), rely on the assumption that evaluativity is an obligatory semantic component of positive constructions (and only positive constructions). That it is obligatory stems from its apparent presence across positive constructions regardless of adjective type (i.e., across antonyms and adjective classes). That it is semantic stems in part from its compositional contribution to truth conditions; the negation of the positive construction amounts to a negation of evaluativity.

(59) a. It's not the case that Adam is tall.
      b. Adam isn't tall.
      c. Adam is not tall.

Each of the sentences in (59) is false in a context in which Adam's height exceeds the relevant standard of tallness. Nor does the evaluative component of positive constructions project from the antecedent of a conditional, as (60) shows.

(60) If Adam is tall, Doug will resent him. ↛ Adam is tall.

Since the 1970s, POS has been the preferred solution to the problems posed by the evaluativity of the positive construction. POS is a null morpheme that, in most formulations, solves the two problems discussed above at once: it requires the degree arguments of gradable adjectives to exceed a standard (the restriction component of

POS); and it existentially binds the degree argument (the quantificational or type-shifting component of POS).

Bartsch and Vennemann (1972) propose that POS is "needed to lexicalize the constituents" (i.e., provide a lexical base for the purported compositional semantics). They do however observe that POS is "usually lexicalized as zero" (p. 175), i.e., is unpronounced. For them, POS has the same semantic status as the comparative, equative, and superlative morphemes, but instead of comparing the subject to an overt object (encoded by a *than*-phrase or an *as*-phrase), it compares the subject to a degree that corresponds to the average of some relevant comparison class along the same dimension.

Cresswell (1976) adopts Bartsch and Vennemann's proposal into a degree-semantic Montagovian semantics. I'll present his treatment in full (from Cresswell 1976: 46) and then translate it into the degree semantics introduced in §2.1.

Our underlying semantic concept for *tall* was in fact "x-much tall." But of course we have sentences like:

[(61)]   Bill is a tall man.

What seems to be meant in a case like this is something like:

[(62)]   Bill is taller than the average man.

I propose to treat the "tall" in [61] as composed of two symbols, *pos* and *tall*. *tall* satisfies [the definition of gradable adjectives], while *pos* conveys "er than the average ————." [...] *pos* makes an ordinary noun modifier, say, ⟨*pos,tall*⟩ out of a modifier like *tall*.

[(63)] $V(pos)^{12}$ is the function η in $D_{\langle\langle\langle 0,1\rangle,\langle 0,1\rangle\rangle,\langle\langle 0,1,1\rangle,\langle 0,1\rangle\rangle\rangle}$ such that where $\zeta \in D_{\langle\langle 0,1,1\rangle,\langle 0,1\rangle,\rangle}$, $\eta(\zeta)$ is the following function: For any $\omega \in D_{\langle 0,1\rangle}$ and $a \in D_1$ and $w \in W, w \in \eta(\zeta)(\omega)(a)$ iff $w \in \omega(a)$ and there is exactly one b such that $\zeta(\omega)(a, b)$; and for that $b, b = \langle u, >\rangle$ (for some $>$ and $u \in \mathcal{F}(>)$) and u is toward the top of the scale determined by $>$ when restricted to those v such that for some $c, w \in \zeta(\omega)(c, \langle v, >\rangle)$ and $w \in \omega(c)$.

Let us see how [the semantics] combine to give us a value for:

[(64)]   ⟨⟨*pos, tall*⟩, *man*⟩

In this case, if we let $V(tall)$ be ζ, $V(man)$ be ω, and $V(pos)$ be η, then $V([64]) = \eta(\zeta)(\omega)(a)$, and [the compositional semantics] give us that $w \in \eta(\zeta)(\omega)(a)$ iff a is a man in w and there is exactly one b such that $b = \langle u, >\rangle$ and $>$ is the greater than relation over spatial distances, and u is the distance between a's extremeties in w, and u is towards the top of the scale determined by $>$ when restricted to those v that are the heights of c's who are men in w.

This is Cresswell's version of POS as a modifier of attributive adjectives; we can assume (for Cresswell and other accounts of POS) that the semantics provides a way

---

12 V is Cresswell's interpretation function, parallel to $[\![\cdot]\!]$. His type notation is different from mine; in it, individuals and degrees are type 1 and truth values type 0, and functions are described from right to left. In (63), the attributive adjective *tall* denotes a function from a property (encoded by the modified nominal) to a relational adjective meaning.

of type-shifting between predicative and attributive versions of all modifiers, including POS.

Translating into our (extensional) lingua franca, we get something like (65), with (65a) the attributive version and (65b) the predicative version (for gradable adjectives $\mathcal{G}$).

(65) a. $[\![\text{POS}]\!] = \lambda \mathcal{G} \in D_{\langle e,\langle d,t\rangle\rangle} \lambda P \in D_{\langle e,t\rangle} \lambda x \exists d[P(x) \wedge \mathcal{G}(x,d) \wedge d > s]$ *attributive*
      b. $[\![\text{POS}]\!] = \lambda \mathcal{G} \in D_{\langle e,\langle d,t\rangle\rangle} \lambda x \exists d[\mathcal{G}(x,d) \wedge d > s]$ *predicative*

These two versions of POS differ from each other in their type and whether they restrict the individual x with respect to the property P (man in the case of the attributive sentence *Bill is a tall man*). They both differ from Cresswell's original formulation in one major way. In §2.1 it was assumed that gradable adjectives, because they are monotonic, map an individual to potentially infinitely many degrees, bounded on one end by the maximum degree to which that individual instantiates the predicate. For example, if Doug's height is 6ft, the adjective *tall* associates him with the interval (0,6ft], as illustrated in (16a). Cresswell, in contrast, characterizes gradable adjectives as relating an individual to a unique maximal height. The difference isn't important for us, but it does require a switch from Cresswell's "exactly one" quantifier to the weaker existential in (65).

Notice that (65) simultaneously solves the extra argument problem and the evaluativity problem, as illustrated in (66). It does this by virtue of the fact that it encodes a semantic restriction (the requirement that $d > s$) and a degree quantifier ($\exists d$). The truth conditions in (66d) predict the sentence is true iff Adam is tall to a degree that exceeds the relevant contextual standard.

(66) Adam is tall.   Cresswell's POS
      a. $[\![\text{tall}]\!] = \lambda x \lambda d.\text{tall}(x,d)$ from (8b)
      b. $[\![\text{POS}]\!] = \lambda \mathcal{G} \in D_{\langle e,\langle d,t\rangle\rangle} \lambda x \exists d[\mathcal{G}(x,d) \wedge d > s]$ from (65a)
      c. $[\![\text{POS}]\!]([\![\text{tall}]\!]) = \lambda x \exists d[\text{tall}(x,d) \wedge d > s]$
      d. $[\![\text{POS}]\!]([\![\text{tall}]\!])([\![\text{Adam}]\!]) = \exists d[\text{tall}(\text{adam},d) \wedge d > s]$

A treatment of evaluativity that combines these two components predicts that evaluativity is present whenever the adjective's degree argument is not overtly manipulated (= saturated by an argument or bound by a quantifier). It also predicts that evaluativity is absent whenever it is. While this second prediction seems to be verified by MP and comparative constructions, it is not true more generally, and this is what motivated the proposal for EVAL, a distinct null evaluativity morpheme (Rett 2007, 2008).

Von Stechow (1984) presents his own version of Cresswell's POS after first discussing the semantics of the comparative and equative, which he does not take to be evaluative (p. 60). In (67), POS denotes a relation between an individual x, adjective meaning $A°$, and comparison class C, so it functions as the glue between the subject, the adjective, and a pragmatic variable corresponding to those individuals against whom the subject is being judged. This formulation is different from Cresswell's in its explicit representation of a contextual argument, but it is similar in that it characterizes POS as a simultaneous solution to the extra argument and evaluativity problems, and thereby predicts that evaluativity occurs only when a degree argument is not overtly bound or valued.

(67) Let $A°$ be any adjective meaning, C be any appropriate property, x be any appropriate individual, and w be any world. Then $w \in [\![POS]\!](A°)(C)(x)$ iff $(\exists d)[d$ is an $A°$-degree & $d >$ average $[A°, C]$ & x has d in $w \in C(x)]$.

Kennedy (1999, 2007) proposes an alternative characterization of POS more directly based on the version in Bartsch and Vennemann (1972). This POS is formulated in the context of a theory in which gradable adjectives are assumed to denote measure functions, functions from individuals to degrees (type $\langle e, d \rangle$). In Kennedy's work, the comparative and POS share a similar syntactic and semantic form:[13]

(69) a. $[\![\text{more}]\!] = \lambda g \in D_{\langle e,d \rangle} \lambda d \lambda x.g(x) > d$
      b. $[\![\text{POS}]\!] = \lambda g \in D_{\langle e,d \rangle} \lambda x.g(x) > s(g)$

The idea is that the constituent [POS Adj] will come to denote an individual property, combining with the subject to denote a proposition, as in (70).

(70) Adam is POS tall.   Kennedy's POS
      a. $[\![\text{POS tall}]\!] = \lambda x.\text{tall}(x) > s_{\text{tall}}$
      b. $[\![\text{Adam is POS tall}]\!] = \text{tall}(\text{adam}) > s_{\text{tall}}$

In this approach, the extra argument problem posed by the positive construction is solved not by binding the degree argument (as Cresswell does) but by supplying the contextual standard for its value. The relational approach POS and the measure function POS have in common that they both predict a one-to-one mapping between the overt manipulation of an adjective's degree variable and a lack of evaluativity.[14]

It's been argued that there is no theoretical difference between characterizing POS as a null morpheme and characterizing it as a type-shifting principle (see also Grano 2012). Kennedy (2007: 7) says of his formulation of POS in (69b):

However, nothing crucial hinges on this assumption: the content of my proposals and argumentation remains the same if we assume instead that 'the positive degree morpheme POS' is really 'the positive type-shifting rule POS'.

---

[13] Kennedy and Svenonius (2006) argue that such an approach additionally requires a null morpheme MEAS to convert the measure function meaning of adjectives to degree-individual relations of type $\langle d, et \rangle$.

(68) $[\![\text{MEAS}]\!] = \lambda g \in D_{\langle e,d \rangle} \lambda d \lambda x.g(x) \geq d$

[14] Another perspective can be found in Kennedy and Levin (2008), who adopt the measure function approach in Kennedy (1999) but say of the relational (type $\langle e, \langle d, t \rangle \rangle$) theory of gradable adjectives: "Our proposals in this chapter can be made consistent with this analysis of gradable adjectives by simply assuming that measure functions correspond not directly to adjective denotations, but rather to more basic units of meaning, which are part of the lexical semantic representation of . . . gradable adjectives . . ." (p. 167).

The phrase "positive type-shifting rule" obscures the fact that degree-semantic approaches to the meaning of gradable adjectives require two distinct fixes: a type fix (addressing the extra argument problem) and a meaning fix (addressing the evaluativity problem). Traditionally, type-shifters only provide type fixes; a type-shifter that affects the truth conditions of a sentence isn't merely a type-shifter. In a compositional theory in which the meaning of a sentence is composed of the meaning of its parts and the rules used to combine those parts, type-shifters fall into the latter category, but POS is a member of the former.

Without a principled way of accounting for why positive constructions receive the meaning they do (why they receive an evaluative interpretation, rather than some other interpretation, say $d < s$), POS remains a stipulation outside of conventions of type flexibility. In Chapter 5 I attempt to provide just this sort of explanation, arguing that the evaluativity of positive constructions can be explained by a combination of existential closure and implicature.

If POS is a semantically contentful null morpheme (rather than a type-shifter) and evaluativity a universal property of adjectival constructions, we would expect that languages would differ on whether POS was a covert or overt operator. In other words, if POS contributes meaning to positive constructions across languages, we might expect this meaning to be (overtly) lexicalized in at least some languages.

Searches for overt versions of POS have, however, come up short. Kennedy (1999) (see also Kennedy and McNally 2005: n. 5) argued that Mandarin positive constructions involve a lexicalized POS, the morpheme *hen*. The evidence, from Sybesma (1999), is reproduced in (71).

(71) a. Zhangsan hen gao.
        Zhangsan *hen* tall
        'Zhangsan is tall.'

     b. Zhangsan bi   ni   (*hen) gao.
        Zhangsan than you (*hen) tall
        'Zhangsan is taller than you.'

The positive construction in (71a) is evaluative. A corresponding sentence without *hen*, however ("Zhangsan gao"), is infelicitous unless the context of utterance allows for a comparative interpretation (in which case the sentence is not evaluative). Kennedy likens *hen* to POS by additionally arguing that *hen* is in complementary distribution with the (null) comparative morpheme in (71b).

The distribution of *hen* does not however seem to directly track evaluativity in Mandarin (Rett 2008; Liu 2010). The equative in (72) is evaluative (as is its English counterpart; see Chapter 3) despite being ungrammatical with *hen* (from Rett 2008: 80).

(72) John he   Mary yiyang (*hen) ai.
      John and Mary same   (*hen) short.
      'John is as short as Mary.'

Liu (2010) and Grano (2012) also observe that positive constructions with overt negation (e.g., *John is not tall*) do not require *hen* but are nevertheless evaluative.

Liu takes data like (72) to indicate that Mandarin employs two distinct versions of POS: a covert version and an overt version *hen*. This is of course not very compelling evidence that POS can have overt counterparts across languages. Furthermore, Grano (2012) argues that Liu's conclusion cannot be right, and that the distribution of *hen* in Mandarin instead tracks a syntactic requirement related to selectional restrictions (see also Grano and Kennedy 2012 for an account of *hen* in comparatives). He thus analyzes POS (following Kennedy 2007) as a "universally available type-shifting operation" (p. 532), although he does not address the evaluativity component of POS or the distribution of evaluativity across adjectival constructions.

After concluding that the only morpheme that has ever been argued to be an overt instantiation of POS is not in fact an overt instantiation of POS, Grano concludes:

> The failure of the putative operator POS to correspond to overt material in language after language—in stark contrast to [comparative markers]—could be taken as evidence that POS does not actually exist and hence that any approach in which positive predication requires a special operator is misguided. Or at minimum, the facts suggest that there is some fundamental and as yet unexplained asymmetry between the way POS and [comparative markers] are realized crosslinguistically.   (Grano 2012: 515)

This is in line with the conclusion above that there is no effective semantic characterization of POS that addresses both the extra argument problem and the evaluativity problem without seeming stipulative. That conclusion aside, POS has proven useful in other types of constructions in addition to the treatment of evaluativity in positive constructions. Before I present an alternative to POS—the null morpheme EVAL, proposed in Rett (2007, 2008)—I will discuss extensions of POS outside of evaluative constructions.

2.3 Extensions of POS in the verbal domain

POS was initially proposed as a way to correct the predicted truth conditions of positive constructions in compositional degree-semantic theories. But POS has proven useful for other purposes as well; it's been co-opted in the semantics of some verb phrases.

To my knowledge, the first proposal of a version of POS in the verbal domain is in Piñón (2005). I'll begin by describing his proposal; I'll then review the treatment of degree achievements in Hay et al. (1999) and Kennedy and Levin (2008).

Piñón (2005) develops two extensions of adjectival POS to account for the distribution of evaluativity in constructions modified by adverbials like *completely* and *partly* (see also Bochnak forthcoming, 2013). Based on evidence that these are event modifiers, he first adds an event argument to adjectival POS to account for cases in which gradable adjectives are modified by *completely* and *partly*. Then, to account for parallel behavior between these constructions and transitive verbs modified by *completely* and *partly*, he proposes a verbal POS. I will present his motivations for each in turn.

Completely differs from *partly* and *half* in terms of what Piñón calls "extensionality":

(73)   a. The glass is completely empty. $\rightarrow$ The glass is empty.
        b. The glass is partly/half empty. $\nrightarrow$ The glass is empty.

While a completely empty glass is necessarily empty, a partially or half-empty glass is not (necessarily) empty. Piñón concludes from this test that modification by *completely* is truth-preserving (for our purposes, evaluativity-preserving), while modification by *partly* or *half* is not. He accounts for this difference by adding an event argument $e \in D_v$ to the measure function account of gradable adjectives, resulting in the type $\langle v, \langle e, d \rangle \rangle$ for gradable adjectives like *empty*. (This reflects the intuition that these modifiers, as adverbials, are event modifiers.)

Piñón's account of the difference in extensionality in (73) involves an event-semantic version of POS—POS_e—along with a weaker null counterpart DEG, which type-shifts but does not contribute evaluativity (pp. 159–61).

(74)   a. $[\![\text{DEG}]\!] = \lambda \mathcal{G} \in D_{\langle v, \langle e, d \rangle \rangle} \lambda d \lambda x \lambda e. \mathcal{G}(e, x) = d$
        b. $[\![\text{POS}_e]\!] = \lambda \mathcal{G} \in D_{\langle v, \langle e, d \rangle \rangle} \lambda x \lambda e. \mathcal{G}(e, x) \geq d_{\text{stnd}}$

The proposal is that *completely*-sentences like (73a) are always evaluative because *completely* selects for POS_e, but *partly*-sentences like (73b) are optionally evaluative because they combine with either DEG or POS_e.

Piñón (2005) also observes that the properties of adverbs of completion illustrated in (73) are replicated when the adverbs modify verbs (p. 153).

(75)   a. Rebecca completely solved the problem. $\rightarrow$ Rebecca solved the problem.
        b. Rebecca partly/half-solved the problem. $\nrightarrow$ Rebecca solved the problem.

To account for this parallel, Piñón proposes versions of DEG and POS for (transitive) verbs, "POS_v" (p. 165). Because Piñón assumes that verbs don't lexicalize degree arguments, his verbal POS relies on another operator δ that maps triples of individuals, events and two-place event relations to degrees representing the extent to which the individual is affected during the event. "For example, if R is the relation of eating between events and objects that are eaten, e is an eating event, and x is an apple, then the value of δ as applied to e, x and R represents how much of the apple is eaten in $e \ldots$" (Piñón 2005: 163).

(76) $[\![\text{POS}_v]\!] = \lambda V \in D_{\langle v, \langle e, \langle e, t \rangle \rangle \rangle} \lambda y \lambda x \lambda e. \delta(e, y, \lambda y' \lambda e'[V(e', x, y')]) \geq d_{\text{stnd}}$

Informally, (76) is a function from transitive verb meanings to their intransitive, evaluative counterparts. Within the relational approach to gradable adjectives, the parallel is clear: Cresswell's POS is a function from relational or two-place gradable adjectives to one-place evaluative individual properties, while Piñón's verbal operator restricts verb meanings to those in which a relatively high degree of progress has been made throughout the event.

However, the verbal POS in (76) does not by itself predict a difference between the two VPs in (75) with respect to evaluativity. To account for this difference, Piñón proposes that the standard associated with a particular modified VP changes depending on which adverb of completion is used. The effect is a (complicated) semantics in which verbs can be associated with degrees, and those degrees (like adjectival degrees) can be restricted relative to some contextual standard by a null morpheme.

While I've glossed over some of the details of Piñón's analysis, it will be helpful to keep in mind the relationship he establishes between evaluativity in the adjectival domain and the verbal domain. He notes that evaluativity seems to correspond to something like event completion—an observation expounded on by Kennedy and Levin (2008)—but also that adverbial modifiers like *completely* and *partly* can determine whether or not a VP is evaluative or telic. The evaluativity parallel between the two domains is relatively easy to capture by enriching the adjectival POS with an event argument or by otherwise type-raising it.

But from Piñón's perspective, evaluativity in the verbal domain differs from evaluativity in the adjectival domain in that it is not an obligatory property of all verb constructions. In this respect, adopting the adjectival POS to the verbal domain makes things more complicated: the adjectival POS was designed to treat the extra argument problem and the evaluativity problem simultaneously, but in the verbal domain, constructions that are not evaluative don't occur with POS and therefore still have an extra argument problem. Piñón addresses this discrepancy by proposing that the verbal POS—but not the adjectival POS—has a non-evaluative, type-shifting null counterpart.

Kennedy and Levin (2008) use a verbal version of POS for a related purpose, the variable telicity of degree achievements. VPs tend to fall into one of two classes: those that are telic, and those that are atelic (Vendler 1957). One test for telicity in English is the distribution of *for-* and *to-*adverbials, which can modify atelic and telic predicates respectively.

(77)   **telic VPs**
    a. Robin slept for/*in an hour.
    b. Robin ate for/*in an hour.

(78)   **atelic VPs**
    a. Robin painted the fence *for/in an hour.
    b. Robin demolished the house *for/in an hour.

Degree achievements, formed with deadjectival verbs, demonstrate both telic and atelic properties (Dowty 1979). A degree achievement construction like those in (79) is therefore ambiguous between a telic and atelic interpretation; (80) and (81) show these readings disambiguated by *to* and *for* adverbials.

(79) **degree achievements**
  a. The soup cooled.
  b. The tailor lengthened the pants.

(80) a. The soup cooled in an hour.   telic/evaluative
  b. The soup cooled for an hour.   atelic/non-evaluative

(81) a. The tailor lengthened the pants in an hour.   telic/evaluative
  b. The tailor lenthened the pants for an hour.   atelic/non-evaluative

As before, the adverbials condition atelic and telic interpretations; these interpretations correspond to non-evaluative and evaluative readings, respectively. Consider (79) in a context in which soup counts as cool if its temperature is between 80°F and 100°F. In this context, (80a) is telic; it entails that the soup cooled. The reading is also evaluative; intuitively, (80a) is true in this context iff the soup went from a temperature above 100° to a temperature between 80°F and 100°F within an hour. As Hay et al. (1999) point out, the standard of comparison relevant for evaluative degree achievement constructions is always the same standard as a positive construction formed with the verb's adjectival root.[15]

In contrast, the atelic version in (80b) is non-evaluative. It is atelic because it does not entail that the soup has cooled. It also, correspondingly, does not entail that the soup is cool (it could have, for instance, cooled from 200°F to 150°F).

Based on these observations, Kennedy and Levin (2008) develop an account of the variable telicity of degree achievements that invokes POS (see also Rett 2008 for a version of this account using EVAL, and Winter 2006 for an analysis that does not rely on the use of either). Like Piñón, Kennedy and Levin assume that gradable adjectives denote measure functions, type $\langle e, d \rangle$, and that these measure functions and POS can be relativized to events. Like Piñón and others, they build into their formal semantics a measure of change function (m_Δ) from an object and event pair to a degree of change.

To account for evaluative interpretations of degree achievements, they adopt a verbal POS, shown in (82a) (Kennedy and Levin 2008: 174). (82b) shows the predicted truth conditions for a degree achievement construction with POS.

(82) a. $[\![POS_v]\!] = \lambda g \in D_{m_\Delta} \lambda x \lambda e . g(x)(e) \geq \mathbf{stnd}(g)$, where m_Δ is a measure of change function mapping an individual/event pair to its degree of change

  b. $[\![$The soup POS cooled (in one hour)$]\!] = \lambda e . \mathrm{cool}_\Delta (\text{the-soup})(e) \geq \mathbf{stnd}(\mathrm{cool}_\Delta)$

---

[15] As we might expect given the discussion in §2.1.3, there is a correlation between the class (relative, absolute) of its adjectival root and its relationship to the relevant bound (Kennedy and McNally 2005; Kearns 2007). I will discuss these differences in greater detail in §5.4.1.

According to (82b), the telic (evaluative) reading of the sentence *The soup cooled* denotes a set of events in which the measure of the soup's change in temperature from the beginning to the end of the event (the measure of change in coolness, i.e., $cool_\Delta$) exceeds the contextual standard for changes in coolness (i.e., $\mathbf{stnd}(cool_\Delta)$).

However, as before, evaluativity in verbal constructions differs significantly from evaluativity in positive adjectival constructions because it seems optional in the verbal domain. To account for this difference, Kennedy and Levin (2008) propose, following Piñón (2005), that POS_v is optional. But POS_v, like its adjectival counterpart, solves two problems at once: it addresses the extra argument problem (here, the d argument of the verb) while contributing evaluativity. In order to allow POS_v to be optional, Kennedy and Levin (2008) also additionally propose a null type-shifting morpheme μ that does not contribute evaluativity (p. 180; see Kennedy and Svenonius 2006 for their version, called MEAS).

That is, Kennedy and Levin (2008) predict that degree achievements are optionally telic because they can occur with POS_v, but optionally atelic because they can instead occur with μ_v. Their account is like Piñón's in this respect.

(83) $[\![\mu_v]\!] = \lambda g \in D_{m_\Delta} \lambda d \lambda x \lambda e.g(x)(e) \geq d$

To sum up this discussion: at least some events seem to have an evaluative interpretation, brought about by a modifier like *completely*, an *in*-adverbial, or by context. Unlike the evaluativity associated with positive adjectival constructions, verbal constructions are not necessarily evaluative. To account for this optional evaluativity while maintaining a parallel with positive adjectival constructions, Piñón (2005) and Kennedy and Levin (2008) have each proposed two null morphemes that occur in free variation in verbal constructions. The POS morpheme values the verb's degree of change over time with a contextually valued standard of change; the other null morpheme (DEG or μ_v) is effectively a type-shifter, with no effect on the truth conditions of the denoted proposition.[16]

2.4 Summary

POS was the first response (and an influential one) to differences between the intuitive truth conditions of positive constructions and the meanings assigned to those constructions in a degree semantics. In particular, the theory predicts that positive constructions do not denote propositions (the "extra argument problem") and are not evaluative ("the evaluativity problem"). POS was designed to solve the two problems at once; the resulting prediction is that evaluativity is directly tied to the positive construction (and only to the positive construction).

---

[16] Bochnak (forthcoming, 2013) presents a recent adaptation of Piñón (2005). See Koontz-Garboden (2011) for a recent adaptation of Kennedy and Levin (2008) and Beavers (2011) for a compelling alternative. Peterson (2013) applies a version of verbal POS to the problem of *again* ambiguities.

There are several reasons to think that evaluativity is part of the (truth-conditional) semantics of the positive construction, and thus that it should be encoded syntactically, as it is in a null morpheme like POS. First, evaluativity in positive constructions is embeddable, scoping under negation and other sentential operators (e.g., *John isn't tall* denies that John's height exceeds a contextual standard). Second, the contextual standard introduced in the evaluative meaning can be bound overtly (e.g., *Everyone in my family is tall*) and restricted overtly (e.g., *Adam is tall for a philosopher*). Finally, if it's true that evaluativity is at work in the variable telicity of VPs, this evaluativity can affect and be affected by other constituents in the sentence, like *for*- and *in*-adverbials, which result in atelic and telic interpretations, respectively.

Several extensions of the basic POS account presented here—those dealing with "optional" evaluativity in the verbal domain—found some reason to divorce the evaluativity component of the original POS from its type-shifting component: namely that evaluativity is optional in some verbal constructions. To preserve the POS account while allowing for this optionality, these theories propose an additional null morpheme (MEAS, δ or $\mathbf{m}_\Delta$) to do the necessary type-shifting work without contributing evaluativity. In these accounts, evaluativity is obligatory in adjectival constructions because the only available type-shifter (POS) contributes evaluativity; in contrast evaluativity is optional in some verbal constructions because these constructions can either use POS_v or a non-evaluative version as a type-shifter.

In the next section, I present further motivation from Rett (2007, 2008) to separate evaluativity from existential quantification or changes in type. This account will form the foundation for the book's proposal to treat evaluativity as a conversational implicature rather than the product of a semantically encoded null morpheme.

3

The null morpheme EVAL

If writers wrote as carelessly as some people talk, then adhasdh asdglaseuyt[bn[pasdlgkhasdfasdf.

Lemony Snicket, *Horseradish: Bitter truths you can't avoid*

In Rett (2007, 2008) I proposed that evaluativity should be encoded in a degree modifier called EVAL, and that the distribution of EVAL should be modulated by a theory of semantic competition informed by markedness considerations. The foundation of this proposal was a new perspective on evaluativity that takes into account a broader range of data. Before I present those data, I will quickly review what evaluativity is and how we can tell whether it is part of a construction's meaning.

3.1 A wider distribution of evaluativity

A construction is evaluative iff it requires that a degree exceed some contextual standard. As discussed in §2.2.1, this means that evaluative constructions are context-sensitive. So far, we have considered only one evaluative adjectival construction: positive constructions, in contrast to MP constructions and comparatives. But the distribution of evaluativity is significantly wider, and systematically so.

3.1.1 The Bierwisch Test

Since positive constructions, as we've seen, are always evaluative, Bierwisch (1989) thus proposed that they be used to test evaluativity in other adjectival constructions. In particular, an adjectival construction is evaluative iff it entails its corresponding positive construction. I have referred to this as the "Bierwisch Test"; (1) uses it to confirm the previously reported intuition that MP constructions and comparatives are not evaluative.[1]

---

[1] Doetjes (2012) argues that some negative antonyms can be modified by MPs, and that these sentences are evaluative. (Her data are in Dutch, and are of attributive MPs; the English *She is 60 years young* is sufficient to illustrate her point, although she considers this predicative use distinct from the attributive one.) She concludes that whether or not a construction is evaluative is independent of whether or not it is MP-modified. I'll return to this point in Chapter 6.

(1) a. Doug is 5ft tall. ⇸ Doug is tall.
b. Doug is taller than Adam. ⇸ Doug/Adam is tall.
c. Doug is shorter than Adam. ⇸ Doug/Adam is short.

The MP construction in (1a) demonstrates that a gradable adjective modified by an MP isn't evaluative; the sentence *Doug is MP tall* can be true even when Doug does not count as tall in that context. Similarly, neither of the comparative constructions in (1b) and (1c)—which differ in the polarity of their antonyms—is evaluative. They describe Doug's and Adam's relative heights in a neutral way; (1b) can be uttered in a context in which neither counts as tall, and (1c) can be uttered in a context in which neither counts as short.

While it is a helpful indicator of evaluativity, the Bierwisch Test is not perfect. Because evaluativity is context-sensitive and contexts can vary across a given utterance, the Bierwisch Test is a little more slippery than it seems at first glance. In Rett (2008) I proposed a more explicit formulation of the Bierwisch Test that took this into account:

(2) **The Bierwisch Test for evaluativity**
A declarative sentence ϕ with subject x and adjective A is evaluative iff for every context c in which ϕ is true, the positive construction "x is A" is true.

As I will show, we will need to use a corrollary to test for evaluativity in questions.

In Lehrer's (1985) version of this test, an adjectival construction is evaluative if it is compatible with the speaker's denial of the corresponding positive construction, as in (3), or the additional assertion of the antonymic positive construction, as in (4).

(3) a. Doug is taller than Adam, but they're not tall.
b. Doug is shorter than Adam, but they're not short.

(4) a. Doug is taller than Adam, but they're both short.
b. Doug is shorter than Adam, but they're both tall.

This test, as well, predicts that the comparatives in (4) are not evaluative because they are both compatible with the speaker's denial of the corresponding positive constructions (that Adam and Doug are not tall, or that they are short).

A major shortcoming of both tests is that they fail to account for the truth-conditionality of evaluativity in positive constructions (as opposed to other constructions, as we'll see shortly). The result is that they incorrectly predict that negated positive constructions, like *John is not tall*, are not evaluative. As we saw in §2.2.2, negated positive constructions are negations of evaluative propositions, which means that negated positive constructions, too, require that the degree exceed a contextual standard.

There is an additional complication involving the context sensitivity of evaluativity, despite the fact that (2) requires holding fixed the context of evaluation. Barker (2002) argues that positive constructions can be used in a context to inform the hearer about the value of the contextual standard (a "metalinguistic" use of the positive construction), rather than to inform about the subject's height. To illustrate this point, Barker describes a context in which Feynman's height is clear, but an interlocutor is interested in knowing what counts as tall in the US. In such a context, the positive construction *Feynman is tall* carries information about "what the prevailing relevant standard for tallness happens to be in our community" (Barker 2002: 2).

If evaluativity can be used in context to *value* the evaluative standard, rather than to merely refer to it, there is reason to think that—at least in some cases—the utterance of an evaluative construction can change what it means to count as evaluative. In a recent experimental investigation of evaluativity (Brasoveanu and Rett 2014), Brasoveanu and I argue that this metalinguistic use of the positive construction can interfere with the Bierwisch Test for evaluativity, at least in discourse-initial contexts. So while the Bierwisch Test can be useful, because evaluativity is context-sensitive it is also important to supplement it by testing speakers' intuitions in particular contexts.

In the next section, I demonstrate that the distribution of evaluativity is wider than the POS theories predict.

3.1.2 *Evaluativity in equatives and degree questions*

As I pointed out in Rett (2007, 2008), certain equative constructions have long been considered evaluative (Lyons 1977; Cruse 1986; Bierwisch 1989, among others).

(5)   a. Doug is as tall as Adam. $\nrightarrow$ Doug/Adam is tall.
      b. Doug is as short as Adam. $\rightarrow$ Doug/Adam is short.

In particular, the positive- and negative-antonym equatives in (5) differ with respect to evaluativity. The positive-antonym equative in (5a) is not evaluative; like the comparative in (1b), it does not entail that Doug or Adam is tall. It can be felicitously uttered in a context in which Doug and Adam are both considered short; it can be felicitously uttered in, e.g., a context in which we are discussing the heights of students in a particular class in which Doug and Adam are the shortest two students.

In contrast, the negative-antonym equative in (5b) is evaluative; it entails that Doug and Adam are short. It is unacceptable in a context in which Doug and Adam are both considered tall, for instance, in a context in which the topic is the height of students in a particular class in which Doug and Adam are the tallest students.

These intuitions are confirmed by the denial test in (6).

(6)   a. Doug is as tall as Adam, but they're both short.
      b. Doug is as short as Adam, #but they're both tall.

The continuation in (6b) is decidedly odd.

As the denial test in (6) suggests, the status of the evaluativity in negative-antonym equatives is slightly different than the status of evaluativity in positive constructions.

As we have seen, evaluativity is truth-conditional in positive constructions. The result is that a denial of the positive construction results in contradiction. (*Adam is tall, #but he is not tall.*)

In contrast, the evaluativity in (5b) and (6b) seems to be encoded in a presupposition or some other not-at-issue content. Standard projection tests confirm this, although only for the internal argument (the *as* clause). In other words, the only evaluativity that projects out of negative-antonym equatives is the evaluativity of the standard (Adam, in this case).

(7)   a. If Doug is as short as Adam, he will not be able to go on the ride.
      b. It's not the case that Doug is as short as Adam.

Both sentences in (7) require that Adam be short (i.e., are only acceptable in contexts in which Adam is short); neither places any requirement on Doug's height.

Based on these projection tests, I will assume that the evaluativity component of negative-antonym equatives is actually associated with the internal argument (the object, or standard of the equative), and is transferred onto the external argument (the subject, or correlate of the equative) via the truth conditions of the equative. (If Adam is short, and Doug is at least as short as Adam, then it follows that Doug is short.) Ideally, an account of evaluativity will account for this asymmetry; as I explain in §3.3, the proposal in Rett (2008) could not.

This evaluativity contrast between antonyms occurs in at least one other construction: degree questions, or degree *wh*-questions. Since questions presuppose rather than assert their content, we will have to discuss their evaluativity in terms of presupposition as well.

(8)   a. How tall is Adam?
      b. How short is Adam?

The positive-polar degree question in (8a) can be uttered in any context regardless of Adam's height or regardless of the speaker's assumptions about Adam's height. In contrast, the negative-polar degree question in (8b) can only be felicitously uttered in contexts in which it is presupposed that Adam is short, or in which Adam's being short is part of the common ground.

There are at least two interesting empirical consequences of this fact. First, because (8b) is evaluative, it cannot be uttered in a neutral context or discourse-initially. Second, only the non-evaluative question can be uttered in a context in which the opposing positive construction has just been asserted, as (9) and (10) show.

(9)   A: John is short.
      B: Huh. How tall is he?

(10) A: John is tall.
      B: #Huh. How short is he?

While B's question in (9) might require a particular intonation pattern (Ljung 1974), (10) is markedly worse, regardless of the intonation pattern.[2]

Important for this test is the idea that because evaluative questions *presuppose* evaluativity, they are only unacceptable in contexts that don't support the intuition. (11) gives an instance of an evaluative degree question that is acceptable because its presupposition is satisfied in the context of utterance.

(11)   A: John is so short that he couldn't join the team.
         B: Well, how short is he?

The same evaluativity difference in quantity questions has led many to argue that the words *many, few, much* and *little* are adjectives, rather than quantifiers, as discussed in §2.1.4 (Bresnan 1973; Hoeksema 1983; Grosu and Landman 1998; Rett 2006, 2008; Solt 2009, 2010). The data above are reproduced here for quantity adjectives; they show that degree questions with *few* (but not *many*) are evaluative. (The same asymmetry holds for the antonym pair *much* and *little*.)

(12)   A: Leopards have few spots.
         B: Huh. How many spots do they have?

(13)   A: Leopards have many spots.
         B: #Huh. How few spots do they have?

(14)   A: Leonard has so few shoes he couldn't possibly participate in the shoe swap.
         B: Well, how few shoes does he own?

The evaluativity of negative-polar equatives is especially surprising in contrast to the lack of evaluativity in negative-polar comparatives in light of standard syntactic and semantic accounts of comparison contstructions. As discussed in §2.1, clausal comparatives are typically analyzed as involving two internal CP arguments, each with a null degree *wh*-operator (Bresnan 1973; von Stechow 1984: among others). (15) is repeated from example (36) in Chapter 2.

(15)   a. Doug is taller than Adam.
         b. $-er([\mathrm{OP}_{d'}$ Adam ~~is d'-tall~~])$([\mathrm{OP}_d$ Doug is d-tall])

Some, including von Stechow, have characterized this operator as a null *how*; in some dialects of English, the operator in the embedded clause can be an overt *what*. If this is right, negative-antonym comparatives would have an underlying form like (16).

(16)   a. Doug is shorter than Adam.
         b. $-er([how/what_{d'}$ Adam ~~is d'-short~~])$([\mathrm{OP}_d$ Doug is d-short])

---

[2] Based on the discussion in Bierwisch (1989), Sassoon (2011) argues that this pattern of evaluativity does not hold for all relative antonym pairs. In particular, she argues that both *heavy* and *light* are evaluative in degree questions. I will return to address this concern in §3.4.3.

From the perspective of (16), the lack of evaluativity in comparative constructions is even more striking, given that the degree question *How short is Adam?* is evaluative. This assumed structural parallel between *than*-clauses and degree questions has proven empirically and theoretically useful, but it does not bode well for an account of evaluativity in which its distribution is syntactically determined, at least at the clausal level.

And while adjectival constructions other than positive constructions must contain a negative antonym in order to be evaluative, the non-evaluativity of *Doug is shorter than Adam* also shows that the correlation does not go in the other direction: a negative antonym can occur without evaluativity. This—along with the evaluativity of positive-antonym positive constructions—suggests that it would be a mistake to encode evaluativity (only) as part of the lexical content of negative-polar antonyms (contra Bartsch and Vennemann 1972: 175).

There is also an antonymy asymmetry in the evaluativity of degree demonstratives (e.g., *that* and *yea*). Positive degree demonstratives are not evaluative, while negative degree demonstratives are. Imagine *A* and *B* are looking at Adam, so his exact height is salient.

(17) A: Adam's really short.
       B: Doug's (about) that tall too.
       B′: Doug's (about) that short too.

(18) A: Adam's really tall.
       B: Doug's (about) that tall too.
       B′: #Doug's (about) that short too.

I will close by mentioning that, to my knowledge, these generalizations about the distribution of evaluativity are cross-linguistically robust, modulo differences across languages in comparison and equative strategies, etc. (for discussion see Kennedy 2009), and modulo differences within types and classes of adjectives (see Bochnak forthcoming, as well as §3.4.3 and §5.4). I will argue that this point is key for choosing between a null operator and an implicature-based account of evaluativity.

3.1.3 *The consequences for POS*

Recall that POS, formulated in either a relational or measure-function semantics of gradable adjectives, was designed to introduce evaluativity into the semantics of positive constructions while binding the degree argument of the gradable adjective. In (19) and (20) I repeat the two variations and their semantics for the positive construction.

(19) **Relational approach**
       (Cresswell 1976; von Stechow 1984)   (from Chapter 2 (65b))
       a. $[\![POS]\!] = \lambda \mathcal{G} \in D_{\langle e, \langle d, t \rangle \rangle} \lambda x \exists d [\mathcal{G}(x, d) \wedge d > s]$
       b. $[\![Adam\ is\ POS\ tall]\!] = \exists d [tall(adam, d) \wedge d > s_{tall}]$

(20) **Measure function approach**

(Bartsch and Vennemann 1972; Kennedy 1999)   (from Chapter 2 (69b))

a. $[\![\text{POS}]\!] = \lambda g \in D_{\langle e,d \rangle} \lambda x.g(x) > s(g)$

b. $[\![\text{Adam is POS tall}]\!] = \text{tall}(\text{adam}) > s_{\text{tall}}$

Both accounts predict that the positive construction denotes a proposition; they differ in that (19) involves quantification over the degree argument, while (20) involves restriction of the degree that results from combining the adjective with its subject argument.

The problem posed by the evaluativity of negative-antonym equatives and degree questions is this: an evaluativity operator that manipulates the degree value/output of a gradable adjective does not leave that argument available for manipulation by a higher degree operator. And we have every reason to believe that the equative morpheme and degree *wh*-words like *how* are degree operators.

In §2.1 I defined the equative morpheme, based closely on previous work on the comparative, as follows (from (39) and (40)):

(21) a. $[\![\text{as}]\!] = \lambda D' \lambda D.\text{Max}(D) \geq \text{Max}(D')$

b. $[\![\text{Doug is as tall as Adam}]\!]$
$= \text{Max}(\lambda d.\text{tall}(\text{doug}, d)) \geq \text{Max}(\lambda d'.\text{tall}(\text{adam}, d'))$

The equative morpheme denotes a degree quantifier, or a relation between sets of degrees corresponding to (in this case) the degrees to which the external argument *Doug* is tall and the degrees to which the internal argument *Adam* is tall. Such an account leaves no room for the introduction of POS, as demonstrated in (22) and (23) for the relational account. (In Test 2 I test just for the internal argument, but the problems remain if we introduce POS in the higher clause.)

(22) **POS Test 1:**

$\text{POS}(as([_{CP}\text{OP}_d \text{ Doug is } d\text{-short}])([_{CP}\text{OP}_{d'} \text{ Adam is } d'\text{-short}]))$

type mismatch: the domain of POS is a gradable adjective; the equative denotes a proposition

(23) **POS Test 2:**

$as([_{CP}\text{OP}_d \text{ Doug is } d\text{-short}])([_{CP}\text{OP}_{d'} \text{ Adam is POS } d'\text{-short}])$

a. $[\![\text{Adam is POS } d'\text{-short}]\!] = \exists d[\text{short}(\text{adam}, d) \wedge d > s_{short}]$

b. $[\![\text{OP}_{d'}(\text{Adam is POS } d'\text{-short})]\!]$ = type mismatch: the domain of the *wh*-operator is a proposition with an open degree variable; its argument contains only a bound degree variable

Because the Bartsch/Vennemann/Kennedy measure function approach to POS also predicts that an application of POS prohibits further binding of a clause's degree argument because it values rather than binds the relevant degree argument their account runs into the same problems.

These predictions of incompatibility between POS and the equative morpheme aren't the result of some trivial type mismatches, potentially fixable with standard, valency-manipulating type-shifters like Currying. They reflect a semantics in which two different operators target the same degree argument. Since POS was introduced to account for the contrast in evaluativity between the positive construction and the comparative or MP construction, this clash is by design. It is the inevitable consequence of any theory of evaluativity which employs a single mechanism to address the extra argument problem and the evaluativity problem.

It might seem tempting to address this problem with POS by loosening the semantic connection between the comparative and equative constructions. If the comparative is more dissimilar semantically to the equative than we had thought, perhaps we can correctly predict the contrast in evaluativity between the two constructions. This is an unappealing solution for several reasons.

First, the comparative and equative just are quite similar, syntactically and semantically, across languages (for typological surveys of the equative, see Haspelmath and Buchholz 1998; Henkelmann 2006), which makes a similar account of the two constructions particularly appealing. Second, the tight syntactic and semantic connection between comparatives and equatives is arguably what allows them to be plausible scalemates for the purposes of implicature calculation, which is crucial for accounting for the semantic properties of equatives. In other words, if the comparative and the equative were substantially different morphologically, we might not expect them to be members of the same Horn scale. (I'll be much more explicit about this in §5.1.1.) And, finally, such an account would not be clearly extendable to other types of comparison constructions that do seem to be evaluative. Some examples of evaluative comparatives are in (24); I return to address these constructions in §5.4 and Chapter 6.

(24) a. The glass is more dirty than the cup.   *absolute comparatives*
      b. Adam is more tall than Doug.   *periphrastic comparatives*
      c. Adam is taller than Doug is short.   *comparisons of deviation*

These comparatives, which have been reported to be evaluative, suggest that we need to divorce the evaluativity component from whatever semantic effect has been tying it exclusively to the positive construction. This is the motivation for EVAL, a null morpheme that encodes evaluativity into a degree modifier that has no effect on type, and therefore has a wide distribution across degree constructions. But such a proposal in isolation also leads to the wrong predictions: it could incorrectly predict that comparatives are evaluative, or fail to predict the asymmetry in evaluativity between antonyms. An account of evaluativity must therefore be supplemented with an account of its distribution outside of the positive construction and the comparative. This is the subject of the next section.

3.2 EVAL and markedness-based competition

3.2.1 *Evaluativity and degree modification*

In the context of the equative and degree question data above, I characterized the approach to evaluativity as follows (Rett 2008: 81): "Instead of asking where evaluativity occurs, the present approach essentially rephrases the question: where *can't* evaluativity occur?" While the distribution of evaluativity is wider than others have assumed, the class of evaluative constructions is not, prima facie, a natural one, as Table 3.1 shows.

Table 3.1 summarizes results for relative adjectives only; I will address other adjective classes in §5.4, and I will address variation within the class of relative adjectives in §3.4.3.[3]

The first move is to divorce the type-shifting component of POS from the evaluativity component in a way that predicts that the distribution of evaluativity is relatively wide. This suggests that evaluativity should be encoded in a function or operator that maps a function to one of the same type, so that the null morpheme doesn't have an effect on semantic type. I called this modifier "EVAL."

(25) $[\![EVAL]\!] = \lambda D\lambda d.D(d) \wedge d > s$

EVAL is a degree modifier; it denotes a relation between sets of degrees D, type $\langle d, t \rangle$. (26) provides a compositional semantic derivation of a positive construction given EVAL.

TABLE 3.1.   The distribution of evaluativity

	EVALUATIVE?	
construction	positive antonym	negative antonym
positive constructions	yes	yes
MP constructions	no	*n/a*
comparatives	no	no
equatives	no	yes
degree questions	no	yes
degree demonstratives	no	yes

---

[3] In Rett (2008), I characterized excessives (e.g., *too tall to join*) and *enough*-constructions (e.g., *tall enough to join*) as non-evaluative, based on the assumption that the standard introduced by overt material in these constructions (how tall someone needs to be to join) need not correspond to the salient contextual standard. The reported intuition is that a sentence like *Adam is too short to join* can felicitously be uttered in a scenario in which John is considered tall. I now think that it is hard to come up with a context in which the salient contextual standard is distinct from the explicit one, so I will just say that these constructions, if evaluative, are evaluative because their truth-conditional meaning entails evaluativity.

(26) EVAL Adam is tall.
   a. $[\![\text{tall}]\!] = \lambda x \lambda d.\text{tall}(x, d)$
   b. $[\![\text{tall}(\text{Adam})]\!] = \lambda d.\text{tall}(\text{adam}, d)$
   c. $[\![\text{EVAL}(\text{tall}(\text{Adam}))]\!] = \lambda d.\text{tall}(\text{adam}, d) \wedge d > s_{\text{tall}}$
   d. $\rightarrow \exists d[\text{tall}(\text{adam}, d) \wedge d > s_{\text{tall}}]$

Because EVAL is a degree modifier, it does not address the extra argument problem, only the evaluativity problem. The open degree argument can be bound at the end of the clause, as illustrated in (26d), via existential closure (Kamp 1981; Heim 1982; Diesing 1992). This approach correctly predicts that a positive construction like (26) denotes a proposition that is true iff there is a degree to which Adam is tall which exceeds the salient contextual standard.

There are two important consequences of this characterization of a null evaluativity morpheme. First, characterizing its domain as a set of degrees, rather than a type corresponding to a gradable adjective, allows for significantly more flexibility in terms of the syntactic object EVAL modifies. As pointed out in Rett (2008), this formulation of EVAL correctly predicts that verbs can have evaluative meanings; it also correctly predicts that verbs are only optionally evaluative. (See §2.3 for discussion.) This seems like a clear improvement over theories that postulate a distinct verbal POS and a non-evaluative null counterpart to POS (Piñón 2005; Kennedy and Levin 2008).

The second consequence is more substantial: encoding evaluativity in a degree modifier suggests that its distribution is significantly wider than we have evidence to support. In the absence of additional theory, (25) predicts that evaluativity is an optional property of any adjectival construction, similar to an adverbial. In contrast we have evidence that it is a necessary property of only a few adjectival constructions, and that its distribution is closely tied to adjectival polarity and the type of adjectival construction. The next section presents a supplement to this theory of evaluativity in adjectival constructions generally based on considerations of markedness and semantic competition.

But I'll first provide an account of EVAL in positive constructions. If EVAL is an optional modifier, then (26) represents one of two semantic interpretations available to positive constructions in this account. (27) represents the second.

(27) Adam is tall. (without EVAL)
   a. $[\![\text{tall}]\!] = \lambda x \lambda d.\text{tall}(x, d)$
   b. $[\![\text{tall}(\text{Adam})]\!] = \lambda d.\text{tall}(\text{adam}, d)$
   c. $\rightarrow \exists d[\text{tall}(\text{adam}, d)]$

This predicts that the positive construction is true iff there is a degree to which Adam is tall. These truth conditions, which reflect another application of existential closure, can be translated as "There is a degree to which Adam is tall."

Importantly, the truth conditions without EVAL assert what they presuppose, given the positive extension presupposition introduced in Chapter 2 and the corresponding characterization of gradable adjectives as partial functions from individuals that exhibit that dimension of measurement. In Rett (2008), this non-evaluative interpretation of positive constructions is characterized as in-principle available but not realized in contexts in which it is uninformative.

In her adaptation of Rett (2008), Bogal-Allbritten (2010) characterizes this component of the theory in terms of what she describes as a neo-Gricean principle, AVOID UNINFORMATIVITY (Stalnaker 1978):

(28)   AVOID UNINFORMATIVITY: Avoid a derivation producing an expression with trivial content or content that can be presumed from general knowledge.

The idea that implicatures are at work in describing the distribution of evaluativity will be explored much more deeply in Chapter 5.

We saw that negated positive constructions are always evaluative; the negation targets an evaluative claim (denying that Adam is tall or short) rather than a non-evaluative claim (denying that Adam has a height). The evaluativity of negated positive constructions, illustrated below for the positive-polar antonym, can be explained along the same lines; the two semantic interpretations are in principle available, but the one without EVAL results in a contradictory sentence (one that denies what it presupposes).

(29)   It is not the case that Adam is tall.
    a. $\neg\exists d[\text{tall}(\text{adam}, d) \land d > s_{\text{tall}}]$ (with EVAL)
    b. $\neg\exists d[\text{tall}(\text{adam}, d)]$ (without EVAL)

This prediction about the truth conditions of (29) requires only the assumption that existential closure is computed under negation, a common assumption (especially in neo-Davidsonian event semantics; Heim 1982; Diesing 1992; Chung and Ladusaw 2004).

3.2.2 Antonymy and markedness

In this section, I'll present the proposal that the distribution of EVAL outside of the positive construction is restricted by considerations of markedness.

Recall from §2.1 that antonyms like *tall* and *short* are associated with the same dimension but with reverse orderings. Among other things, this accounts for entailment patterns like (30) (from (14) in Chapter 2).

(30)   Doug is taller than Adam. $\longleftrightarrow$ Adam is shorter than Doug.

The point made in Rett (2007, 2008), and maintained throughout the rest of this book, is that positive and negative antonyms are not merely mirror images of each other; negative antonyms are the negation of positive antonyms, and are as a result marked relative to their positive counterparts. (Sassoon 2010a characterizes negative antonyms as *transformed* or *reversed* linear mapping functions.) As Lyons (1977: 275) observes, "We tend to say that small things lack size, that what is required is less height, and so on, rather than that large things lack smallness and that what is required is more lowness."

That negative adjectives are negated (and thereby marked) versions of their positive antonyms is morphologically realized on many antonym pairs, as shown in (31).

(31)   a. possible / impossible
       b. responsible / irresponsible
       c. kind / unkind

Cruse (1986: 173) observes that this difference in markedness has clear linguistic consequences: "*long* is unmarked with respect to *short* because it occurs in a variety of expressions from which *short* is excluded." For instance, positive antonyms, but not negative ones, can form nominals (Waugh 1982).

(32)   a. length / *shorth
       b. height / *lowt(h)
       c. width / *narrowth

Lehrer (1985) offers an extensive list of other distributional and semantic differences.

A difference in markedness also predicts that negative antonyms are learned later than positive ones (Clark and Clark 1977), that they are more complex in processing terms, and that, if a language has only one member of antonym pairs, it will be the positive member.

Croft and Cruse (2004) also point out that the factor modifiers *twice* and *half* affect different antonyms differently. The two sentences in (33) have distinct meanings: (33a) is true iff Adam is shorter than Doug, while (33b) is true iff Adam is taller than Doug.

(33)   a. Adam is half as tall as Doug.
       b. Adam is twice as tall as Doug.

In contrast, the two sentences in (34) seem synonymous: they both describe Adam as shorter than Doug. (The acceptability of these modifiers with negative antonyms is subject to dialectical variation; for example, Lehrer 1985 talks about the relative markedness of negative antonyms by stating that sentences like (34) are ungrammatical.)

(34)   a. Adam is half as short as Doug.
       b. Adam is twice as short as Doug.

The difference between (33) and (34) seems potentially related to the difference in evaluativity between positive-antonym and negative-antonym equatives (see Sassoon 2012 for related discussion).

There is another apparent semantic difference between antonyms that is arguably related to their difference in markedness. Rullmann (1995), Kennedy (2001), and Heim (2007) argue that negative-polar antonyms involve implicit negation because they exhibit ambiguity in some sentences where their positive-polar counterparts do not. The difference is illustrated in (35) and (36) (see also Beck 2012; Rett 2012).

(35)   The helicopter was flying lower than a plane can fly.
  a. **min reading:** The helicopter was lower than the minimum a plane can fly.
  b. **max reading:** The helicopter was lower than the maximum a plane can fly.

(36)   The helicopter was flying higher than a plane can fly.
  a. **#min reading:** The helicopter was higher than the minimum a plane can fly.
  b. **max reading:** The helicopter was higher than the maximum a plane can fly.

While the *than*-clause in the negative-antonym comparative can be associated with either its upper or lower bound, the *than*-clause in the positive-antonym comparative can only be associated with its upper bound. Rullmann and Heim argue that this difference is predicted as a scope ambiguity in a theory in which negative-polar adjectives are semantically composed of a positive-polar meaning and negation or some other scopable negative operator. While this is not a necessary assumption for what follows, it is a compelling one.

3.2.3 *Markedness and semantic competition*

The characterization of negative adjectives as marked relative to their positive antonyms is the key to explaining the distribution of evaluativity in adjectival constructions. (So much so that Lehrer's 1985 term for an evaluative use of an adjective was its "marked sense.") The theory governing the distribution of EVAL presented in Rett (2007, 2008) is as follows: EVAL can optionally occur in any adjectival construction, but it occurs obligatorily in constructions with marked (negative) antonyms whenever an unmarked (positive) antonym could have been used. This "could have been used" notion is termed "polar variance" in Rett (2008). Effectively, it amounts to the claim that those adjectival constructions that are evaluative only with negative antonyms are those for which the positive-polar and negative-polar versions are mutually entailing.

Rett (2008) invokes a principle of markedness-related competition:

A theory of markedness suggests that when two forms differ only in χ, then the form with the least marked value of χ ([$-\chi$], say, rather than [$+\chi$]) is less marked overall. If these two meanings are synonymous, it seems reasonable to conclude that the marked meaning will be blocked by its unmarked counterpart. (pp. 97–8)

Bogal-Allbritten (2010) recasts this principle, too, in terms of a constraint "AVOID SYNONYMY":

(37) AVOID SYNONYMY: Avoid a derivation producing an expression that has the same truth conditions as a competing derivation containing a less marked adjective.

So while the formulation of EVAL in (25) predicts that all adjectival constructions are in principle ambiguous between an evaluative and a non-evaluative interpretation, this optionality is suspended by a general prohibition against marked forms in adjectival constructions that could have been formed with the positive, unmarked antonym.

This is the difference between comparative and equative constructions: the comparative, according to Rett (2008), is polar-variant, which means that the polarity of the antonym that forms the comparative always affects the truth conditions. In contrast, the equative is polar-invariant: the polarity of the adjective doesn't affect the truth conditions.

This difference in polar (in)variance is illustrated by the contrast in (38), assuming that the equative is uttered in a context which supports its being strengthened to an "exactly" interpretation:

(38)   a. Adam is as short as Doug. $\rightarrow$ Adam is as tall as Doug.
       b. Adam is shorter than Doug. $\nrightarrow$ Adam is taller than Doug.

Essentially, there is an entailment relationship between an equative with a negative-polar antonym and its positive-antonym counterpart. This asymmetrical entailment pattern reduces to their difference in evaluativity: if the negative-polar antonym didn't additionally require that Adam and Doug be short, then the two constructions would be mutually entailing.

In contrast, there is no entailment relationship between the sentences in (38b). This difference between the comparative and equative constructions is a direct result of their relative strength and weakness: the comparative is strict, while the equative is non-strict, so the truth conditions of the two sentences in (38a) overlap.

In a neutral context, the equative is strengthened to a punctual, "exactly" interpretation. In these contexts, the meaning of the equative is supplemented with a scalar implicature, as in (39a), resulting in truth conditions like (39b).

(39)   Adam is as tall as Doug.
       a. $\text{MAX}(\lambda d.\text{tall}(\text{adam}, d)) \geq \text{MAX}(\lambda d'.\text{tall}(\text{doug}, d'))$
          $\wedge \neg\text{MAX}(\lambda d.\text{tall}(\text{adam}, d)) > \text{MAX}(\lambda d'.\text{tall}(\text{doug}, d'))$
       b. $\rightarrow \text{MAX}(\lambda d.\text{tall}(\text{adam}, d)) = \text{MAX}(\lambda d'.\text{tall}(\text{doug}, d'))$

In a context in which the scalar implicature associated with the equative is not cancelled, then, the EVAL account predicts that the two equatives below are in principle associated with at least two possible semantic interpretations.[4]

---

[4] I will return in §3.3 to discuss the other two, one with EVAL in the external, correlate clause (associated with Adam) and the other with EVAL in both clauses.

(40) Adam is as tall as Doug.
   a. $\text{Max}(\lambda d.\text{tall}(\text{adam}, d)) = \text{Max}(\lambda d'.\text{tall}(\text{doug}, d') \wedge d' > s_{\text{tall}})$

(with EVAL)

   b. $\text{Max}(\lambda d.\text{tall}(\text{adam}, d)) = \text{Max}(\lambda d'.\text{tall}(\text{doug}, d'))$

(without EVAL)

(41) Adam is as short as Doug.
   a. $\text{Max}(\lambda d.\text{short}(\text{adam}, d)) = \text{Max}(\lambda d'.\text{short}(\text{doug}, d') \wedge d' > s_{\text{short}})$

(with EVAL)

   b. $\text{Max}(\lambda d.\text{short}(\text{adam}, d)) = \text{Max}(\lambda d'.\text{short}(\text{doug}, d'))$ (without EVAL)

According to (40), positive-antonym equatives can receive either an evaluative or a non-evaluative interpretation. This predicts they are effectively ambiguous between a strong (evaluative) and a weak (non-evaluative) interpretation. This is completely consistent with the observed data, reported in §3.1.2, that positive-antonym equatives are non-evaluative, i.e., that they do not require or entail an evaluative interpretation. Because EVAL is null, the interpretation of a positive-antonym equative can never be reliably disambiguated, so we predict that the strong, evaluative reading will never be the only reading available.

However, as we've seen, the non-evaluative interpretation of negative-antonym equatives (41b) is not available. And this is where the principle of markedness-related competition comes in. Notice that the two non-evaluative interpretations, (40b) and (41b), are synonymous, or mutually entailing. If Adam's maximum degree of tallness (i.e., his height) is exactly the same as Doug's, then Adam's maximum degree of shortness (also his height) is necessarily the same as Doug's. This is illustrated in (42) in a context in which Doug's height is 6ft.

(42) a. $\text{Max}(\{d : \text{Doug is } d\text{-tall}\}) = \text{Max}(\ (0{,}6\text{ft}]\ ) = 6\text{ft}$
   b. $\text{Max}(\{d : \text{Doug is } d\text{-short}\}) = \text{Max}(\ [6\text{ft}, \infty]\ ) = 6\text{ft}$

The switch from POS to EVAL, coupled with a notion of markedness-based semantic competition, thus predicts that the marked (i.e., negative-antonym) non-evaluative equative will be blocked by its unmarked counterpart when the equative receives an "exactly" interpretation. (In the next section I'll discuss the predictions of this account for contexts in which the equative is not strengthened to its "exactly" interpretation.)

The maximality operator used to define the comparative and equative morphemes in §2.1 is characterized as a definite, i.e., a partial function that is undefined in a context in which there are no degrees satisfying the description.

(43) $\text{Max}(D) = \iota d[d \in D \wedge \forall d' \in D[d' \neq d \to d' < d]]$ (from Chapter 2 (37))

This correctly predicts that the evaluative equatives in (40a) and (40b) will be undefined in a context in which Doug is not tall or short in an evaluative sense, which is consistent with the intuition that evaluativity in equative constructions is encoded in a presupposition or not-at-issue content.

Because the comparative morpheme encodes a strict linear ordering, it forbids overlap between its two arguments, so semantic equivalences like the one between (40b) and (41b) are not possible for comparative constructions. The EVAL account predicts that the two comparatives below are associated with at least two possible semantic interpretations.

(44)　Adam is taller than Doug.

　　a. $\text{Max}(\lambda d.\text{tall}(\text{adam}, d)) > \text{Max}(\lambda d'.\text{tall}(\text{doug}, d') \wedge d' > s_{\text{tall}})$

　　　　　　　　　　　　　　　　　　　　　　　　　　　　(with EVAL)

　　b. $\text{Max}(\lambda d.\text{tall}(\text{adam}, d)) > \text{Max}(\lambda d'.\text{tall}(\text{doug}, d'))$　　(without EVAL)

(45)　Adam is shorter than Doug.

　　a. $\text{Max}(\lambda d.\text{short}(\text{adam}, d)) > \text{Max}(\lambda d'.\text{short}(\text{doug}, d') \wedge d' > s_{\text{short}})$

　　　　　　　　　　　　　　　　　　　　　　　　　　　　(with EVAL)

　　b. $\text{Max}(\lambda d.\text{short}(\text{adam}, d)) > \text{Max}(\lambda d'.\text{short}(\text{doug}, d'))$　　(without EVAL)

The two non-evaluative interpretations in (44b) and (45b), as demonstrated in (38b), are not synonymous (in fact, they entail each other's negation). They therefore do not qualify as competitors for a given meaning, and their contrast in markedness is consequently irrelevant. As a result, both the evaluative and non-evaluative interpretations of these antonymic comparative constructions are licensed and available in principle to the hearer. As with the positive-antonym equative in (40), this means that they are ambiguous between a non-evaluative and an evaluative interpretation, which means they are effectively non-evaluative.

Importantly, the principle of markedness-based competition invoked here operates at a relatively high syntactic level. If the relevant level for a markedness-based competition were the lexical (adjectival) level, we would erroneously predict that the unmarked, positive antonym would always beat out the marked, negative antonym.

Recall that evaluativity in degree quantifier constructions like the equative seems to be encoded in a presupposition, and also seems to be asymmetrically associated with the internal argument. This evidence comes from projection data, repeated in (46) (from (7a)).

(46)　If Doug is as short as Adam, he will not be able to go on the ride.

　　presupposes Adam is short.

　　does not presuppose Doug is short.

This asymmetry was reflected (but not accounted for) in (40) and (41), where EVAL is associated with the internal argument (but not the matrix clause). That the content is presuppositional comes from the fact that EVAL is embedded under the equative morpheme, and from the assumption that the maximality operator is undefined over empty sets. But the account above does nothing to explain why EVAL isn't (ever) associated with the matrix clause of an equative construction. In addition to the two interpretations discussed in (40) and (41), the EVAL account predicts two other potential semantic interpretations of the equative.

(47)   Adam is as tall as Doug.
   a. $\text{MAX}(\lambda d.\text{tall}(\text{adam}, d) \wedge d > s_{\text{tall}}) = \text{MAX}(\lambda d'.\text{tall}(\text{doug}, d'))$

                                                      (main clause EVAL)
   b. $\text{MAX}(\lambda d.\text{tall}(\text{adam}, d) \wedge d > s_{\text{tall}}) = \text{MAX}(\lambda d'.\text{tall}(\text{doug}, d') \wedge d > s_{\text{tall}})$

                                                                (2 EVALs)

(48)   Adam is as short as Doug.
   a. $\text{MAX}(\lambda d.\text{short}(\text{adam}, d) \wedge d > s_{\text{short}}) = \text{MAX}(\lambda d'.\text{short}(\text{doug}, d'))$

                                                      (main clause EVAL)
   b. $\text{MAX}(\lambda d.\text{short}(\text{adam}, d) \wedge d > s_{\text{short}}) = \text{MAX}(\lambda d'.\text{short}(\text{doug}, d')$
      $\wedge d > s_{\text{short}})$ (2 EVALs)

While these positive- and negative-polar interpretations are not in competition with each other—by virtue of the fact that they are evaluative, and thus invoke distinct standards—they do pose a slight complication for the EVAL account as presented above. The story was that for negative-antonym equatives, the non-evaluative interpretation is blocked by their positive-antonym counterparts. This leaves available three other predicted interpretations: one with EVAL in the main clause, one with EVAL in the subordinate *as*-clause, and one with EVAL in each clause. Yet it seems from projection tests that only the subordinate-clause interpretation is available.

   To attempt to explain the asymmetry illustrated in (46), I proposed in Rett (2008) that the semantic competition resulting in the suppression of non-evaluative readings of negative-antonym equatives didn't take place at the sentential level, but instead at some more local clausal level. This proposal was admittedly quite stipulative, and I do not intend to endorse it in what follows. But it is worth presenting here to highlight how challenging this internal-argument asymmetry is for a theory of evaluativity.

   The fact, demonstrated in (46), that evaluativity only seems to be a property of the embedded clauses of equatives suggests that the markedness competition that leads to evaluativity in this approach should be localized to that clause. To control the syntactic level at which the markedness competition applies, I recast polar (in)variance as a property of degree quantifiers (as opposed to propositions, as the comparison in (40) and (41) suggests). The corrollary of (in)variance at the degree quantifier level is called "(non-)directionality".

   It defines "(non-)directionality" in terms of generalized entailment between two generalized degree quantifiers.

(49)   For any $Q \in D_{\langle\langle d,t\rangle,\langle\langle d,t\rangle,t\rangle\rangle}$, Q is non-directional iff for any $D, D' \in D_{\langle d,t\rangle}$ such that $\text{MAX}(D) = \text{MAX}(D') \wedge D \cap D' = \{\text{MAX}(D)\}$, $Q(D) \Rightarrow Q(D')$; otherwise, Q is directional.

(50) Generalized entailment $=_{def} \forall f, g \in D_{\langle \sigma, t \rangle} : f \Rightarrow g$ iff $\forall x \in D_\sigma, f(x) \rightarrow g(x)$

According to (49), a degree quantifier construction is non-directional iff the maximum value of its internal argument equals the maximum value of the internal argument of its antonymic counterpart, and that is their only point of overlap. According to this, the "exactly" interpretation of the equative morpheme denotes a degree quantifier that is non-directional, while the comparative is directional. The theory stipulates that markedness considerations only come into play for non-directional degree quantifiers, and so as a result only sentences with negative antonyms and non-directional degree quantifiers are evaluative.

This variation of the EVAL account is summarized in (51).

(51) A sentence S with a degree quantifier Q and adjective A is **evaluative** iff:
   a. Q is non-directional; and
   b. A is marked relative to its antonym.

The definition in (49) extends appropriately to degree questions if we assume that degree *wh*-phrases like *how* denote generalized degree quantifiers (Karttunen 1977). The EVAL theory predicts that each of the questions in (52) and (53) will be associated with two semantic interpretations.

(52) How tall is Adam?
   a. $\lambda p \exists d[p(w^@) \wedge p = \lambda w.\text{tall}(w)(\text{adam}, d) \wedge d > s_{\text{tall}}]$ (with EVAL)
   b. $\lambda p \exists d[p(w^@) \wedge p = \lambda w.\text{tall}(w)(\text{adam}, d)]$ (without EVAL)

(53) How short is Adam?
   a. $\lambda p \exists d[p(w^@) \wedge p = \lambda w.\text{short}(w)(\text{adam}, d) \wedge d > s_{\text{short}}]$ (with EVAL)
   b. $\lambda p \exists d[p(w^@) \wedge p = \lambda w.\text{short}(w)(\text{adam}, d)]$ (without EVAL)

As before, the two non-evaluative interpretations in (52b) and (53b) are mutually entailing. In a world in which Adam's height is 6ft, the set of propositions denoted by the positive-antonym question is (54a), and the set of propositions denoted by the negative-antonym question is (54b).

(54) a. $\{p = \lambda w.\text{tall}(w)(\text{adam},1\text{ft}), p = \lambda w.\text{tall}(w)(\text{adam},2\text{ft}),$
   $..., p = \lambda w.\text{tall}(w)(\text{adam},6\text{ft})\}$
   b. $\{p = \lambda w.\text{short}(w)(\text{adam},6\text{ft}), p = \lambda w.\text{short}(w)(\text{adam},7\text{ft}),$
   $..., p = \lambda w.\text{short}(w)(\text{adam}, \infty)\}$

While these are distinct sets of propositions, they are equally informative, insofar as the fact that 6ft is the maximum degree in one entails that 6ft is the maximum degree in the other, and vice versa (Beck and Rullmann 1999). Given our assumptions about markedness-based semantic competition, we can predict that the non-evaluative interpretation of negative-antonym degree questions (e.g. (53b)) is unavailable.

This addresses the difference in evaluativity between comparatives and equatives, and the evaluativity of degree questions; I will end this section by discussing the treatment of MP constructions in the EVAL account.

In Rett (2007, 2008) I treated MPs as degree names, denoting objects of type d. Given this assumption, the only way an MP can combine with EVAL is as follows:

(55)   Doug is 6ft tall.   (with EVAL)
    a. $[\![\text{tall}]\!] = \lambda x \lambda d.\text{tall}(x, d)$
    b. $[\![\text{tall}(\text{Doug})]\!] = \lambda d.\text{tall}(\text{doug}, d)$
    c. $[\![\text{EVAL}(\text{tall}(\text{Doug}))]\!] = \lambda d.\text{tall}(\text{doug}, d) \wedge d > s_{\text{tall}}$
    d. $[\![6(\text{EVAL}(\text{tall}(\text{Doug})))]\!] = \text{tall}(\text{doug}, 6\text{ft}) \wedge 6\text{ft} > s_{\text{tall}}$

This means MP constructions, like the comparative, are optionally evaluative. Rett (2008: 108) says:

MP constructions are therefore not evaluative for the same reasons a comparative construction is not evaluative: it has the potential to receive an evaluative interpretation, but the hearer will presumably not assign it one unless he has reason to do so (to think that Adam is 6ft tall and that 6ft is significantly tall).

However, as discussed in Chapter 2, there's reason to think that the semantics of MPs is more complicated. The characterization of MPs as generalized degree quantifiers, type $\langle \langle d, t \rangle, t \rangle$ (repeated in (56)), leaves open the possibility of this "evaluative" interpretation, as in (57) (in addition to one without EVAL):

(56) $[\![6\text{ft}]\!] = \lambda D \in D_{\langle d, t \rangle}.6\text{ft}(D)$

(57)   Doug is 6 ft tall.   (with EVAL)
    a. $[\![\text{tall}]\!] = \lambda x \lambda d.\text{tall}(x, d)$
    b. $[\![\text{tall}(\text{Doug})]\!] = \lambda d.\text{tall}(\text{doug}, d)$
    c. $[\![\text{EVAL}(\text{tall}(\text{Doug}))]\!] = \lambda d.\text{tall}(\text{doug}, d) \wedge d > s_{\text{tall}}$
    d. $[\![6\text{ft}(\text{tall}(\text{Doug}))]\!] = 6\text{ft}(\lambda d.\text{tall}(\text{doug}, d) \wedge d > s_{\text{tall}})$

The truth conditions in (57d) can be read as, "the set of degrees to which Doug is tall that exceed the contextual standard measures 6ft," or "the space between Doug's height and the contextual 'tall' standard measures 6ft." These are the right truth conditions for the sentence *Doug is 6ft taller than average*, but not for the MP construction in (57) (under any reading). Clearly, the prediction in (57d) is incorrect. There is, however, nothing immediately obvious in the EVAL account to prevent it.

3.3 Discussion

The EVAL account improves on the traditional POS in a number of ways. Because it treats evaluativity as a property independent of whether an adjective's degree argument is overtly manipulated (by MPs or by degree quantifiers), it predicts that evaluativity can exist outside of the positive construction. And because it incorporates assumptions about the relative markedness of negative-polar adjectives, along with a notion of markedness-based semantic competition, it can account for the fact that there is a polarity asymmetry in the evaluativity of only a strict subset of adjectival constructions.

Rett (2008) also includes discussion of several extensions of the account: to the verbal domain, where EVAL correctly predicts the optional evaluativity evident in degree achievements; to other adjective classes (e.g., absolute adjectives), where the pattern of evaluativity is more widespread across adjectival constructions; and to cross-linguistically robust differences in evaluativity between analytic and synthetic comparatives, as illustrated in (58).

(58) a. Adam is shorter than Doug. $\nrightarrow$ Adam/Doug is short.
      b. Adam is more short than Doug. $\rightarrow$ Adam/Doug is short.

The account proposed in Chapter 5 preserves some important aspects of the EVAL approach and consequently makes roughly the same predictions with respect to these extensions, so I will put off discussing them until Chapter 6.

But it should be clear that there are some problems with the EVAL account. The previous section highlighted two: first, in order to account for the internal argument asymmetry—the fact that negative-antonym equatives presuppose that the internal argument (but not the external argument) is evaluative—the account switched from an intuitive, propositional-level semantic competition to a more stipulative competition at the level of the internal argument of a degree quantifier. This would place syntactic restrictions on what is intuitively a pragmatic process, with no explanation of the interplay between the syntactic, semantic, and pragmatic levels.

And second, the tension between independently motivated semantic treatments of MPs and the semantic predictions of EVAL, as illustrated in (57). It seems hard to maintain both a type-flexible characterization of MPs and to explain why MP constructions can't receive an interpretation in which they measure the size of a set of evaluative degrees (degrees of deviation from a salient standard).

Furthermore, the explanation of evaluativity in the equative—that the non-evaluative interpretation of an equative with a marked antonym is synonymous with the non-evaluative interpretation of its unmarked counterpart—takes for granted that the equative is strengthened, receiving an "exactly" interpretation. But the evaluativity of negative-antonym equatives seems to persist even when the relevant scalar implicature is cancelled, as (59) shows. Even more worrisome is that it persists even when the equative is overtly modified by *at least* (as well as when it is modified by *exactly*), (60).

(59) Adam is as short as Doug, in fact he's shorter. $\rightarrow$ Adam/Doug is short.

(60)   a. Adam is at least as short as Doug. $\rightarrow$ Adam/Doug is short.
        b. Adam is exactly as short as Doug. $\rightarrow$ Adam/Doug is short.

There really seems to be no way of accounting for the evaluativity of these constructions while maintaining the intuitive notion of markedness-based semantic competition the account relies on. In Rett (2008) I discuss several possible solutions, none of which is particularly satisfying.

The EVAL theory can predict that evaluativity in equatives is a presupposition because EVAL can modify a degree argument (in the *as*-clause, for instance) before that clause combines with the equative morpheme, and is thus embedded under a MAX operator. As a result, the EVAL theory correctly predicts a contrast in truth-conditionality between positive constructions and evaluative equatives.

But it also predicts (or seems to predict) that the blocking of the non-evaluative interpretations of negative-antonym equatives is part of some extra-linguistic markedness competition, conducted after the truth conditions of the equative's possible LFs have been calculated. If this is right, depending on the details of this markedness competition, we might predict that the evaluativity of negative-antonym equatives could not have truth-conditional import. But evidence from equative modifiers (from Croft and Cruse 2004, repeated from (33) and (34)) suggests that this might be an incorrect prediction.

(61)   a. Adam is half as tall as Doug. $\nleftrightarrow$ Adam is twice as tall as Doug.
        b. Adam is half as short as Doug. $\leftrightarrow$ Adam is twice as short as Doug.

Finally, by virtue of the fact that it encodes evaluativity in a null morpheme, the EVAL account prompts the same worry as the POS account did: if natural languages, across the board, demonstrate similar patterns of evaluativity (citing Hale's 1971 work on Walbiri, Lehrer 1985 suggests that they do), why do none of them encode evaluativity in a phonologically overt morpheme? Grano's (2012) complaint about POS, repeated below, applies just as much to EVAL.

The failure of the putative operator POS to correspond to overt material in language after language—in stark contrast to [comparative markers]—could be taken as evidence that POS does not actually exist and hence that any approach in which positive predication requires a special operator is misguided. Or at minimum, the facts suggest that there is some fundamental and as yet unexplained asymmetry between the way POS and [comparative markers] are realized crosslinguistically.   (Grano 2012: 515)

In Chapter 5, I argue that a number of these worries are resolved in an adaptation of the EVAL account into a theory of evaluativity as a conversational implicature. Among other things, such an approach has the benefit of placing evaluativity in the schema of a larger empirical phenomenon. Before I present the details of the account, I'll review other phenomena that seem to involve markedness-based semantic competition, and other treatments of the phenomena (Chapter 4). But I'll end this chapter by briefly reviewing a few other approaches to evaluativity.

3.4 Some alternatives to POS and EVAL

There are to my knowledge three other semantic accounts of evaluativity. The first two, which I present in §§3.4.1 and 3.4.2, differ from the Cresswellian POS, but nevertheless characterize a counterpart of POS because they predict that evaluativity is incompatible with degree quantifiers or other overt morphology, contrary to the evidence in §3.1. The third type, which I present in §3.4.3, focuses on the evaluativity of relative adjectives other than *tall/short* and *old/young*, and takes as its starting point the claim that the empirical generalizations introduced in §3.1 are not as universal as they are presented as being. These accounts will help inform the implicature-based approach to evaluativity proposed in Chapter 5.

3.4.1 Evaluativity as quantifier domain restriction

Schwarzschild (2012) proposes an analysis of comparatives in Hindi and Navajo in which standard clauses equivalent to English *than* clauses function like quantifier domain restrictors (see also Francez and Koontz-Garboden forthcoming; Bogal-Allbritten 2013; Schwarzschild 2010). This perspective is based in part on Cresswell's (1976: 272) interpretation of the positive construction *Bill is a tall man* as predicating of Bill that he is "tall enough to make it sensible to distinguish Bill from other men" (see also Kennedy 2009).

Schwarzschild takes as his empirical focus the observation that comparatives in Hindi and Navajo are formed with standard markers that are homophonous with spatial postpositions. His analysis, effectively, treats comparatives like (62a) in parallel with path PP constructions like (62b).

(62) a. anu raaj se lambii hai.
Anu Raj FROM tall-FEM PRES-SG
'Anu is taller than Raj.'

b. anu us baRe kamre se niklii.
Anu that-OBL big-OBL room-OBL FROM came-out-PERF-FEM
'Anu came from/out of that big room.'

Following Zwarts (1997), Schwarzschild analyzes spatial propositions like (62b) as involving vectors, or strictly ordered points in space. He adopts a parallel characterization of degree scales, or intervals. In his approach, the morpheme common to both sentences in (62), *se*, is a "quantifier domain adverbial." It restricts intervals or vectors introduced elsewhere in the sentence.

In Schwarzschild's approach, comparative markers combine with their arguments to define an interval D whose upper bound is the external argument's measure (in (62a),

Anu) and whose lower bound is the internal argument's measure (in (62a), Raj). The truth conditions of (62a) are presented in (63).[5]

(63)   [anu raaj se lambii hai] = $\exists D$[tallness(D) $\wedge$ START(D) = raj $\wedge$ END(D) = anu]

The truth conditions in (63) can be interpreted informally as, 'There is a positive gap between Anu's height and Raj's height.' This gap can be modified by overt differentials, as in *Anu is 2 in taller than Raj*.

In the equation in (63), the standard phrase [*raaj se*] restricts the bottom of the scale described by the comparative clause. Schwarzschild characterizes a null evaluativity operator POS in the same vein, as shown below (for a relation R between sets of degrees and individuals and for an assignment function g, which will play a role in the characterization of evaluativity).

(64)   [tall]^g = $\lambda D\lambda x$.END(D) $\wedge$ tallness(D)

(65)   [POS]^g = $\lambda R\lambda x \exists D \in C[R(D)(x)]$

(66)   [Anu is tall]^g = $\exists D \in C[$END(D) = anu $\wedge$ tallness(D)$]$

Informally, (66) characterizes the sentence as being true iff there is a (non-empty) set of degrees in the context of utterance C along the "tall" scale whose endpoint is Anu's height. Schwarzschild includes a constraint on POS's value:

(67)   Constraint on the assignment of values to C in strucure POS$_C$ by function g supplied by discourse Δ: $\forall D[D \in g(C) \rightarrow$ START(D) and END(D) are individuals on what counts in discourse Δ as the top end of the scale $<_\sigma]$

In this characterization of POS, the null operator binds a degree argument associated with the adjective and introduces a dependence on context. A positive construction *My older sister is tall* is true iff "my older sister is on what counts in Δ as the top end of the height scale" (p. 72).

Schwarzschild's motivation for characterizing POS as a quantifier is to account for the lack of evaluativity in comparative constructions in these languages (effectively, the contrasting distribution of POS and standard phrases, p. 72). And while his version of POS and his semantics of standard phrases are significantly different from those POS accounts found in Bartsch and Vennemann (1972), Cresswell (1976), von Stechow (1984), and Kennedy (1999), the proposal is nevertheless still susceptible to the problems discussed in §3.1; namely, the account predicts that evaluativity is just as absent in equatives and degree questions as it is in the comparative, and this is not

---

[5] Instead of sets of degrees or intervals, Schwarzschild uses as his primitives 'directed scale segments' σ which are defined in terms of their endpoints, order and dimension of measurement. For our purposes, these are equivalent to the intervals in Schwarzschild and Wilkinson (2002) and the sets of degrees (or scales) we've been dealing with, so I've converted his truth conditions to our more familiar formalism.

the case, at least, for Navajo—one of the languages he intends to account for (Bogal-Allbritten 2013).

3.4.2 *Evaluativity and dynamic update*

Barker (2002) proposes what is effectively an adaptation of Klein's (1980, 1982) semantics of adjectival constructions within a dynamic-semantic framework (see also Moltmann 1992, 2009). His main empirical motivation is the ability of positive constructions like *Feynman is tall* to be used metalinguistically, as described in §3.1.1. Relevant for this use is a context in which the speaker and hearer are both looking at Feynman, and so know his height, but in which the hearer is asking about the relevant standard of tallness for physicists, or Americans, or whatever the salient comparison class is. In this context, an utterance of the sentence *Feynmann is tall* has a metalinguistic use in which it serves to inform the hearer of the nature of the relevant contextual standard.

To account for this reading, Barker argues, we must treat gradable adjectives dynamically, as update functions on contextual standards. His proposal for the semantics of positive constructions is in (68) given a relational account of gradable adjectives like *tall* (pp. 7–8).

(68)   a. $[\![tall]\!] = \lambda x \lambda C.\{c \in C : c \in \mathsf{tall}(\mathsf{d}(c)([\![tall]\!]), x)\}$
       b. $[\![Feynman\ is\ tall]\!] = \lambda C.\{c \in C : c \in \mathsf{tall}(\mathsf{d}(c)([\![tall]\!]), \mathsf{feynman})\}$

(68a) depicts the meaning of *tall* in a positive construction as taking two arguments: an individual (corresponding to the subject) and a contextual set C (corresponding to the common ground at the time of utterance). Its range is a set of contexts c—a subset of C—in which the individual x is tall to some contextual standard which is valued contextually, just like the standard s in POS and EVAL accounts.

Barker's account differs from POS and EVAL accounts in that he characterizes MPs and degree quantifiers like the comparative as also manipulating this standard (Klein following 1980, 1982). His definitions of MPs and of the comparative morpheme are below.

(69) $[\![two\ meters]\!] = \lambda \alpha \lambda x \lambda C.\{c \in C : c[2\mathsf{m}/\alpha] \in \alpha(x)\}$

(70) $[\![-er]\!] = \lambda \alpha \lambda x \lambda y \lambda C.\{c \in C : \exists d.(c[d/\alpha] \in \alpha(y)) \wedge (\neg c[d/\alpha] \in \alpha(x))\}$

The measure phrase functions as a "modified delineation function," effectively valuing the standard in the lexical meaning of the adjective α. Barker describes its effect on the compositional semantics of an MP construction (p. 11): "[T]he sentence *Mary is two meters tall* is true just in case Mary would count as tall if the standard for tallness were set to two meters." In this account, instead of evaluating Mary's height with respect to a contextual standard, MP constructions evaluate Mary's height with respect to the MP. It appropriately predicts that MP constructions are not context-sensitive (or evaluative), in contrast to positive constructions, although it assigns MP constructions an 'at least' semantics.

Barker's analysis of comparatives is similar: comparatives bind the pragmatic variable lexicalized by the gradable adjective. He says of (70) (p. 12): "This meaning quantifies over degrees: for each degree d, the truth conditions evaluate an expression based on the absolute meaning of the adjective with respect to a candidate in which the relevant standard has been temporarily set to d." A comparative like the one in (71), therefore, denotes a set of contexts in which Feynman is associated with some degree of tallness with which Bill is not associated.

(71) $[\![$Feynman is taller than Bill$]\!]$
$= \lambda C.\{c \in C : \exists d.(c[d/[\![tall]\!]] \in [\![tall]\!](\text{feynman})) \wedge (\neg c[d/[\![tall]\!]] \in [\![tall]\!](\text{bill}))\}$

This analysis, too, correctly predicts that comparatives, in contrast to positive constructions, are not context-sensitive (or evaluative). But, like POS accounts, it predicts a direct correlation between evaluativity and the lack of overt degree morphology (i.e., MPs or degree quantifiers) in an adjectival construction. Barker does not discuss equatives, but (72) seems to be a clear extension of his account of comparatives (see Schwarzschild 2008 for a discussion of the semantics of equatives in "A-not-A" approaches, like the one in (71)).

(72) $[\![$Feynman is as short as Bill$]\!]$
$= \lambda C.\{c \in C : \exists d.(c[d/[\![short]\!]] \in [\![short]\!](\text{feynman})) \wedge (c[d/[\![short]\!]] \in [\![short]\!](\text{bill}))\}$

Because (72) characterizes the equative morpheme as existentially binding the only source of context sensitivity available to gradable adjectives in the account (the degree argument d), it incorrectly predicts that evaluativity is impossible in degree quantifier constructions like the equative. Therefore Barker's account, while extremely useful in terms of accounting for the metalinguistic use of positive constructions, is subject to the same criticisms as POS approaches when it comes to an account of evaluativity, modulo a more radical characterization of the equative.

3.4.3 *Evaluativity and other relative adjectives*

Sassoon (2011) and Breakstone (2012) propose alternatives to the EVAL approach in part based on worries that the adjectives *tall* and *short* are not particularly representative of the class of relative adjectives as a whole. These data come from Sassoon (2011: 532) but are also discussed in Breakstone (2012).

(73) a. ?This ice cream is as warm as that one.
b. ?How warm is the ice cream?
c. ?How cold is the fire?

Sassoon and Breakstone take the data in (73) to show that the antonym pair *warm* and *cold*, despite being relative adjectives, do not pattern like *tall* and *short* in terms of evaluativity. The empirical argument demonstrated in (73) requires the controversial assumption that ice cream counts as cold in all contexts and fire counts as warm in all contexts.

Generalizing from *tall* and *short*, we would expect that only *cold* would be evaluative in equatives and degree questions. This is supported by the unacceptability of (73c), given the assumption that fire can never count as cold. But the data in (73a) and (73b) suggest that *warm* is also evaluative in equatives and degree questions. The claim is that these sentences are unacceptable because the constructions are evaluative (and because ice cream does not count as warm). The conclusion is that the EVAL account might be right for relative adjectives like *tall* and *short*, but that it would be a mistake to extend it to all relative antonym pairs.

Sassoon (2011) and Breakstone (2012) (see also Sassoon 2010a) are also worried about the inability of the semantic account in Rett (2007, 2008) to predict the incompatibility of MPs and negative antonyms. They argue that the two phenomena seem related, and that ideally an account of one phenomenon would explain the other (see also Winter 2005 and Doetjes 1997 for accounts of the general incompatibility of MPs and negative antonyms). However, they propose very distinct solutions to these problems. I'll describe them briefly in turn.

Sassoon's (2011) account relies on a characterization of gradable adjectives (originally proposed in Sassoon 2010a) in which the negative antonym is a transformed or reversed version of the positive one. In addition to replicating some version of the markedness contrast assumed in the EVAL account, this allows for an explanation of the difference between *tall/short* (which she terms "neutral" adjectives based on the non-evaluativity of their comparative forms) on the one hand and *warm/cold* (which she terms "norm-related" based on the evaluativity of their comparative forms) on the other. The explanation has to do with how the adjectives treat their minimal endpoint, zero. She says (p. 537):

> What, then, distinguishes neutral adjectives (like English *tall* and *old*) from norm-related ones (*fat, rich, warm* and negative antonyms in general)? In the former, the zero is absolute. It marks complete absence of height, width, age, etc. Conversely, in the latter, the zero is relative. The 'out of the blue' context fails to determine precisely which entities cease to have any amount of the measured properties.

Sassoon's account of the difference between neutral (e.g., *tall*) and norm-related (e.g., *fat*) adjectives translates to a difference in evaluativity between the two types of adjectives because it predicts that the degree value of norm-related adjectives is (relatively) high even in non-evaluative constructions. But it still offers no explanation for the evaluativity of negative "neutral" adjectives like *short* in questions and equatives.

It also seems to equate the class of "neutral" adjectives with those adjectives for which we have conventional scales of measure and corresponding measure terms (like *meters* or *grams*). For every gradable adjective associated with a measure noun—including spiciness, whose unit of measure is a Scoville (Schwarzschild 2006b)—the dimension of measurement has a minimum bound of zero units. For gradable adjectives that aren't measure adjectives, the minimum bound is indeterminate. If this is right, Sassoon predicts that all adjectives whose dimensions have units of measurement behave like *tall*, while all other gradable adjectives are "norm-related," and behave like *fat*.

This, however, doesn't seem to be the case. The adjectives *warm* and *cold* are associated with the dimension of temperature, and therefore have a variety of different units, including degrees Fahrenheit, Celsius, and Kelvin. Yet these adjectives are "norm-related" (i.e., demonstrate a different evaluativity pattern than *tall* and *short*) according to her tests (p. 532; see also (73)).

(74) a. How warm is the pizza? $\rightarrow$ The pizza is warm.
      b. The pizza is as warm as the pie. $\rightarrow$ The pizza is warm.

(75) a. How cold is the pizza? $\rightarrow$ The pizza is cold.
      b. The pizza is as warm as the box. $\rightarrow$ The pizza is cold.

In short, while Sassoon's account is an improvement on the EVAL account in that it allows for some flexibility within the class of relative adjectives, it's not clear that the account is explanatory, or if it is, that it provides the right explanation. It also doesn't seem to be able to address the difference in evaluativity between comparatives and equatives.

Breakstone's (2012) proposal is effectively the reverse of the EVAL account; in it, all adjectives are treated as lexically evaluative, as in (76), but constructions involving MPs and the comparative lack evaluativity due to the distribution of a null morpheme that cancels their evaluative interpretation.

(76) a. $[\![\text{tall}]\!] = \lambda d \lambda x.\text{height}(x) \geq d \wedge d > s$
      b. $[\![\text{short}]\!] = \lambda d \lambda x.\text{height}(x) \leq d \wedge d < s$

Instead of providing an account of where evaluativity is blocked, then, the Breakstone account is tasked with explaining where the cancellation of evaluativity is blocked. While I've been assuming that evaluative constructions with negative antonyms require that the relevant degree exceed the standard on the negative scale (e.g., $d >_{\text{short}} s_{\text{short}}$), Breakstone assumes that the evaluativity associated with negative antonyms requires that the relevant degree be below the standard on the positive scale ($d <_{\text{tall}} s_{\text{short}}$). This difference seems trivial, but it is an important component of Breakstone's account.

He proposes that the semantics includes a freely-occurring "Standard Shifting Morpheme (SSM)", interpreted relative to some context c:

(77) $[\![\text{SSM Adj}]\!]^{c} = [\![\text{Adj}]\!]^{c_0}$; where context $c_0 \equiv c$, except that $s_{c_0}(\text{Adj}) = 0$

This morpheme has the effect of cancelling the evaluativity of a construction that invokes a contextual standard; it resets the pragmatic variable s_{c_0} (in a context c_0) to zero.

Breakstone's account of the evaluativity of positive constructions is the same as it is in the EVAL account: positive constructions are evaluative (are not formed with an SSM) because if they weren't, they'd be uninformative. He derives the non-evaluativity of MP constructions by characterizing them as degree quantifiers that measure sets of degrees, as in Schwarzschild (2005) (see §2.1.4), but as undefined over vague sets of degrees, as in (78). If an MP construction is not formed with SSM, Breakstone assumes that the set of degrees measured by the MP is vague because it is bounded by a contextual variable. The result is a presupposition failure, presumably preventing the availability of the evaluative reading.

(78) $[\![n\ \text{units}]\!] = \lambda D_{\langle d,t \rangle} : D$ is not vague. $n(D)$

Breakstone's explanation of the evaluativity contrast in degree questions has to do with the contrast in the characterization of antonyms in (76): since *short* forms a set of degrees that are *below* the standard, and since SSM resets the standard to zero, the derivation of [How SSM short is John?] results in a question about degrees below zero, and is hence undefined.

In contrast, he argues, antonyms like *early* and *late* are both evaluative in degree questions because there is no extension gap between the antonyms (see also Ljung 1974): it's possible, he argues, to be neither tall nor short, but it's impossible to be neither late nor early. (His example is #*John is neither late nor early, but somewhere in between*, which seems acceptable to me.) He argues that, in these cases, the set of degrees associated with an individual's value is always a point instead of an interval, so "SSM is vacuous and evaluativity always obtains" (p. 8).

This characterization of the difference between *tall/short* and *late/early* is a little unsettling. It's easy to imagine a context in which John is neither late nor early but right on time; furthermore, Breakstone's characterization of the difference between Sassoon's "neutral" and "norm-related" antonym pairs doesn't extend comfortably to *warm/cold* (given *lukewarm* or Goldilocks' *just right*) or *heavy/light*.

In sum, the accounts of evaluativity in Sassoon (2011) and Breakstone (2012) offer important counterexamples to the empirical generalizations in Rett (2007, 2008); it does indeed seem like a mistake to assimilate pairs like *tall/short* and *old/young* with pairs like *warm/cold* and *rich/poor*. But these approaches seem to fall short in other respects; in particular, they make strong predictions about which pairs of relative adjectives will be evaluative in degree questions and which will not, and it is not clear that these predictions hold up across antonym pairs (or across languages; see Murphy 2006). I will offer a new perspective on these data in §5.4.

3.4.4 Summary

Semantic accounts of evaluativity fall into roughly two categories: those that associate evaluativity with the positive construction, and those that aim to include a broader range of data under the label of evaluativity. The POS account is a prominent member of the first category, and the EVAL account is clearly a member of the second category.

The differences between these types of theories is, plausibly, a consequence of at least one significant difference between evaluativity as it is manifested in the positive construction, on the one hand, and elsewhere. As we've seen, evaluativity in positive constructions is part of the at-issue or asserted content of the sentence; it can be directly denied in discourse, as demonstrated in (79), and it can be embedded under sentential operators like negation. In contrast, evaluativity in negative-antonym equatives is part of the not-at-issue or presupposed content of the sentence; it cannot be directly denied in discourse, as demonstrated in (80), and it projects out of sentential operators like negation.

(79) A: Doug is tall.
      B: That's false, Doug is not tall.

(80) A: Doug is as short as Adam.
      B: #That's false, Adam is not short.

It's not clear which construction degree questions pattern with. On the one hand, in degree questions like (81), evaluativity is presupposed. On the other hand, questions typically presuppose content that would be asserted in their declarative-sentence counterparts, as shown in (82).

(81) How short is Adam?

(82) a. Adam ate a pizza.
      b. Who ate a pizza?

Putting aside degree questions for a moment, a proponent of the standard POS approach to evaluativity could defend the approach in the face of data like (80) by arguing that the truth-conditional difference between evaluativity in positive constructions and in negative-antonym equatives is sufficient to suggest that there are two "types" of evaluativity, and that POS is a successful treatment of one type, but that the theory needs to be supplemented to account for the second type.

In contrast, the EVAL approach takes for granted that the "exceeds a standard" interpretation the two types of constructions have in common is sufficient to warrant a parallel treatment. It therefore seeks to account for the truth-conditional difference between evaluativity in positive constructions and in degree quantifier constructions by appealing to the fact that the theory predicts EVAL is unembedded in the former and semantically embedded in the latter. As we saw, there were problems with this approach: it can predict that EVAL is semantically embedded, but not that it is only semantically embedded in the internal argument of the equative. And if EVAL (or POS) is a semantic operator, why is it covert across languages?

The rest of this book is devoted to presenting a theory of evaluativity as Gricean conversational implicature. In doing so, it avoids the pitfalls of postulating a null operator to encode evaluativity; it predicts that evaluativity is universal, but not that it should be explicitly represented.

The theory differentiates between positive constructions and other degree constructions; evaluativity arises in the former as the result of a Quantity implicature, and in the latter as a Manner implicature. It uses independent considerations of discourse prominence to explain differences in truth-conditionality. And it draws on independent observations about the degree domain to explain why it is that the conversational implicatures associated with degree constructions amount to evaluativity (Bolinger 1972).

In many respects, the treatment of the positive construction in this approach is similar to the POS approach, especially those who consider POS to be an intuitive type-shifter (see also Lassiter and Goodman 2013). And the treatment of constructions in which evaluativity is tied to the marked antonyms is similar to the EVAL approach, especially insofar as it relies on markedness competition to affect the interpretation of these degree constructions. I argue that the standard markedness competitions invoked by (neo-)Gricean theories of Manner implicature are a much more intuitive treatment of the association of evaluativity with negative antonyms than encoding evaluativity in a semantic operator, as the EVAL approach does.

There are therefore two components of this implicature-based approach to evaluativity: one in which evaluativity arises as a Quantity implicature, and another in which it arises as a Manner implicature. Before presenting the proposal in detail, I will review what I have in mind when I talk about semantic competition and about conversational implicatures. In anticipation of the account in Chapter 5, the review will focus on two relatively understudied aspects of conversational implicature: Manner implicature, and the interaction between conversational implicature and Questions Under Discussion.

4

Implicature: A brief review

Brevis esse laboro; obscurusfio. 'I strive to be brief; I become obscure.'

Horace, *Ars Poetica*, quoted in Horn 2008

The goal of this chapter is to introduce and motivate several distinctions that will underpin the account in Chapter 5. I begin with a general presentation of Grice's (1975) distinction between what is said and what is implicated (§4.1.1). I will then adopt Horn's (1984) Q and R Principles, and his notion of the division of pragmatic labor, to address Quantity and Manner implicature (§4.1.2). I then review several instances of Manner implicatures, which are often overlooked in the conversational implicature literature.

I will depart from Grice (1975, 1989) and others (e.g., Hirschberg 1991) to argue that cancellability is not a necessary condition of conversational implicatures, but rather a property of implicatures (like Quantity implicatures) that are based on the meaning rather than the form of an utterance (§4.2). Finally, I present evidence that the (not-)at-issue status of implicatures is a function of discourse prominence and related properties (§4.3; van Kuppevelt 1995; van Rooij and Schulz 2004; Mayol and Castroviejo 2013).

4.1 A theory of implicature

4.1.1 Grice's taxonomy of signification

Grice (1975) famously introduced the phenomenon of implicature to formal theories of meaning. He characterizes the **total signification of an utterance** as composed of **what is said** and what is implicated. The distinction comes from his observation that (p. 43) "while it is no doubt true that the formal devices are especially amenable to systematic treatment by the logician, it remains the case that there are very many inferences and arguments, expressed in natural language and not in terms of these devices, that are nevertheless recognizably valid." His system of maxims is intended to offer some way of identifying and explaining these inferences.

Grice's taxonomy of signification, or the total signification of an utterance, is in (1).

(1)   TOTAL SIGNIFICATION of an utterance

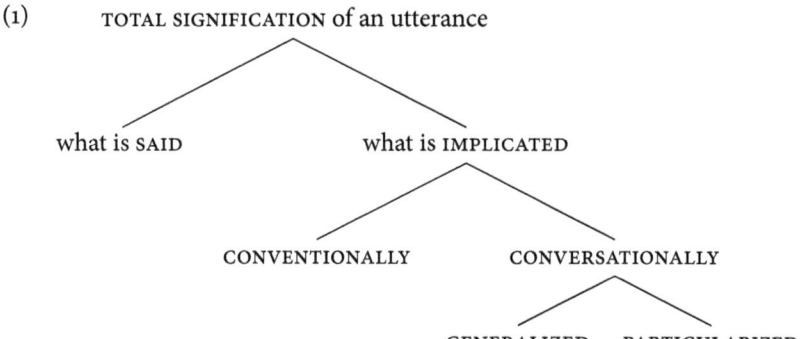

The first distinction, the distinction between what is said and what is implicated, can be roughly characterized in terms of the difference between explicitly encoded or literal meaning and non-literal meaning (Recanati 1989, Bach 1994). This difference is often construed in terms of truth-conditional content—those aspects of meaning that contribute to the truth value of a proposition—although I'll argue in §4.3 that some implicated content is (in fact, must be) truth-conditional.

What remains is what is implicated. Grice distinguishes between two types of implicature: that which seems to be encoded lexically, or conventionally—always occurring with a particular word, and never defeasible—with those that seem to be the result of a hearer reasoning about the utterance relative to the utterance context, or conversation. Grice's example of the former is *therefore* (1975: 44–5):

> If I say (smugly), *He is an Englishman; he is, therefore, brave*, I have certainly committed myself, by virtue of the meaning of my words, to its being the case that his being brave is a consequence of (follows from) his being an Englishman. But while I have said that he is an Englishman, and said that he is brave, I do not want to say that I have *said* (in the favored sense) that it follows from his being an Englishman that he is brave, though I have certainly indicated, and so implicated, that this is so. I do not want to say that my utterance of this sentence would be, *strictly speaking*, false should the consequence in question fail to hold. So *some* implicatures are conventional . . . .

Other examples are *even*, *too*, and *only* (Karttunen and Peters 1979). Each of these words seems to carry two different types of meaning, corresponding to what is said (a conjunctive, $p \wedge q$ meaning in the case of *therefore*) and what is implicated (for *therefore*, that *p* follows from *q*).

I will treat the term "conventional" as synonymous with "fully lexicalized," characterizing conventional implicatures as inextricably tied to the lexical items that introduce them, a part of the meaning of any sentence that contains the lexical item or phrase. A consequence of this complete lexicalization is that the conventional implicature associated with *therefore* cannot be cancelled (negated in discourse, in this case by *In fact . . .*).

(2)   He is an Englishman, therefore he is brave. *In fact, there is no clear connection between being English and being brave.

In contrast to conventionally or lexically encoded implicature are conversational implicatures ("CIs"), based on the particulars of what is uttered and when it is uttered. Instead of being inextricably tied to a lexical item, these implicatures are more loosely derived from what is said, and appear or disappear across contexts.

Grice (1975) described conversational implicatures "as being essentially connected with certain general features of discourse" (p. 45). He attributes to language users the recognition of particular rational, cooperative efforts in their attempts to achieve "a common purpose or set of purposes, or at least a mutually accepted direction" (p. 45). This assumption is encoded in his general principle of conversation, the Cooperative Principle, and its subprinciples (pp. 45–6).

(3)   **The Cooperative Principle**
Make your conversational contribution such as it is required, at the stage at which it occurs, by the accepted purpose or direction of the talk exchange in which you are engaged.

(4)   **Quantity**
1. Make your contribution as informative as required (for the current purposes of the exchange).
2. Do not make your contribution more informative than is required.

(5)   **Quality**
1. Do not say what you believe to be false.
2. Do not say that for which you lack adequate evidence.

(6)   **Relation**
Be relevant.

(7)   **Manner**
1. Avoid obscurity of expression.
2. Avoid ambiguity.
3. Be brief (avoid unnecessary prolixity).
4. Be orderly.

Grice developed these maxims to explain what he took to be a tendency of conversational participants to strive for "a maximally effective exchange of information" (p. 47). The maxims are generally followed but are occasionally flouted. Flouting a maxim allows a speaker to exploit these principles of communication and thereby conversationally implicate something.

A good example is a flouting of the Relation maxim, which exhorts speakers to say only that which is relevant to the conversation. In the exchange in (8) ("at a genteel tea party," p. 54), *B* fails to obey this maxim.

(8)   A: Mrs *X* is an old bag.
      B: The weather has been quite delightful this summer, hasn't it?

In doing so, she implicates something that is directly related to the maxim she flouts: that she does not want to address *A*'s statement. To understand this, *A*'s reasoning might proceed like this: "I know *B* is a cooperative conversational participant, and it's cooperative to say things that are relevant to the topic of conversation. Since her response is not relevant, it must be because she cannot or does not want to say anything relevant."

I will discuss some of these submaxims in more detail in §4.2.1 and §4.2.2. For now, I'll say a little more about the relationship between conversational and conventional implicature, which I take to be less categorical than Grice does.

The tree in (1) as it stands makes three distinctions under the heading of "what is implicated": conventional implicatures; generalized conversational implicatures; and particularized conversational implicature. As we've seen, conventional implicatures are inextricably tied to some lexical item, while conversational implicatures are determined in particular contexts based on the intentions of the speakers and hearers. I will do my best to present some idea of what Grice had in mind when he made these distinctions, but I will ultimately assume that there is a continuum from conventionalized to particularized conversational implicature based on the varying extent to which an implicature is grammaticized ("conventionalized") in a lexical entry or phrase.

Grice listed five properties of conversational implicature (in contrast to conventional implicature), none of which have survived the test of time as necessary conditions of CIs. I'll present the least controversial ones here.

First is **cancellability**: Grice claims that conversational implicatures (but not conventional implicatures) can be cancelled in discourse by the speaker, commonly with a cancellation signifier like *in fact* . . . . (9) illustrates that the scalar implicature typically associated with numerals—i.e. *n* but not *n* + 1—is cancellable, in contrast to the conventional implicature in (2).

(9)   John has two children . . . in fact, he has three.

Hirschberg (1991) points out that it is odd to think of cancellability as a property of CIs given that CIs are defined almost entirely in terms of the speaker's intentions. She instead recommends focusing on "consistent semantic meaning," determined by the question (p. 28): "Can [a sentence] be felicitously uttered in a context in which [its CI] is denied or clearly false?" This does indeed seem to be a better test of CIs, but I will nevertheless use the traditional *in fact* test to approximate conditions for consistent semantic meaning.

It is generally recognized that cancellability is not a *sufficient* property for CIs; Sadock (1978) argues that the cancellability test can be used to disambiguate ambiguous sentences, for instance, in the absence of CIs. And there is some sense in which presuppositions pass something that looks like the *in fact* test, as demonstrated in (10).

(10)   John didn't take his sister to the airport . . . in fact, John doesn't have a sister.

The resulting conclusion, made by many (see, for instance, Hirschberg 1991: 32), is that cancellability is a *necessary* condition of conversational implicature.

Yet there are at least two types of counterexamples to this claim. First is that the cancellability test works better for scalar implicatures than it does for even other types of Quantity implicatures. One of the canonical examples of CIs comes from Grice's example of the letter writer: (p. 52): "*A* is writing a testimonial about a pupil who is a candidate for a philosophy job, and his letter reads as follows: 'Dear Sir, Mr. *X*'s command of English is excellent, and his attendance at tutorials has been regular. Yours, etc.'" In this example, *A* feels compelled to write something true, and this is the most cooperative thing he can say. The implicature, therefore, is that he cannot truthfully say that Mr. *X* is good at philosophy; therefore that *A* thinks that Mr. *X* is not good at philosophy.

This implicature doesn't seem easy to cancel, as suggested in (11) (Huitink and Spenader 2004).

(11)   Mr. *X*'s command of English is excellent, and his attendance at tutorials has been regular. ??In fact, he is quite good at philosophy.

Even less natural is the cancellation of at least some Manner implicatures, based on the Manner maxim in (7), as the example of periphrasis in (12) (in part from Grice 1989: 37) shows.

(12)   Miss *X* produced a series of sounds that correspond closely with the score of "Home Sweet Home." #(In fact,) She has a beautiful voice.

In (12), the speaker used a circumlocution to describe an event of Miss *X* singing. This wordy description therefore carries the Manner implicature that the speaker cannot truthfully describe the event as one of Miss *X* singing, and therefore that the speaker does not think Miss *X* has a nice voice. The reasoning is similar to the Quantity case: if the speaker had thought that Miss *X* had a nice voice, he would directly have said so more directly.

Horn (1989) and Levinson (2000), in their discussion of Quantity and Manner implicatures, suggest that the two differ in cancellability because the former is calculated on content, but the latter on form. I will make this assumption as well; it will be motivated further in my more in-depth discussion of Manner implicatures in §4.2.

Another class of counterexamples to the claim that CIs are cancellable are those examples in which properties of the discourse seem to block cancellation. An example is in (13) (from Mayol and Castroviejo 2013: 85, based on data from van Kuppevelt 1995); it represents a canonical scalar implicature, based on the Quantity maxim: that an utterance of *some* carries the implicature "not all".

(13)   A: How many exams did John pass?
        B: Some. #In fact, he passed all of them.

This suggests that, even amongst CIs that are generally recognized as cancellable (e.g. scalar implicatures like the one associated with *some* in (13)), cancellability is subject to discourse considerations. I discuss this complication in more detail in §4.3.

A second property that Grice attributes to CIs (in contrast to conventional implicatures) is **detachability**: the extent to which an implicature can be divorced from a particular form. Conventional implicatures are non-detachable by virtue of the fact that they are lexicalized by a particular word or phrase. In contrast, CIs are tied to what is said—the semantic meaning of the utterance as a whole. In particular, Grice describes the test of detachability as follows: "*insofar as the manner of expression plays no role in the calculation*, it will not be possible to find another way of saying the same thing, which simply lacks the implicature in question" (p. 58, emphasis mine). Detachability is thus generally recognized, by Grice and others (Walker 1975; Sadock 1978) as a property of CIs "other than those arising via the maxim of Manner" (Hirschberg 1991: 34–5).

Because the detachability test only holds for a strict subset of CIs, it, too, cannot be considered a necessary property of CIs.

This puts us in an odd position, theoretically speaking. It is generally recognized that conversational implicatures are a real force in communication; scalar implicature is in particular thought to play an important semantic role (Chierchia et al. 2009). And it's generally recognized that Grice was right to treat different types of CIs under the same umbrella of cooperation. But since this apparent natural class of phenomena lack any common core properties, it is hard to productively extend Grice's theory to non-canonical phenomena in a systematic, falsifiable way. In other words, in the absence of any necessary conditions for conversational implicatures, we are left with a situation in which we know a CI when we see it, but we can't provide incontrivertible evidence for the claim.

The goal of the analysis in Chapter 5 is to argue that evaluativity is a conversational implicature that arises in some cases as a Quantity implicature and in other cases as a Manner implicature. While e.g. scalar implicatures are generally cancellable, we've seen that other Quantity implicatures and Manner implicatures are less clearly so. If

CIs are a real and compelling phenomenon, and there is a general consensus that they arise from (or, at least, can be approximated by) Grice's maxims, then in the absence of necessary conditions for CIs the best evidence I can bring to bear for such a claim is to show clear parallels between evaluativity and established CIs, and to provide some explanation of how evaluativity could result from Grice's maxims. This is what I will do.

In the rest of this section, I will introduce Grice's generalized/particularized CI distinction, and defend the claim that the relationship between these and conventionalized implicature is less categorical than Grice had thought. In §5.4, I will use this graded notion of conventionalization to try to explain differences in evaluativity within the class of relative adjectives.

There is a sense in which Grice's distinction between generalized and particularized conversational implicature (GCI and PCI, respectively), modeled in the tree in (1), reflects some gradience of conventionalization. Grice describes the distinction as follows (1975: 56, original emphasis):

> I have so far considered only cases of what I might call particularized conversational implicature—that is to say, cases in which an implicature is carried by saying that p on a particular occasion in virtue of special features of the context, cases in which there is no room for the idea that an implicature of this sort is *normally* carried by saying that p. But there are cases of generalized conversational implicature. Sometimes one can say that the use of a certain form of words in an utterance would normally (in the *absence* of special circumstances) carry such-and-such an implicature or type of implicature.

Grice (1975) gives only one example of a GCI, one that he "hope[s] may be fairly noncontroversial" (p. 56); he argues that the sentence *X is meeting a woman this evening* carries a generalized implicature that restricts its truth-conditional content.

(14)   Doug is meeting a woman this evening.
    a. truth conditions: $\exists x[\mathrm{woman}(x) \wedge \mathrm{meeting}(\mathrm{doug}, x)]$
    b. generalized implicature: $\ldots \wedge \neg\mathrm{related}(\mathrm{doug}, x)$

Specifically, its truth conditions are consistent with Doug meeting his mother that evening, but the use of the indefinite *a woman* (in contrast to, e.g., the definite *his mother*) carries a generalized implicature that the woman Doug is meeting is not, e.g., his mother.

According to this, GCIs are like PCIs in that they are calculable from conversational principles, but differ in that PCIs are calculated from context to context, while GCIs come about relatively automatically. Atlas and Levinson (1981: 5) say (see also Lewis 1969; Brown and Levinson 1978; Karttunen and Peters 1979):

> The generalized implicature is "conventional" in the sense that it is not calculated at each occasion of use of a sentence. There is a (defeasible) shared assumption that the implicata obtain in the context unless they are explicitly suspended or cancelled (see Harnish 1976: 353). Conversational inferences may well have degrees of conventionalization.

This distinction is summarized elsewhere as follows (Levinson 2000: 16):

(15)   **The distinction between PCIs and GCIs**

    a. An implicature *i* from utterance *U* is **particularized** iff *U* implicates *i* only by virtue of specific contextual assumptions that would not invariably or even normally obtain.

    b. An implicature *i* is **generalized** iff *U* implicates *i* *unless* there are unusual specific contextual assumptions that defeat it.

There is a tension here between the apparent empirical need for such a distinction— i.e., the observation that conversational implicatures seem to differ in the extent to which they are detachable or cancellable—and what seems to be the complete lack of gradability in the categories of conversational and conventional implicature. Specifically, if we think of a conventional implicature as one that is encoded lexically (see Lewis 1969), and a conversational implicature as one calculated on the fly, it seems incoherent to think that an implicature could be halfway in between.

Levinson (2000) admits that "the distinctions are tortuous" (p. 373); Grice himself has to revert to a diachronic perspective to be precise about the relationship between conventional and conversational implicature.

To speak approximately, since the calculation of the presence of a conversational implicature presupposes an initial knowledge of the conventional force of the expression the utterance of which carries an implicature, a conversational implicatum will be a condition that is not included in the original specification of the expression's conventional force. Though it may not be impossible for what starts life, so to speak, as a conversational implicature to become conventionalized, to suppose that this is so in a given case would require special justification. So, initially at least, conversational implicata are not part of the meaning of the expressions to the employment of which they attach.   (Grice 1975: 58)

The distinction between conventional implicatures, GCIs, and PCIs is even less helpful given that cancellability is of no help in testing for the difference. Instead of differentiating between GCIs and PCIs, I will follow Atlas and Levinson (1981) in assuming that there are varying extents to which an implicature is conventionalized. But I acknowledge that this perspective is more diachronically than synchronically useful. While it seems unlikely that a GCI would be partially lexicalized in an individual's mental lexicon, it might be possible that it is lexicalized in the mental lexicons of only part of a linguistic community, at least at some point in time, and that this could result in the effects we see in GCIs.

In sum, Grice makes very clear-cut distinctions between the different types of meaning that seem to contribute to the total significance of the utterance. He differentiates between what is said and what is implicated, and then between conventional implicatures and generalized and particularized implicatures.

In Grice's discussion, conversational implicatures differed from conventional implicatures in being cancellable and detachable. However, detachability is not a universal property of CIs, because Manner implicatures are tied to form and by nature non-detachable. And cancellability, too, seems to be a property of only some CIs (e.g., scalar implicatures) and in only some discourse contexts. In §4.2 I'll have a little more to say about how non-canonical CIs behave, and in §4.3 I'll say more about the relationship between cancellability and discourse.

In the absence of clear tests to differentiate between conventional and conversational implicatures, Grice's contrast between GCIs and PCIs, too, doesn't seem to hold up particularly well. It does seem useful to talk about the extent to which a conversational implicature is conventionalized—i.e. associated with a particular lexical item or phrase—but (following Grice 1975; Atlas and Levinson 1981) varying degrees of conventionalization seem more appropriately a diachronic rather than synchronic property of words or phrases. I will come back to this observation, too, to address the differences in evaluativity across adjectives highlighted in Sassoon (2011) and Breakstone (2012).

Since Grice, there have been several revisions of the Gricean program. Below I will review one particular implementation: Horn's division of pragmatic labor, which highlights the contrasts between Grice's maxims of Quantity and Manner, and will therefore be particularly useful for an account of evaluativity.

4.1.2 Horn's division of pragmatic labor

In a series of papers (Horn 1984, 1989, 1991a), Horn brings together McCawley's treatment of periphrasis and related constructions with Atlas and Levinson's (1981) treatment of generalized or conventional implicature. He reconceptualizes Grice's maxims into two opposing forces, representing the speaker's and hearer's processes of reasoning, respectively—a theory generally referred to as Horn's "division of pragmatic labor." I will adopt Horn's implementation of Grice's program because it highlights the tension between considerations of Quantity and Manner, which are both crucial for the account presented in Chapter 5.

Horn's empirical focus, like McCawley's (1978), are phenomena in which linguistically marked (in the sense of Jespersen 1965) elements seem to take on marked interpretations. Horn's work can be seen as an adaptation of Grice, but he argues that the correlation between simple phrases and simple meanings goes back to Zipf's (1949) Principle of Least Effort, which is a principle of human behavior at odds with its antithesis, the Force of Diversification.

Horn (2008) calls the application of Zipf's principles to natural language "the Zipfian character of the implicata generating indirect speech acts," and suggests that the first connection between the two was made by Searle (1965: 234–5; see also Martinet 1962):

I think this condition is an instance of the sort of phenomenon stated in Zipf's law. I think there is operating in our language, as most forms of human behaviour, a principle of least effort, in this case a principle of maximum illocutionary ends with minimum phonetic effort, and I think [this] condition is an instance of it.

I'll first present Horn's theory—a recasting of Grice (1975) into two opposing principles corresponding to Zipf's, which he elsewhere dubs "Zipfo-Gricean" (Horn 1991a: 85)—and then present his treatment of manner implicature phenomena.

Horn's observation, inspired by Zipf, is that certain implicata are best characterized as the result of a tension between the speaker's motivations and the hearer's. He encodes this tension in two distinct principles; his Q Principle is a recasting of the first principle of Grice's Quantity Maxim (4), and his R Principle is a recasting of Grice's Relation and Manner maxims as well as the second principle of the Quantity Maxim.

(16)   **The Q Principle (Hearer-based):** (Horn 1984: 13):
       Make your contribution sufficient (cf. Quantity$_1$)
       Say as much as you can (given R)
       Lower-bounding principle, inducing upper-bounded implicata

(17)   **The R Principle (Speaker-based):** (Horn 1984: 13):
       Make your contribution necessary (cf. Relation, Quantity$_2$, Manner)
       Say no more than you must (given Q)
       Upper-bounding principle, inducing lower-bounded implicata

The Q Principle is responsible for phenomena like scalar implicature. An utterance of the sentence *Some of my friends are Buddhist* results in an implicature corresponding to "some but not all" because the speaker is bound by the Q Principle, which exhorts her to say as much as she can. Horn characterizes the Q Principle as a "lower-bounding" one because it places a lower bound on the information the speaker provides (effectively, "the speaker must communicate at least p"). The result are "upper-bounded implicata," so-called because the resulting implicature restricts the information on the opposite end of the informativity spectrum (effectively, "the speaker doesn't know more than p").

The R Principle is the antithesis of the Q Principle. Horn offers indirect speech acts as the canonical example of R implicata. He says (p. 14): "[I]f I ask you whether you can pass me the salt, in a context where your abilities to do so are not in doubt, I license you to infer that I am doing something more than asking you whether you can pass the salt—I am in fact asking you to do it." In this case, the implicatum is lower-bounded (effectively, "the speaker must mean at least p").

Horn's pragmatic division of labor results in a clash between the Q and R Principles. As Horn says (p. 15), "A speaker obeying only Q would tend to say everything she knows on the off-chance that it might prove informative, while a speaker obeying only R would probably, to be on the safe side, not open her mouth." He draws an example of a potential clash from a discussion between a husband and wife collected in Tannen (1975):

(18)   Wife: Bob's having a party. You wanna go?
        Husband: OK.
        Second exchange (later):
        Wife: Are you sure you want to go?
        Husband: OK. Let's not go. I'm tired anyway.
        Post-mortem:
        Wife: We didn't go to the party because you didn't want to.
        Husband: *I* wanted to. *You* didn't want to.

In (18), the husband calculates from the wife's utterance (*Are you sure you want to go?*) the implicature that she does not want to go, based on (Horn suggests) a consideration of the R Principle ("say no more than you must"). The wife, in contrast, might believe she is obeying the Q Principle ("say as much as you can"), sacrificing a speech act just to make sure her husband is still interested in attending.

The particular relevance of Horn's pragmatic division of labor for evaluativity comes from his examination of R implicata across several different types of data. I'll review one phenomenon here—the treatment of the alternation between PRO and pronouns—but will ultimately focus on other data, discussed in §4.2.2, as a foundation for the treatment of evaluativity in Chapter 5.

One account of the use of coreferential PRO in sentences like (19) has been the suggestion that speakers avoid overt pronouns when the same referential relationship can be established without overt material ("Avoid Pronoun", Chomsky 1981).

(19)   a. John$_i$ would much prefer [PRO$_i$ going to the movie]
        b. John$_i$ wants to [PRO$_i$ win]

Chomsky makes the connection to Grice's pragmatic principle but flags the phenomenon as unique in its ties to the syntax.

[The Avoid Pronoun principle] might be regarded as a subcase of a conversational principle of not saying more than is required, or might be related to a principle of deletion-up-to-recoverability, but there is some reason to believe that it functions as a principle of grammar.   (Chomsky 1981: 65)

This same principle, Horn argues, can be recast in terms of the division of labor between the Q and R Principles ("an equilibrium"). He claims that the two conspire to produce a principle of least effort, (20), via a series of steps.

(20)   **Horn's Principle of Least Effort** (Horn 1984: 22)
        The use of a marked (relatively complex and/or prolix) expression when a corresponding unmarked (simpler, less "effortful") alternate expression is

available tends to be interpreted as conveying a marked message (one which the unmarked alternative would not or could not have conveyed).

First, the speaker utters an expression E' with marked ("extra") material (relative to E). The hearer reasons about the necessity of the extra material. If it was unnecessary, the speaker would be in violation of the R Principle. So, assuming the speaker is cooperative, the material must be necessary. Two different implicata come about as the result of this conclusion:

The unmarked alternative E tends to become associated (by use or—through conventionalization—by meaning) with unmarked situation s, representing stereotype or salient member of extension of E/E' (R-based inference, cf. Atlas and Levinson 1981). The marked alternative E' tends to become associated with the complement of s with respect to the original extension of E/E' (Q-based inference). (Horn 1984: 22)

We can therefore recast Chomsky's Avoid Pronoun as follows. In the sentences in (21), both PRO and the overt pronoun are assumed to be able to refer in principle to either the subject or some other salient individual. However, if a speaker utters (21b) (with "extra" linguistic material, the pronoun) when he could have uttered the less marked (21a), the hearer infers that the speaker intends the special interpretation, the one in which it is not bound by the subject. This is an R implicatum, the result of the speaker's compulsion to say no more than she must.

(21)   a. John$_i$ would much prefer PRO$_{i/j}$ going to the movie.
       b. John$_i$ would much prefer him$_{i/j}$ going to the movie.

If, instead, a speaker utters (21a) (the unmarked option), the hearer infers that the speaker intends the bland, unmarked meaning; in this case, the coreferential reading. This is a Q implicatum, calculated based on the hearer's trust that the speaker is saying as much as she can.

Note that Horn appeals to conventionalization to account for the apparent semantic reality of what he claims is ultimately a pragmatic concern. This notion of conventionalization is a diachronic one: Horn assumes that, if a particular form is generally associated with a Manner implicatum, this added meaning can be grammaticized over time. This diachronic perspective on the semantics/pragmatics boundary will be important for the account of evaluativity in Chapter 5, and I discuss it briefly below.

4.2 Empirical predictions

Grice's account, and Horn's Q and R Principles, make several predictions for several different kinds of implicata. I'll review two distinct types here: Quantity implicature (which will form the basis for my treatment of evaluativity in positive constructions) and Manner implicature (which will form the basis for my treatment of evaluativity in constructions in which it tracks antonymy). I'll argue here that the Quantity and Manner implicatures most relevant to evaluativity don't behave exactly the way Grice predicts they will; namely, they're not cancellable or detachable, and they are (in some cases) truth-conditional. This will form an important part of the discussion in Chapter 5.

4.2.1 *What Quantity implicatures look like*

Canonically, Quantity implicatures are those that involve lexical items (Grice's "formal devices") that are ordered along a scale of informativeness (a Horn scale, or a Q scale). Three examples are in (22).

(22)   a. ⟨*some, all*⟩
       b. ⟨1, 2, 3, 4, 5, . . .⟩
       c. ⟨*as, -er*⟩

We've already seen the predictions made by Quantity or the Q Principle on the pair in (22c): an utterance of the equative in (23a) carries with it the Quantity implicature in (23b) (or possibly something weaker; Russell 2006). The result is that the equative is strengthened from its compositional semantic "at least" interpretation to its total signification in (23c): that Adam is exactly as tall as Doug.

(23)   a. Adam is as tall as Doug.
       b. $\neg$ Adam is taller than Doug.
       c. $\leadsto_Q$ Adam is exactly as tall as Doug.

These canonical Quantity implicatures behave just the way Grice expects them to: they are cancellable and detachable. The cancellability of the implicature is apparent in (24). In (24a), the *in fact* clause, which is thought to signal cancellation of an implicature, is inconsistent with the "exactly" interpretation.

(24)   a. Adam is as tall as Doug; in fact, he's taller than Doug.
       b. Adam is not as tall as Doug, he's taller.

Perhaps more compelling evidence is in (24b), in which the equative is negated. The negated sentence in (24b) shows not only that the equative can carry an "exactly" implicature, but that this implicature can be embedded under a logical (truth-conditional) operator. These are referred to as local or embedded or intrusive implicatures, and will be significant in what follows. I'll address them further in §4.4.

That the Quantity implicature associated with the equative is detachable can be verified by an utterance of the equative in a context that supports the compositional, "at least" interpretation (or, alternatively, does not support the calculation of the implicature). Imagine a roller coaster ride at an amusement park that carries a height requirement, with a cardboard cut-out next to it asking, *Are you as tall as this bear?* In this context, the question is most naturally interpreted as asking whether riders are at least as tall as the bear (not exactly as tall). This illustrates that, in addition to being cancellable, the scalar implicature associated with the equative is detachable, i.e., not particularly grammaticized by the equative construction.

That the quantity implicature is resistant to conventionalization is also potentially supported by the (tentative) observation that equative degree quantifiers across languages carry this "at least"/"exactly" ambiguity (Henkelmann 2006). The Gricean story is that while equative morphemes tend to mean "exactly as", due to CI, this meaning isn't conventionalized.

I will end this section by describing one other phenomenon also treated as a Quantity implicature: the strengthening (or "narrowing," Geurts 2011) of truisms or tautologies. I will refer to them as **uninformativity-based Quantity implicatures**, in contrast to scalar implicatures, which could be thought of as *under*-informativity-based.

Here is Grice's example of an uninformativity-based Quantity implicature (1975: 52):

Extreme examples of a flouting of the first maxim of Quantity are provided by utterances of patent tautologies like *Women are women* and *War is war*. I would wish to maintain that at the level of what is said, in my favored sense, such remarks are totally noninformative and so, at that level, cannot but infringe the first maxim of Quantity in any conversational context. They are, of course, informative at the level of what is implicated, and the hearer's identification of their informative content at this level is dependent on his ability to explain the speaker's selection of this *particular* patent tautology.   (original emphasis)

Geurts (2011: 183) discusses the content of the implicature a little more explicitly, in regard to the example in (25):

(25)   Bankers are bankers.

If both occurrences of *bankers* had the same meaning, [(25)] would be a tautology, which it is not, or at least, not necessarily. One way of bringing an utterance of [(25)] in line with the Quantity maxim is by suppposing that the second occurrrence of the noun is restricted in its application to individuals exhibiting greed, lack of moral fibre, or what have you.

The idea is that the first principle of Grice's Quantity maxim—effectively, Horn's (1984) Q Principle, "Make your contribution sufficient"—can also be used to strengthen or supplement the meaning of otherwise meaningless or uninformative utterances. The result is a uninformativity-based Quantity implicature.

There are several different ways in which these Quantity implicatures differ from the scalar implicatures exemplified by the equative in (24a). First they are indeterminate. ("[T]here may be various possible specific explanations" of why a maxim was violated, and "the conversational implicatum in such cases will be a disjunction of such specific explanations . . ." Grice 1975: 58.) Their interpretation is affected much more by world knowledge than scale-based Quantity implicatures. Second, they don't seem to be cancellable, as suggested by (26).

(26) a. War is war . . . #in fact, violence is avoidable in war.
      b. Bankers are bankers . . . #in fact, many bankers are lovely.
      c. Boys will be boys . . . #in fact, they often behave unpredictably.

The first point—that these uninformativity-based Quantity implicatures are indeterminate—complicates the second. I have chosen natural interpretations of these tautologies in (26), but the *in fact* cancellations in (26) do not represent an exhaustive test for whether the Quantity implicatures are cancellable. Nevertheless, I take (26) to be indicative that other implicatures in other contexts would also not be cancellable.

It should not be a surprise, given the discussion in the previous section, that uninformativity-based Quantity implicatures are not cancellable. While they differ from scalar implicatures in this respect, they are not the first instance of a non-cancellable Quantity implicature we've seen; (11) demonstrated that it is hard to cancel the implicature in Grice's letter writer case, which is an instance of a non-scalar underinformativity-based Quantity implicature.

I will argue in §5.3 that the evaluativity in positive constructions results from an uninformativity-based Quantity implicature, so this distinction will be important in what follows. I'll also make the case that other instances of evaluativity are the result of a Manner implicature; other examples of this phenomenon are reviewed below.

4.2.2 *What Manner implicatures look like*

Grice's original Manner maxim is repeated below.

(27) **Manner**
      1. Avoid obscurity of expression.
      2. Avoid ambiguity.
      3. Be brief (avoid unnecessary prolixity).
      4. Be orderly.

Accounting for apparent markedness-based semantic competition within the general framework of Gricean pragmatics has one very notable primary challenge: an account of how a process seen as extra-linguistic can interact with syntactic, semantic, and possibly morphological levels. McCawley (1978) took up the task directly, and his treatment of core data forms a very solid foundation for the account presented in Chapter 5. I will start by summarizing his work and related work in Atlas and Levinson (1981) before presenting Horn's adaptations and extensions.

McCawley's opening discussion, highlighting the relevance of Grice for considerations of linguistic markedness, is worth quoting in full (1978: 245):

What is conversationally implicated by an utterance depends not only on the utterance but on what other utterances the speaker could have produced but did not. For example, a declarative sentence *A or B* conveys that the speaker doesn't know whether *A or B* is the case because if he did know which of *A* and *B* was the case, he would have been in a position to say *A* or to say *B*, as the case may be, and thus he could have said something more informative than *A or B* with less linguistic effort (Grice 1967, 1975). Because the speaker expended the extra effort, he is taken as not having been in a position to (cooperatively) assert *A* or assert *B* and is thus taken as not knowing whether *A* or *B* is the case.

Of course, the linchpin in this process of reasoning is the notion of "less linguistic effort" (and, correspondingly, the calculation of "what other utterances the speaker could have produced but did not"). This is where linguistic markedness fits in. McCawley acknowledges the challenge of defining linguistic effort objectively, but argues that the empirical phenomena he addresses provide compelling evidence that, at least in some cases, the relevant notion of markedness can be reduced to the property of being "more complex in surface syntactic structure, as well as containing more phonological material" (p. 246). I'll review some examples of these cases.

First, McCawley examined something akin to the lexical blocking addressed in Kiparsky (1973): the contrast between *pale green* and *?pale red* or **pale black* (the observation is attributed to Householder 1971). The intuitive explanation is that *pale red* and *pale black* sound more unnatural than *pale green* because they (in contrast to *pale green*) have lexical counterparts, specifically *pink* and *grey*.

A corollary, based on Grice's prediction that the marked strategy will carry a marked meaning, is that *pale red* (and, presumably, *pale black*) means something slightly different than we'd predict compositionally. As McCawley summarizes (p. 246), "Thus, an analysis in terms of conversational implicature allows one to define *pink* as 'pale red,' show why *pink* and *pale red* are not interchangeable, and show why *pale red* refers to shades of red that are nowhere near as pale as the shades of green, blue, and yellow that one refers to as *pale green, pale blue,* and *pale yellow.*"

Here is another situation in which we seem to be able to account for the distribution of two elements in terms of a special/general semantic relationship, as with the Avoid Pronoun data in §4.1.2. But it is perhaps our first exposure to a case where a special or marked meaning corresponds to a special or marked element. This is the hallmark of Manner implicature phenomena, as explicitly predicted by Horn's Principle of Least Effort, and I will ultimately argue that it captures the interaction between evaluativity and markedness perfectly.

McCawley gives several other examples of phenomena in which marked meaning is correlated with marked form (and unmarked meaning with unmarked form). Another is the contrast in meaning between lexical and periphrastic causatives. He cites Shibatani's (1973a,b) work on Japanese causatives, but the empirical observations are just as appropriate for English (see also Fodor 1970; Katz 1970; Shibatani 1976).

It has been tempting, historically, to provide a lexical semantics for the verb *to kill* in terms of "to cause to die," called a **periphrastic** causative (from the Greek roots for "to speak" (*phrasis*) and the PP "around" (*peri*)). But the two sentences in (28) (from Katz 1970) seem to have slightly different meanings.

(28)   a. He caused the sheriff to die.
       b. He killed the sheriff.

While the two VPs are in principle synonymous, (28) illustrates that they do not have the same meaning in use. *Kill*, the unmarked VP, is associated with the typical interpretations of the verb's meaning: an event of intentional, direct killing. The marked VP, in contrast, is associated with more unconventional interpretations. McCawley (1978: 249) says: "It would be more correct to say [(28a)] than [(28b)] of someone who has tampered with the sheriff's gun with the result that in a shoot-out with an outlaw the sheriff's gun fails to fire and the outlaw is thus able to shoot the sheriff to death." In this perspective of the sentences in (28), the two VPs differ in terms of markedness (the result of a contrast in morphological complexity), and this difference has a semantic consequence (association with a non-canonical interpretation).

McCawley's main contribution is the introduction of these phenomena under the umbrella of the Gricean program; he does not offer a detailed proposal for how to account for them. He summarizes his argument as follows (pp. 257–8): "I have argued that the lack of interchangeability between the lexical item and its periphrastic equivalent are [*sic*] due not to idiosyncratic restrictions that must be incorporated into the relevant dictionary entries, but rather are consequences of general principles of cooperative behavior."

One other prominent example of Manner implicatures comes in the form of litotes, the stacking of two negations which seems to carry meaning above and beyond what is said in Grice's sense. In presenting this phenomenon, I will focus on the work in Horn (1991a), but a Gricean treatment of litotes can also be found in Bolinger (1972), Atlas and Levinson (1981), Brown and Levinson (1978), and Horn (1989).

In his discussion of these data, Horn (1991a) makes two observations that are relevant to the study of Manner implicature. The first has to do with the truth-conditional extension of the negation of negated predicates or of negative antonyms like *not unhappy*.

The foundations of this observation are illustrated in Figure 4.1, where I have adopted Klein's (1980, 1982) term "extension gap" to refer to the value that falls between the predicates *happy* and *unhappy*; Sapir (1944) called this, perhaps more memorably,

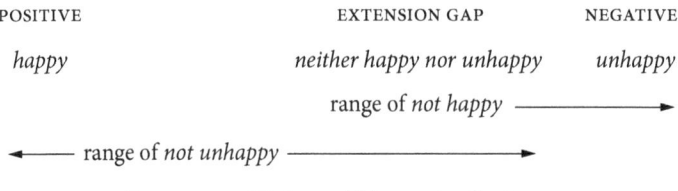

FIGURE 4.1. Litotes and Manner implicatures

the "zone of indifference." Litotes—the negation of negative predicates like *unhappy*—should in theory correspond to the complement of the negated predicate, and so mean something like "either happy or neither happy nor unhappy." This is the bottom arrow in Figure 4.1. But in actuality, they seem to pick out only the extension gap. As Jespersen (1965) puts it (p. 332):

[T]wo negatives, however, do not exactly cancel one another out so that the result [*not uncommon, not infrequent,*...] is identical with the simple *common, frequent*; the longer expression is always weaker: "this is not unknown to me" or "I am not ignorant of this" means "I am to some extent aware of it," etc. The psychological reason for this is that the *détour* through the two mutually destructive negatives weakens the mental energy of the listener and implies . . . a hesitation which is absent from the blunt, outspoken *common* or *known*.

This is, as Horn suggests, is a "metaphysical (and somewhat Victorian)" (p. 31) version of the Principle of Least Effort. He characterizes the phenomenon of double negation as "an especially clear correlation between the stylistic naturalness of a given form, its relative brevity and simplicity, and its use in stereotypic situations (via R-implicature)" (p. 31).[1]

The second observation is that litotes tend to have two different interpretations. One reading corresponds to Jespersen's description above: as Horn puts it, "a doubly negated adjective is perceptibly weaker, more hesitant than the corresponding simple positive" (1991a: 84). The other reading seems to be the opposite, in that it seems stronger than we'd expect given Figure 4.1. For this reading, Horn quotes Erasmus:

This point would not have been lost on Erasmus, who—under the heading *Commuta in Negationem* ("Change it into a Negative") in his *Colloquia*—recommends the use of double negation as a discreet means for conveying a strong positive, e.g. *non ineloquens* for the blatant and overdirect *eloquentissimus*, "Your letter was no small joy", "Wine pleases me not a little".

In other words, Horn (1991a) notes, the sentence in (29) can mean, depending on context, 'I was damn well aware of it' (p. 90, the stronger than expected, or "exceptional reading") or something like "I had a very slight awareness of the problem" (the weaker than expected, or "gap reading").

(29) I was not unaware of the problem.

Horn (1989, 1991a) argues that these readings cannot be treated semantically (contrary to, e.g., Frege 1919 and Geach 1972), but are rather the result of the Principle of Least Effort, in Hintikka's (1968: 42) terms, "the pragmatic pressure not to use circumlocutions without some specific purpose." He argues that the two distinct possible

---

[1] See Horn (1991a,b) and Levinson (2000) for more explicit treatments of litotes in terms of Manner implicatures. More recently, Krifka (2007) supplements these theories where they concern doubly negated gradable adjectives with an explicit semantics of vagueness.

interpretetations are the result of two distinct possible implicature calculations, similar to the scenario in (18) in which the husband and wife miscommunicate.

Recall that Horn's Q Principle places a lower bound on the informational content of an utterance, while his R Principle places an upper bound. He claims that the (more natural) gap reading is the result of the application of the R Principle, which restricts the more marked form (*not unhappy*) from being associated with typical situations (i.e., the "happy" extension). The Q Principle can thus optionally apply to this outcome, restricting the meaning "to those situations outside the stereotype, for which the unmarked expression could not have been used appropriately" (Horn 1991a: 85). The result is the exceptional reading, meaning something like "very happy".

(Levinson 2000: 145) endorses this approach:

But the consensus (or at least that extracted by Horn) is that the inference may go either way: (a) it may suggest that the property described falls short of the positive or (b) that it exceeds the positive or that the positive needs emphasizing.... The learned commentary suggests indeed that the (b) use is parasitic on the (a) use: by asserting "I am not an ungenerous man" I might implicate that I am something less than fully generous, but because modesty would be reason for that, I may in fact implicate something less modest. Thus polite understatement may be a factor in the extreme value readings.

This perspective on litotes suggest that these Manner implicatures are indeterminate, as Grice (1975) predicted they would be. But how do Manner implicatures fare in terms of the other features Grice attributed to implicatures? They do generally seem to be cancellable, at least somewhat. But, unlike scale-based Quantity implicatures, manner implicatures seem to be not particularly context-dependent, and fairly conventionalized. I will discuss these points in turn.

The "unconventional interpretations" Horn and others predict are associated with marked forms due to the R Principle appear to be cancellable, at least somewhat. This is illustrated below; (30a) tests for the Manner implicature, discussed in Grice (1975: 38), that an indefinite like *a woman* carries an implicature in opposition to a more specific description like *his wife*.

(30) a. Doug met a woman at the bar . . . ?in fact, he met his wife.
      b. Adam caused the sheriff to die . . . ?in fact, he killed him outright.
      c. Helicopters are not uncommon here . . . ?in fact, they're somewhat common.

Their ability to be cancelled is clearly improved when there is some discourse-related reason for the speaker to have used the marked form in the first place. (Van der Sandt 1992 refers to this as an "anaphoric link"; I will discuss it in more detail in §4.3.)

(31) A: I saw Doug leave for the bar. Did he go to meet a woman?
      B: Yes (Doug met a woman at the bar), in fact he met his wife there.

(32)　A:　I just saw an ambulance leave Adam's apartment carrying the sheriff's body. Did Adam somehow cause the sheriff to die?

　　　B:　Yes (Adam caused the sheriff to die), in fact he killed him outright.

(33)　A:　Goodness, that's the fourth helicopter I've seen this afternoon. It gives me the impression that helicopters are not uncommon in Venice. Is that right?

　　　B:　Yes (helicopters are not uncommon here), in fact they're somewhat common.

A's initial use of these marked forms carries an implication of politeness in (32) and (33) (Brown and Levinson 1978, 1987; Leech 1983), and perhaps something like caution in (31). So while A's utterances of these marked forms might carry different implicatures, based on differences in the words or phrases that trigger it, the interpretations of the same phrases in B's responses show that these implicatures and others can be cancelled.

While this indicates that the *type* of Manner implicature available to a marked form is in principle context-dependent (in Grice's words, is indeterminate), it also suggests that any use of these periphrastic constructions carries some implicature or another, except possibly when they're cancelled in discourse. This raises questions about the extent to which these conversational implicatures are really just conventionalized implicatures, possibly grammaticized via some diachronic process.

Horn (1984) assumes a grammaticization process explicitly for certain phenomena related to McCawley's (1978) lexical blocking phenomena, explaining, for instance, how *cow* might have come to exclude bulls from its normal use, and *finger* to exclude thumbs. In the periphastic cases above, this process of conventionalization or grammaticization would need to apply to a phrase instead of a word. In this case, phrases like *not uncommon* (and other litotes or periphrastic expressions) would be associated with a conventionalized or generalized implicature.

4.2.3　*When Quantity and Manner interact*

In presenting Grice's program and various adaptations of it, I have suggested that a given utterance could carry multiple implicatures from multiple sources. It stands to reason that these implicatures could in principle be incompatible with one another. This is a concern of Levinson's (2000), who argues that the different types of conversational implicature form a hierarchy with respect to one another. For our purposes, it is sufficient to note that he predicts that Quantity implicatures will be calculated prior to Manner implicatures, and therefore that all sentences that could potentially carry a conflicting pair of Quantity and Manner implicature will only carry a Quantity implicature.

This conclusion will be important for (and, I believe, better supported by) the evaluativity discussion in Chapter 5, so I will present his argument here, while admitting it is not as strong as it could be. One of his two examples of an utterance carrying a conflicting Quantity and Manner implicature is in (34) (from p. 160).[2]

(34)   It's not unlikely that Giant Stride will win the Derby, and indeed I think it likely.

The relevant Manner implicature is potentially contributed by the litote in the first conjunct; we would predict that it would contribute to the utterance an implication like "It's less than fully likely." The relevant Quantity implicature is potentially contributed by the embedding verb *I think* in the second conjunct; the claim is that *think* is on a Horn or Q-scale with *know* and its use carries the CI "¬ know." Levinson's claim (p.160) is that the "Q-inference . . . defeats the inconsistent M-inference," resulting in the meaning that the speaker thinks it's likely that Giant Stride will win.

Levinson argues that the relative priority of Quantity over Manner implicatures is connected with the extent to which these implicatures are defeasible and, consequently, the likelihood that they will be generalized. By way of explanation, he offers (p. 161): "The relative priority of the Q-Principle over the [R]-Principle is presumably attributable to the relative importance of informational content over expression modulation." While I do not feel comfortable endorsing this attribution, the idea that Manner implicatures are more generalized than, less defeasible than, and secondary to Quantity implicatures will be borne out in the discussion of evaluativity in Chapter 5.

I have presented claims that there are conversational implicatures, calculable from a series of conversational principles, the Q- and R-Principles among them. I've presented Grice's claims that these CIs are in principle cancellable, context-dependent, etc., and are a part of what is implicated rather than what is said, but I have ultimately concluded that there is no clear necessary condition for conversational implicature generally. In the next section I'll explore in closer detail another complication to Grice's taxonomy: that the presence of conversational implicature (and its cancellability) seems to be sensitive to discourse properties. I will focus in particular on the ability of discourse topic to affect the extent to which implicatures can be an entailment (rather than an implication) of an utterance.

4.3 Discourse sensitivity

As originally characterized by Grice (1975), conversational implicatures are like presuppositions in many ways: they do not affect a sentence's truth value, and so are

---

[2] Levinson's other example invokes disjunction:

i. Cortes caused the death of Montezuma, or indeed he killed him outright with his own hands.

Levinson notes (p. 160) that the sentence "clearly lacks the potential Manner implicature . . . and this is obviously due to the content of the first disjunct." But this disjunction seems to be behaving more like a discourse particle than logical negation (Asher and Txurruka 2007), so I think it's better to put this example aside.

not entailments of the sentence.[3] There is however reason to think that this feature of CIs is sensitive to certain properties of discourse. I'll begin by describing some arguments made in van Kuppevelt (1996) and related observations. I'll then discuss recent claims that the projectability of conventional implicature and presupposition can be discourse-sensitive as well (Simons et al. 2011).

The first discussion of the discourse sensitivity of conversational implicatures, to my knowledge, comes from work in Campbell (1981) and Fretheim (1992), formalized in van Kuppevelt (1996). Van Kuppevelt argues that while scalar implicatures are usually cancellable (35), they are sometimes not (36).

(35) A: Who bought four books?
     B: <u>Harry</u> bought four books. In fact he bought seven.

(36) [Harry did a lot of shopping this afternoon.]
     A: How many books did he buy?
     B: He bought <u>four</u> books. #In fact he bought seven.

The underlining in (35) and (36) indicates the comment in the sentence. Van Kuppevelt defines a **topic** as "that which is being questioned by means of a contextually induced explicit or implicit question Q" and the corresponding **comment** "that which is asked for by Q" (p. 396). The observation is that the comment structure of the answer *Harry bought four books* changes depending on what question it is a response to, and this difference affects the cancellability of the scalar implicature.

Specifically, in (36), "exactly four" seems to be an entailment of *B*'s response, rather than an implicature.

First, it demonstrates that the cancellation of an upper bound inference cannot, as is generally assumed, be an essential property of scalar Quantity-(i) implicatures. Example [(36)] shows that the cancellation of such an inference may be blocked. Second, it demonstrates that if cancellation is not possible it is blocked by a contradiction which implies that the upper bound inference that Harry bought no more than four books is *entailed* by the first part of the answer.

(original emphasis; van Kuppevelt 1996: 412)

This claim is supported by the acceptability of *C*'s response in (37), where *C*'s response seems to be a denial of the strengthened, "exactly" interpretation of the numeral in *B*'s response, a property typically associated with truth-conditional content.

---

[3] Although it is worthwhile noting that presuppositions don't perfectly instantiate this description, either. To quote Chierchia and McConnell-Ginet (1990: 136), there is "a whole class of presuppositions that are no more defeasible than entailments are."

(37)   [Harry did a lot of shopping this afternoon.]
    A: How many books did he buy?
    B: He bought <u>four</u> books.
    C: No he didn't, he bought five!

This suggests that the same sort of meaning that Grice explicitly classified as part of what is implicated can, depending on the discourse, be a part of what is said.

Van Kuppevelt concludes (citing Campbell 1981) that "only when cardinals are in comment position do they always give rise to an 'exactly n' interpretation," or that "only if a cardinal belongs to the background (topic part), is its upper bound pragmatically provided by conversational implicature" (p. 407). And instead of treating conversational implicatures as non-truth-conditional, we must characterize them as entailments, depending on the properties of the discourse.

To do so, Van Kuppevelt (1996) proposes a theory of implicature in which scalemates are defined in terms of their informativity (they must be partially ordered with respect to informativity) and their coherence: they must all be satisfactory answers to the implicit or explicit question driving the discourse (see also Horn 1992). Scalar implicature is calculated at a discourse level, and where "at least" interpretations of numerals are prohibited (when that numeral is the comment), the implicature is non-defeasible.

Roberts (1996) makes a similar proposal on a larger scale, adapting what she calls "intentional structure" into a Stalnakerian theory of information structure (Stalnaker 1978). She argues that, in discourse, an interlocutor can make one of two moves: a set-up, which requests information, and a payoff, which addresses it (see also Carlson 1983). Set-ups establish the **question under discussion** (QUD), and payoffs either restrict that question into a **subquestion** or answer the question. As Roberts argues, the QUD (be it implicit or explicit) can determine prosodic focus (and corresponding focus alternatives) and could possibly be used to extend the proposals in Thomason (1990) and Welker (1994) to treat conversational implicature.

In recent work, Simons et al. (2011) have expanded the potential empirical significance of the QUD to make claims about the relationship between truth conditionality and relevance to the QUD. Traditionally—including throughout Grice's program—meaning has been divided into two categories. A sentence's entailments form its truth-conditional content, and can thus be embedded under truth-conditional operators like negation, and can be denied in discourse, etc. A sentence's projective content—canonically presuppositions, but also plausibly CIs—projects outside of truth-conditional operators and can generally not be denied or addressed in discourse (excepting, for instance, von Fintel's 2004 *Hey, wait a minute!* test). Simons et al. indicate that the sort of meaning encoded by a word or phrase could change depending on the relationship between that content and the QUD. I'll review their proposal briefly here.

Simons et al. differentiate between at-issue content and not-at-issue content (defined in terms of the QUD) to account for when a projected proposition can function as an entailment. "$?p$" should be read as "whether p."[4]

(38)   A proposition p is **at-issue** relative to a question Q iff $?p$ is relevant to Q.

They relate this to the truth-conditional status of implicatures as follows: "All and only those implications of (embedded) sentences which are not-at-issue relative to the Question Under Discussion in the context have the potential to project," by which they mean project outside of truth-conditional operators, the sort of behavior we typically associate with presupposition.

To illustrate this, they contrast the meaning of the appositives in (39) and (40). The meaning encoded in appositives is typically thought of as projecting, as demonstrated in (39), outside of presupposition filters like the antecedent of conditionals (Karttunen 1977; Potts 2012; Anderbois et al. 2010, 2013).

(39)   If Bob, a big drinker, is here, we'll have fun.

That the appositive content projects is evident in the intuition that (39) as a whole carries the implication that Bob is a big drinker, while the encoded, truth-conditional content of the embedded clause (that Bob is here) is embedded under *if*.

Contrast this with the appositive *who probably won't be able to come* in (40):

(40)   A: Who's coming to the dinner tonight?
       B: Well, I haven't talked to Charles, who probably won't be able to come, but I
          did talk to Sally, who is coming.

Here, *B*'s response seems to be a felicitous answer to *A*'s question, despite the fact that the relevant information is encoded in an appositive. Simons et al. take this to indicate that appositives can, in the right context, be entailments (rather than implications) of an utterance. This happens whenever the relevant information addresses the QUD.

However, as they note, at-issue appositive content still seems to project. This is illustrated by the epithet in (41).

(41)   A: What do you think of Bob?
       B: I've never met the son-of-a-bitch.

Epithets, like conventional implicatures, tend to be not-at-issue and tend to project (Potts 2012). (41) shows that epithets can be at-issue, by virtue of the fact that *B*'s

---

[4] Their revised definition takes into consideration speaker intention:

i.   **Revised definition of at-issueness**
     a. A proposition p is at-issue iff the speaker intends to address the QUD via $?p$.
     b. An intention to address the QUD via $?p$ is **felicitous** only if $?p$ is relevant to the QUD, and the speaker
        can reasonably expect the addressee to recognize this intention.

response seems to be a felicitous answer to A's question. But they seem to nevertheless encode projected content; that Bob is a son-of-a-bitch still seems to project outside of the negation in *B*'s utterance, if we assume that *never* has the potential to target the content encoded in the epithet.

In sum: there is evidence that canonically projective content—like conversational implicature, conventional implicature, presupposition, and epithets, etc.—can sometimes be an entailment of an utterance. Their (non-)projective status seems to depend on their (not-)at-issue status, which is defined in terms of the goals of the discourse, and in particular the Question Under Discussion (see also Thomason 1990; Roberts 1996). Despite this change in discourse function, they still seem to project outside of the logical operators that are typically seen as filters for presupposition.

There is evidence that, despite the fact that these meanings seem to function at a different level than standard compositional semantics (Grice's "what is said"; Karttunen and Peters 1979; Potts 2012), these projective meanings can nevertheless affect compositional semantics in particular ways. Anderbois et al. (2010, 2013) discuss whether appositives can condition anaphora, ellipsis, and more. Two examples are below; see also Farkas and Bruce (2010); McCready (2010); Murray (2010).

(42)   a. John, who had been kissed by Mary, kissed her too.
       b. So Lalonde, who was the one person who could deliver Trudeau, did.

Murray (2010) and Anderbois et al. (2010, 2013), based on these and other data, call for a formal semantics that can account for this semantic interaction (this "mixed content") between at-issue, truth-conditional semantics (what is said) and not-at-issue, projective, (conventionally) implicated content. At the very least, then, the relationship between content that has traditionally been characterized as entailments and as projective is much less black-and-white than previously thought, and clearly seems to track at least whether or not the content addresses the QUD.

I will summarize the conclusions of this section briefly. Grice differentiated between what is said and what is implicated, and between conventional and conversational implicature. Each of these distinctions takes for granted that content is either truth-conditional or projective, but it seems as though this is not the case. There is evidence that, at least, the projective status of a conversational implicature can change if its content is at-issue in the discourse, i.e., pertinent to the QUD. And there is evidence that, e.g., conventional implicatures can affect truth-conditional content despite the fact that these meanings often project outside of logical operators.

These observations are relevant for evaluativity because, while I argue that evaluativity arises as a Quantity or Manner implicature, it behaves in many cases like an entailment. In presenting my case, I will rely on parallels between evaluativity and some of these other phenomena.

4.4 Discussion

There is a general consensus that utterances carry meaning above and beyond what we might expect given their compositional semantics, and that at least some of this meaning can be explained in terms of Grice's Cooperative Principle and its submaxims (or, from another perspective, Horn's Q and R Principles and his Zipfian division of pragmatic labor). I've given a few reasons to think that CIs can differ in the extent to which they're cancellable: some, like Manner implicatures and the Quantity implicatures associated with tautologies, don't seem to be as naturally cancellable as scale-based Quantity implicatures. And the extent to which scale-based Quantity implicatures are cancellable is itself sensitive to properties of discourse.

I will end this chapter by briefly mentioning a debate about the extent to which CIs are context-dependent and global. Grice defines CIs as calculated (in part) on what is said. This appears to require an implementation of CIs in which they are calculated globally, at utterance level, as a function of the entailments of the sentence ("what is said") and other considerations of the discourse. There is, however, a great deal of evidence that CIs are calculated (in fact, must be calculated) in local, embedded contexts where they can be manipulated by truth-conditional operators. These are called local, embedded, or intrusive implicatures.

There is an ongoing and exciting debate about the extent to which the existence of these intrusive implicatures are damaging to the Gricean picture. In particular, some argue that intrusive implicatures can be fully accounted for with the assumption that CIs are calculated at the level of utterance (Soames 1982; Sauerland 2004; Russell 2006; Simons 2010; Geurts 2011; Simons 2014), while others have argued that they require a theory in which CIs are triggered by an operator in the syntax (Fox 2003; Chierchia 2004; Klinedinst 2007; Magri 2011; Gajewski and Sharvit 2012).

An example of an intrusive implicature is in (43) (from Chierchia 2004: 44). The relevant implicature is scalar, triggered by the quantifier *some* (which is a weak member of a Q scale with *every*).

(43) John believes [$_{CP}$ that some students are waiting for him.]
    a. It is not the case that John believes that every student is waiting for him.
    b. John believes that not every student is waiting for him.

One interpretation of Grice's program, in which CIs are calculated at the utterance level, incorrectly predicts that the utterance will carry the implicature in (43a), the negation of the sentence containing *every*, or something similar. Instead, intuitively, the utterance seems to carry the implicature in (43b). This makes it seem as though the implicature is calculated in the embedded CP, under the scope of the embedding verb *believe*.

The phenomenon of intrusive implicatures can be considered independent of the observation that scalar implicatures behave differently in downward-entailing contexts, as in (44).

(44) Adam isn't as tall as Doug.
    a. . . . In fact, he's taller.
    b. #. . . Because they're the same height.

The continuation in (44a) reflects that object of negation is an "exactly" interpretation of the equative; the unacceptability of the continuation in (44b) shows that the object of negation is not the "at least" interpretation. The absence of the "at least" interpretation is arguably attributable to the observation that what counts as "more informative" is reversed in downward-entailing contexts (Harnish 1976; Atlas and Levinson 1981; Hirschberg 1991; Horn 1989).

Those who argue that the Gricean program is consistent with examples like (43) offer interpretations of pragmatic CI calculation in which the speakers' knowledge, intentions, and goals in the discourse are better controlled for; those who argue that these phenomena are syntactic claim that their treatment requires a null syntactic operator to calculate SIs in particular environments, similar to *only* in, e.g., *John believes that only some students are waiting for him.*

I could not possibly do this debate justice in the space I have here. I would instead like to offer a perspective on it that, I believe, will make the study of evaluativity more simple: the examples that form the foundation of this debate all involve scale-based or scalar Quantity implicatures like *some*, *or*, or numerals like *two*. And the mainstream syntactic proposals encode this specifically in an operator that is specific to scale-based Quantity implicatures. There are, as far as I know, no arguments that uninformativity-based Quantity implicatures (such as the ones associated with tautologies) or Manner implicatures are syntactically encoded. And these are the only CIs relevant to the discussion in Chapter 5.

Furthermore, the debate doesn't really even translate to a discussion of uninformativity-based Quantity implicatures and Manner implicatures. One argument in favor of a silent scalar operator is the observation that it can be overt in, e.g., *only*; there is, as far as I can tell, no lexical item that is to Manner implicature what *only* is to scalar implicature; such a word would mean something like *I'm being periphrastic but do not intend to implicate anything by it.*

The Quantity implicature associated with tautologies like *Bankers are bankers* seems to scope under embedding verbs, as in (45), but this is arguably because uninformativity-based Quantity implicatures are not defeasible in the same way as scale-based Quantity implicature, and/or are conventionalized to some extent.

(45) A: Adam seems remarkably unfazed by the fact that he is the victim of a
        pyramid scheme.
      B: Well, you know, Adam has always believed that bankers will be bankers.

Manner implicatures seem to be optionally embeddable, depending on context. On one interpretation of (46), the periphrasis could be the result of the speaker using the periphrastic form for reasons of politeness or delicacy, perhaps to inform the sheriff's family about the sheriff's cause of death. This is an interpretation in which the Manner implicature seems to be interpreted globally.

(46) The judge believes that Adam caused the sheriff to die.

On another reading of (46), the Manner implicature seems to be able to scope under the embedding verb. This reading is especially natural in a context in which Adam is being acquitted of murder charges after it came out that Adam tampered with the sheriff's gun before the sheriff's shootout with an outlaw.

While there is clearly a lot to consider in analyzing these examples, they do give reason to think that scalar implicatures are special, for some reason, in that they are generally cancellable and locally calculable, but that we should be cautious in extending this generalization to other CIs. Certainly, given (46), it would be a mistake to argue that Manner implicatures are *necessarily* calculated locally, although it seems reasonable to think that they might be calculated slightly differently depending on which clause they are interpreted in.

I will return to other examples of Manner implicatures affecting the truth conditions of sentences in §5.2. For now, I will take these considerations as a license to sidestep the issue of intrusive implicatures and the possibility that Grice's program might need to be supplemented with other (possibly syntactic) aspects.

In the following chapter, I will argue that at least some instances of evaluativity are the result of Horn's (1984) Principle of Least Effort, which uses the R Principle to account for why marked forms tend to be associated with marked meaning. But there are some alternative accounts of markedness-based semantic competition in other independently motivated formal systems; Grice isn't the only game in town, and there are plenty of options for those who appreciate the empirical parallels I will draw but are squeamish about Gricean implicature.

Blutner (2000) translates the theory in Horn (1984) into a dynamic-semantic Optimality-Theoretic (OT) framework (Prince and Smolensky 1993). He reinterprets Horn's Q and R Principles into (violable) constraints, and modifies the foundations of OT so that the theory is bidirectional, treating both the speaker's and hearer's perspectives. The model for this bidirectionality is the game-theoretic notion of equilibrium, in which a successful communication is one that satisfies both the speaker's and the hearer's needs and expectations. He refers to this as "superoptimality," the optimal candidate according to both the speaker's and hearer's constraint rankings. In (47), A ranges over semantic forms, σ over contexts of utterance and τ over updated contexts. Gen_σ is the set of ordered pairs of forms and output contexts generated by the context of utterance.

(47) **Bidirectional OT (weak version)** (Blutner 2000: 203)
     (Q) $\langle A, \tau \rangle$ satisfies the Q-principle iff $\langle A, \tau \rangle \in \text{Gen}_\sigma$ and there is no other pair $\langle A', \tau \rangle$ satisfying the I-principle such that $\langle A', \tau \rangle > \langle A, \tau \rangle$.

(I) $\langle A, \tau \rangle$ satisfies the I-principle iff $\langle A, \tau \rangle \in \mathbf{Gen}_\sigma$ and there is no other pair $\langle A', \tau \rangle$ satisfying the Q-principle such that $\langle A, \tau' \rangle > \langle A, \tau \rangle$.

$\langle A, \tau \rangle$ is called *superoptimal* iff it satisfies both the Q-principle and the I-principle.

Effectively, (47) predicts that a meaning (here, context change potential) will be paired with a form A iff the form is optimal (the Q-principle) and the meaning is optimal (the I-principle). The result is a theory, like Horn's, in which unmarked forms are associated with unmarked meanings (and so forth for marked forms).

In a similar vein, Schaden (2009) offers a treatment of the interpretation of present-perfect aspect relative to simple past tense in an OT-based system of markedness competition.

Van Rooij (2004) argues that the conventions described in Horn (1984) are the result of evolutionary factors, and reformulates the Manner implicatures in the more universal framework of game theory, as a signalling game (see also Skyrms 2010; McCready 2012). He argues that conventionalized Manner implicatures arise when a speaker and hearer achieve a Nash Equilibrium; in this theory, competition is between form/action pairs associated with the speaker and hearer, respectively. The notion of markedness is recast in terms of utility (p. 308): "Let us call a strategy *strictly efficient* if in interaction with itself it has a higher utility than any other strategy β in selfinteraction: $U(\alpha, \alpha) > U(\beta, \beta)$."

While I have not spent a great deal of time investigating these alternatives, it is my tentative prediction that they would be just as effective for a Manner-implicature-based account of evaluativity as the relatively informal frameworks in Horn (1984) and Levinson (2000) (see also multi-tiered semantics as in Potts 2012; McCready 2010; Murray 2010, 2014; Anderbois et al. 2010, 2013).

5

Evaluativity as implicature

Is and Isn't produce each other.
Hard depends on easy,
Long is tested by short,
High is determined by low,
Sound is harmonized by voice,
After is followed by before.

Lao Tzu, *Tao Te Ching* (translated by
Stephen Addiss and Stanley Lombardo)

Recall the distribution of evaluativity across adjectival constructions from Table 3.1:

TABLE 5.1. The distribution of evaluativity

construction	EVALUATIVE?	
	positive antonym	negative antonym
positive constructions	yes	yes
MP constructions	no	n/a
comparatives	no	no
equatives	no	yes
degree questions	no	yes
degree demonstratives	no	yes

As noted in Rett (2007, 2008), evaluativity is often, but not always, associated with negative adjectives. There are some constructions, like the comparative, in which neither of a relative antonym pair seems to receive an evaluative interpretation. And there are some constructions, like the positive construction, in which both antonyms are associated with an evaluative interpretation.

In this chapter, I present a proposal wherein evaluativity arises in every case as a conversational implicature. I argue that it always arises in positive constructions for reasons related to the maxim of Quantity, and that it arises in with negative antonyms in some degree quantifier constructions for markedness reasons, thereby as a result of the maxim of Manner. (In this respect, the account has many parallels with the EVAL account.)

This conversational implicature approach to evaluativity raises at least two important questions: why is it evaluativity that is implicated in these cases (especially as the result of two different maxims)? And how can the characterization of evaluativity as an implicature account for its apparent truth-conditional status in positive constructions (and its apparent non-truth-conditional status in other constructions)? I will address these questions in §5.1.2 and §5.2 respectively.

I will also argue that casting evaluativity as an implicature can explain why evaluativity seems to be asymmetrically associated with the internal clause of equatives. I'll suggest that the concept of generalized or conventionalized conversational implicature can lend some insight into why relative adjectives can differ with respect to their evaluativity (as Sassoon 2011 argued; §5.4). Finally, I'll argue that characterizing evaluativity as an implicature is the best way of predicting that it is not overtly lexically encoded cross-linguistically (§5.5).

There are as far as I know two accounts that mention evaluativity that are framed within a program that is loosely described as "neo-Gricean," notably Bogal-Allbritten (2010) and Lassiter and Goodman (2013). But these theories do not provide an account of the full distribution of evaluativity nor answers to the questions posed above.

The chapter proceeds as follows. I will first (in §5.1) adapt Horn's (1989) version of Grice's Cooperative Principle into a more formal framework, borrowed from Katzir (2007), that makes more explicit what elements count as scalemates of others (and what elements count as marked scalemates of others). In formalizing the approach, I also present a discussion of general properties of the degree domain (based on work in Bolinger 1972) to attempt to explain why an implicature associated with a degree construction amounts to evaluativity (§5.1.2).

§5.2 presents the evaluativity data I attribute to the Manner maxim, effectively encoding the EVAL account in this (neo-)Gricean framework. §5.3 presents the evaluativity data I attribute to the Quantity maxim, and §5.4 discusses how this approach could be extended to account for different evaluativity patterns across adjective classes (i.e. the relative/absolute distinction), within adjective classes (i.e. Sassoon's observations about differences amongst relative adjectives), and across languages.

5.1 Preliminaries

In this section I'll argue that evaluativity is a Manner implicature by showing that it falls under the category of "marked form, marked meaning" phenomena. I'll also address the question of why marked meaning, in the case of degree constructions, amounts to evaluativity (as opposed to some other type of non-conventionality; §5.1.2). I'll begin by formalizing Horn's (1984) Principle of Least Effort.

5.1.1 A recasting of markedness competition

What follows is Horn's (1984) discussion of an addressee's process of reasoning upon hearing a speaker utter a marked expression E' (p. 22; see also example (20) in Chapter 4):

The speaker used marked expression E' containing "extra" material (or otherwise less basic in form or distribution) when a corresponding unmarked expression E, essentially contrastive with it, was available. Either (i) the "extra" material was irrelevant and unnecessary, or (ii) it was necessary (i.e. E could not have been appropriately used). [(i)] is in conflict with the R Principle and is thus (ceteris paribus) to be rejected. Therefore, [(ii)], from [the premise and rejection of [(i)], by modus tollendo ponens.

The unmarked alternative E tends to become associated (by use or—through conventionalization—by meaning) with unmarked situation s, representing stereotype or salient member of extension of E/E' (R-based inference, cf. Atlas and Levinson 1981). The marked alternative E' tends to become associated with the complement of s with respect to the original extension of E/E' (Q-based inference).

In this section, I'll incorporate recent work by Katzir (2007) and others to formalize this idea at least preliminarily. To do so, I'll need to say a little more about the relevant scale for Manner implicatures, and a little more about what it means to be the typical extension of a predicate. I'll start by reproducing Horn's (1984) Q and R Principles:

(1) **The Q Principle (Hearer-based)** (Horn 1984: 13):
 Make your contribution sufficient (cf. Quantity$_1$)
 Say as much as you can (given R)
 Lower-bounding principle, inducing upper-bounded implicata

(2) **The R Principle (Speaker-based)** (Horn 1984: 13):
 Make your contribution necessary (cf. Relation, Quantity$_2$, Manner)
 Say no more than you must (given Q)
 Upper-bounding principle, inducing lower-bounded implicata

I interpret Horn (1984) to have in mind something like the following difference between Quantity and Manner implicatures:

(3) **Quantity implicatures**
 a. involve Q scales, which hold fixed markedness (i.e. morphological or syntactic complexity) and order elements with respect to informativity
 b. are calculated relative to the Q Principle

(4) **Manner implicatures**
 a. involve M scales, which hold fixed informativity and order elements with respect to markedness (i.e. morphological or syntactic complexity)
 b. are calculated relative to the R Principle (when a marked form is used) or the Q Principle (when an unmarked form is used)

There are a number of reasons to think that Q scales must control for markedness or complexity in the same way that M scales must control for informativity; a common example is in (5) (based on Fox 2006).

(5)   Adam is as tall as Doug.
    a. Adam is taller than Doug.
    b. Adam is exactly as tall as Doug.

I've been assuming that the strong, "exactly" interpretation of the equative in (5) comes about as the result of its competition with its stronger scalemate, the comparative in (5a). The reasoning is, loosely, 'If the speaker had had evidence that Adam is taller than Doug, he would have uttered (5a) instead, so it must be the case that Adam is not taller than Doug.'

But this reasoning falls apart if the hearer also (or instead) considers the overtly modified equative in (5b) as a relevant alternative to (5) (Fox 2003). This would erroneously predict that Quantity implicatures would result in an "at least" interpretation of the equative in (5). The reasoning would be, loosely, 'If the speaker had evidence that Adam is exactly as tall as Doug, he would have uttered (5b) instead, so it must be the case that Adam is not exactly as tall as Doug.'

This undesirable result has led some to argue that Q scales must be stipulated, for instance, in the lexicon (Horn 1972; Gazdar 1979) and others to develop significantly more complicated definitions of scales (Hirschberg 1991; see Matsumoto 1995 for an overview). In contrast, Katzir (2007) argues that many of these relatively basic problems with the implementation of the Q Principle can be avoided if we use structural complexity to restrict Q scales. I'll present his implementation of this idea briefly and then show how it can be helpful in the characterization of evaluativity as a conversational implicature.

Katzir (2007) defines structural complexity on parse trees, syntactic trees formed step by step. He characterizes structural alternatives—potential Q scalemates—in terms of structural complexity, as in (7) (p. 679).

(6)   STRUCTURAL COMPLEXITY
    Let ϕ, ψ be parse trees. If we can transform ϕ into ψ by a finite series of deletions, contractions, and replacements of constituents in ϕ with constituents of the same category taken from $L(\phi)$, we will write $\psi \lesssim \phi$. If $\psi \lesssim \phi$ and $\phi \lesssim \psi$ we will write $\phi \sim \psi$. If $\psi \lesssim \phi$ but not $\phi \lesssim \psi$ we will write $\psi < \phi$.

(7)   Q-ALTERNATIVES
    Let ϕ be a parse tree. The set of **Q-alternatives** for ϕ, written as $A_{Qstr}(\phi)$, is defined as $A_{Qstr}(\phi) := \{\phi' : \phi' \lesssim \phi\}$.

He redefines the Q Principle in terms of this definition of scalar alternatives as in (8).

(8) THE Q PRINCIPLE

Do not use ϕ if there is another sentence $\phi' \in A_{Qstr}(\phi)$ such that both:

a. $[\![\phi']\!] \subset [\![\phi]\!]$, and

b. ϕ' is weakly assertable.

Where "[a] structure ϕ is said to be **weakly assertable** by a speaker S if S believes that ϕ is true, relevant, and supported by evidence" (p. 672). The preamble in (8) invokes the set of Q-alternatives; (8a) refers to the relative informativity of ϕ and ϕ'.

This definition correctly predicts that the comparative in (5a) is a more informative Q-alternative to the quative in (5), resulting in a Quantity implicature, because the two are equally complex. It also correctly predicts that the *exactly* equative in (5a) is not a Q-alternative to the unmodified equative; the modified equative is more informative than the unmodified one, but is also more complex.

Parallel treatment of Horn's R Principle requires a correlate to (7), as in (9), which is my adaptation of Katzir's informal suggestions for Manner implicatures (p. 680). (10) restricts the speaker from using a marked form ϕ when its unmarked version ϕ' would have been acceptable.

(9) M-ALTERNATIVES

Let ϕ denote a semantic object of type $\langle \omega, t \rangle$. The set of **M-alternatives** for ϕ, written as $A_{Mstr}(\phi)$, is defined as $A_{Mstr}(\phi) := \{\phi' : [\![\phi']\!] \subseteq [\![\phi]\!]\}$.

(10) THE M PRINCIPLE

Do not use ϕ if there is another sentence $\phi' \in A_{Mstr}(\phi)$ such that both:

a. $\phi' < \phi$, and

b. ϕ' is weakly assertable.

Of course, the primary concern here is a formulation of M-alternatives in which a contrast in antonymy results in a contrast in markedness. In terms of the definition of structural complexity in (6), Katzir says that simplifying transformations could involve deletion or contraction. I will adopt the working assumption that translating Horn's "prolixity" into subsets/supersets of morphemes requires, at least, encoding the markedness of e.g. *short* in the morphologically complex "not-tall." I presented some preliminary evidence for this in §3.2.2 (see also Heim 2007), but will nevertheless view this as more of a theoretical convenience than an empirical claim.

We can thus reformulate Horn's Principle of Least Effort into what I'll call the "Marked Meaning Principle." This describes the effect of the R Principle on marked constructions.

(11) **The Marked Meaning Principle** *(informal)*

Marked forms are associated with marked meaning.

(12)   **The Marked Meaning Principle** *(formal)*

For sentences (or parse trees) ϕ, ϕ' such that $\phi' \in A_{Mstr}(\phi)$ and $\phi' < \phi$, ϕ carries the Manner implicature: "$\wedge$ atypical($[\![\phi]\!]$)"

The property "atypical" in (12) is one way of characterizing Horn's description of marked forms as "conveying a marked message" (Horn 1989: 22) or as being associated with a marked situation. A priori, there are a number of different ways an adjective like *tall* or a degree quantifier like *as tall as* can be manifested in an atypical way. In §5.1.2 I will present an explanation of why atypical($[\![\phi]\!]$), for adjectival or degree constructions, always amounts to evaluativity. But first I will demonstrate how (12) can help predict the evaluativity of some adjectival constructions. I'll focus on degree questions for now and will return to discuss e.g. degree quantifier constructions in §5.2.

Consider the (non-evaluative) truth conditions for antonymic degree questions, repeated from examples (52) and (53) in Chapter 3.

(13)   a. $[\![\text{How tall is Adam?}]\!] = \lambda p \exists d[p(w^{@}) \wedge p = \lambda w.\text{tall}(w)(\text{adam}, d)]$
b. $[\![\text{How short is Adam?}]\!] = \lambda p \exists d[p(w^{@}) \wedge p = \lambda w.\text{short}(w)(\text{adam}, d)]$

As discussed in §3.2.3, these questions denote distinct sets of propositions, so they fail to count as M-alternatives to one another given the definition in (9).

But if we instead analyze questions as denoting the most informative true proposition in the set (Beck and Rullmann 1999), they do: the fact that d is the maximum degree in one set entails that d is the maximum degree in the other, and vice versa.

The equivalence is perhaps easier to see in a framework in which degree questions denote properties (in this case, degree properties; Groenendijk and Stokhof 1989; George 2011).

(14)   a. $[\![\text{How tall is Adam?}]\!] = \lambda d \lambda w.\text{tall}(w)(\text{adam}, d)$
b. $[\![\text{How short is Adam?}]\!] = \lambda d \lambda w.\text{short}(w)(\text{adam}, d)$

If we treat *wh*-phrases as relativizers, on at least some level, then these degree questions denote the set of degrees to which Adam is tall and short, respectively. As I discussed in Chapter 2 (example (16), repeated below), these sets are always mutually entailing; whenever Adam's tallness is capped at 6ft, his shortness is capped (on the opposite end of the scale) by 6ft; both entail that Adam's height is 6ft.

(15)   a. $\{d : \text{Adam is } d\text{-tall}\} = \{1\text{ft}, 2\text{ft}, 3\text{ft}, 4\text{ft}, 5\text{ft}, 6\text{ft}\} = (0,6\text{ft}]$
b. $\{d : \text{Adam is } d\text{-short}\} = \{6\text{ft}, 7\text{ft}, 8\text{ft}, 9\text{ft}, \ldots, \infty\} = [6\text{ft}, \infty)$

Thus within a natural framework for the semantics of *wh*-questions, these antonymous degree constructions satisfy the Marked Meaning Principle in (12): they are, assuming that they are strengthened to their maximal or most informative proposition in the set, mutually entailing; and the *short* question is more marked than the *tall* question. Therefore, we can predict that *How short is Adam?* carries the Manner implicature "$\wedge$ atypical($[\![\text{How short is Adam?}]\!]$)."

This is the basic form that the argument will follow in my treatment of those degree constructions for which evaluativity is attached to the negative antonym. I will develop it further in §5.2. But first, I'll address the relationship between evaluativity and the requirement that the relevant content be atypical.

5.1.2 Why evaluativity?

The Marked Meaning Principle associates marked forms with marked meanings; in particular, (12) predicts that a marked construction will carry an additional restriction that ϕ's content is atypical. For the meaning in (13b) of the question *How short is Adam?*, "atypical" could in principle mean a lot of things: that Adam is significantly short (i.e. evaluativity) but also, for instance, that he is short for an unusual or unnatural reason.

This indeterminacy is highlighted in Kennedy's (2007: 17) discussion of the contextual standard associated with evaluativity:

> For Bogusławski (1975), the standard of comparison is the minimal degree of the measured property that is "conspicuous", "noteworthy" or "sufficient to attract attention" for a comparison class in the context of utterance; for Graff (2000), it corresponds to an interest-relative, "significant" degree of the measured property for a comparison class in the context.

In other words, there are a lot of ways in which someone's shortness can be noteworthy, conspicuous, attention-attracting, or atypical. An optimal account of evaluativity, given what was said in Chapters 2 and 3, would ensure that the atypical restriction in (12) included all and only worlds in which Adam is short to a high degree (see also Szabó 2001).

In this section, I'll address the question of why the atypicality property in degree constructions is always manifested as evaluativity. I will first argue that, where gradable antonyms are concerned, evaluativity is the most natural way of interpreting a Manner implicature's atypicality requirement. I'll then review a significant amount of evidence from Bolinger (1972) that there is a general tendency in natural language for potentially underinformative degree constructions to receive a (strengthened) evaluative interpretation.

Recall from the discussion of litotes in §4.2.2 that there is an extension gap between the positive, evaluative interpretations of gradable antonyms, as shown in Figure 5.1.

As it stands, the gradable antonyms *tall* and *short* are semantically defined so that they can be used to describe an individual at any point in the spectrum. (This allows *Adam is taller than Doug* to be acceptable in a context in which they're both significantly short.) But what happens when predications involving *tall* and *short* are restricted with respect to atypicality?

According to Figure 5.1, both of the antonyms have in common that their typical instantiations involve individuals of average height, those in the extension gap. To be typical (or not atypical) in the case of the application of a degree predicate is to instantiate that predicate to an average degree. Atypical uses of each antonym, then, don't include the extension gap; to instantiate the predicate *short* atypically is to not be in the extension gap.

This predicts that the evaluative uses of *tall* and *short* will not include the extension gap, but it fails to restrict *tall* to only those individuals whose height exceeds the "tall" standard (and *short* to only those individuals whose height exceeds the "short" standard on the opposite scale). Specifically, if atypical shortness just means "not of average height," why can't *Doug is as short as Adam* carry the implicature that Adam is taller than average?

I will assume that there is, in determining what counts as atypical for a specific adjective (and therefore the relevant standard of comparison), a compulsion for the stronger or more informative interpretation.[1] As Figure 5.1 depicts it, *tall* and *short* could both in principle carry the implicature "not of average height," a relatively weak meaning. The antonyms differ in terms of which end of the scale is more informative on the ordering they associate with; so they are plausibly associated with implicatures that are strengthened relative to one another in a way that draws on this difference.

From this perspective, there are a priori two different ways to instantiate atypical shortness: to be above or below the extension gap. The same is true for atypical tallness. But note that there is only one way to be atypically short *relative to the short scale*, as illustrated in Figure 5.2. Since a gradable adjective comes to carry its Manner implicature only in consideration of its antonym, the implicature is calculated with respect to its antonym. This is, in effect, Grice's calculability assumption:

The presence of a conversational implicature must be capable of being worked out; for even if it can in fact be intuitively grasped, unless the intuition is replaceable by an argument, the implicature (if present at all) will not count as a conversational implicature.... To work out that a particular conversational implicature is present, the hearer will rely on the following data: (1) the conventional meaning of the words used, together with the identity of any references that may be involved; (2) the Cooperative Principle and its maxims; (3) the context, linguistic or otherwise, of the utterance; (4) other items of background knowledge; and (5) the fact (or supposed fact) that all relevant items falling under the previous headings are available to both participants and both participants know or assume this to be the case.   (Grice 1975: 31)

POSITIVE	EXTENSION GAP	NEGATIVE
significantly tall	neither tall nor short	significantly short

FIGURE 5.1. The height dimension

---

[1] This can be thought of as very similar to Kennedy's (2007) **Interpretive Economy** principle (p. 36): "Maximize the contribution of the conventional meanings of the elements of a sentence to the computation of its truth conditions." I'll return to discuss this in §5.4.1.

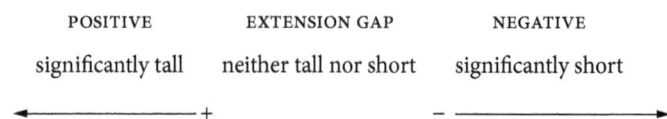

FIGURE 5.2. Atypical degree predication

In other words, the Marked Meaning Principle defines marked meaning relative to the markedness alternatives. The property atypical is therefore shorthand for "atypical given what the speaker *could have* said."

In sum, then: when an adjectival or degree construction is associated with an implicature that strengthens its meaning, it is strengthened from a typical extension to an atypical one. There are, a priori, two different ways of being atypically associated with 'tall' degrees: one in which the individual is less tall than average, and another in which (s)he is more tall than average (the evaluative interpretation). These logical possibilities are arguably divided up between two antonyms, with each antonym taking on the most informative of the two atypical extensions as its strengthening implicature. As a result, a positive antonym like *tall* is associated with the implicature "taller than average," while a negative antonym like *short* is associated with the implicature "shorter than average."

There is independent evidence that neutral or unmodified degree constructions are interpreted with respect to only a strengthened, intensified subset of its extension in contexts in which the extension itself is too weak. Bolinger (1972) argues that degree constructions or other gradable constructions systematically receive intensified readings where they are logically compatible with other interpretations.

Degree modifiers can either intensify or do the opposite (following Bolinger, I will use the word "diminish"), as shown in (16).

(16) a. The gesture was much appreciated.   intensifier
      b. The gesture was little appreciated.   diminisher

Neutral degree modifiers like *so, such,* and *how* only receive intensifying interpretations.[2] There is plenty of reason to treat *so, such, as,* and *how* as in principle neutral, i.e. as not carrying an intensifying or diminishing interpretation. When they combine with non-gradable predicates, they receive the interpretation "in that way or manner," as (17) shows (see also Rett 2013). (Examples cited with just page numbers are from Bolinger 1972.)

(17) a. John danced as Sue danced.   'in the same way/manner'
      b. John danced how Sue danced.   'in the same way/manner'
      c. I'll explain it so as not to shock you.   'in a way that' (p. 178)
      d. It was just such a place (as yours was).   'similar' (p. 177)

[2] Bolinger lists (p. 22) several other lexical adjectival detensifiers, like *a bit, a little, least, less, somewhat, kind of, sort of,* and *-ish*.

Yet when these "neutral" modifiers occur with gradable predicates, they become intensifiers, never diminishers. (18) lists some adjectival examples; (19) verbal; and (20) nominal.

(18) a. I was calm as calm.   (Kirchner 1955: 106)
      b. How calm he is!
      c. I wish he wouldn't bungle so.   (p. 16)

(19) a. He improved so (much) that he looked like a different person.[3]   (p. 194)
      b. He frightened me so!   (p. 189)
      c. How he frightened me!

(20) a. Such a telescope is hard to find.   (p. 62)
      b. #Such a telescope was in the window.   (p. 62)
      c. She manifested grief such as would have destroyed another.   (p. 65)
      d. What a telescope it is!   (p. 69)
      e. What attempts they made!   (p. 69)
      f. Such mollycoddling!   (p. 69)

Many of Bolinger's examples involving neutral modifiers amount to exclamatives, which could be thought of as combining an evaluative interpretation with an expression of speaker surprise (Rett 2011). The relevant observation is that these examples all unambiguously involve intensification despite the fact that they are formed with modifiers whose literal meaning, given (17), seems to be neutral or not evaluative.

Bolinger (1972) cites several other types of phenomena that support his claim that in-principle neutral elements tend to signify intensification. The reduplication of adjectives, for instance, could be redundant or could, in principle, water down the meaning of the adjective. But these examples receive intensified readings (21), at least in English (cf. Cusic 1981).

(21) It's a long, long way.   (p. 248)

The modifiers *quite* and *well* could, in principle, receive something other than an intensity reading; (22a) could mean something like "an idiot in every aspect of his life" instead of "an extreme idiot," and (22b) could mean something like "stylishly" instead of "extremely." Instead, they both function as intensifiers.

(22) a. John is quite an idiot.   (p. 16)
      b. a well-travelled person.   (p. 33)

There is no reason to think that indefinite DPs would receive any sort of gradable interpretation. Nevertheless there is a fairly productive use of indefinites, like those in (23), in which the indefinite denoting a property ϕ is interpreted instead as meaning

---

[3] Cf. *He recovered so (*much) that he looked like a different person.*

something like "instantiates ϕ to a high degree," i.e. an intensified or evaluative interpretation.[4]

(23) a. John owns a number of shoes.
     b. Mary likes men of a certain age.
     c. That was some party.

It is perhaps surprising that these DPs receive a degree interpretation at all; it is important for the point here that they can never mean "instantiates ϕ to a low degree." I'll return to discuss these "evaluative DPs" in §6.3.

Bolinger additionally points out that, where English has constructed idioms or generic equatives (p. 19; see also Rett 2013), these receive intensifying (rather than diminishing) readings.

(24) a. She cried her heart out.
     b. It floated with all the buoyancy of a lead balloon.
     c. He is mad as a hatter.
     d. It was clean as a whistle.
     e. She is spoiled rotten.

Bolinger's semantic observations have some morphological and syntactic corrollaries: he notes that while "*such* with nonpredicative nouns [has] the value 'so great'" (p. 80), there is no counterpart to *such* which means "so little." And, in contrast to intensifying modifiers like *very* or *quite*, diminishing modifiers like *a bit* and *a little* can't be used attributively.[5]

(25) a. Your dress is very/a bit tight.   (p. 50)
     b. She owns a very/*bit tight dress.

This syntactic observation pops up elsewhere: Nakanishi and Rullmann (2009), Cohen and Krifka (2011), Coppock and Brochhagen (2013), and Biezma (2013) observe that the superlative modifier *at least* receives what they term a "concessive" or evaluative interpretation when it occurs sentence-initially, as demonstrated in (26).

(26) a. Mary is at least an associate professor.   "epistemic"
     b. At least Mary is an associate professor.   "concessive"

While the modifier in (26a) seems to set a lower bound on the range of epistemic possibilities, in (26b) its use entails the proposition that Mary is an associate professor and additionally associates that proposition with something positive.

---

[4] Thanks to David Wolfsdorf (p.c.) for emphasizing the relevance of these examples.
[5] This restriction bears a curious relationship to the "Position Generalization" in Morzycki (2009: 179): "Degree readings of size adjectives [as in *an enormous idiot*—JR] are possible only in attributive positions (in English, prenominally)."

I have provided an account of evaluativity in which adjectival constructions can in principle be associated with marked adjectival expressions with atypical meaning. While an atypical application of a gradable predicate could theoretically amount to something other than evaluativity (or an extreme or intensified interpretation), there is independent evidence that, for whatever reason, natural language closely associates atypical gradability with a high degree (as opposed to a low degree, or some other unusual circumstance). In other words, while there are many notable ways to dance (e.g. gracefully, with Sue), there is only one salient way to be tall, and that is to be tall in an evaluative sense. I've suggested that this is due to the fact that the evaluative interpretation of these in-principle neutral terms is the most informative way of strengthening their meaning, due to the monotonicity of the underlying predicates.

In sum, in this section, I argue that degree predicates whose meaning is supplemented with implicature are supplemented with evaluativity. That the strengthening takes the form of evaluativity arises from the nature of antonymy: antonyms are natural competitors because they differ only in their ordering, which means that this ordering is extremely salient for implicature calculation. To instantiate a gradable predicate to an atypical degree therefore means to exceed (rather than fall below) that antonym's contextual standard, the more informative of the possible interpretations. The tendency for strengthened meaning to result in or correspond to intensity or evaluativity, as opposed to other logical possibilities, has been shown by Bolinger (1972) to be the norm both for degree constructions and even constructions that are formed with only non-gradable predicates.

This claim is distinct from recent work that argues expressives like the epithet *fucking* can receive either a positive or negative interpretation (reflecting the speaker's positive or negative opinion; e.g. Potts 2007; Schroeder 2008; Constant et al. 2009; McCready 2010, 2012). This flexibility is demonstrated in (27) (from McCready 2012: 247).

(27) a. Fucking Mike Tyson won another fight. He's wonderful.
      b. Fucking Mike Tyson got arrested again for domestic violence. #He's wonderful.

But notice that, when these expressives modify gradable predicates, the ambiguity is absent; (28) means that Adam's height exceeds the "tall" standard to an impressive degree (see also Morzycki 2011, 2012).

(28) Adam is fucking tall.

In what follows, I'll discuss how this account can be extended to predict the presence or absence of evaluativity in other constructions. In light of the above discussion, I will represent atypical instances of degree predication using the evaluative requirement $\wedge$ $d > s$, for some contextual standard s.

5.2 Antonym-sensitive evaluativity

The characterization of evaluativity as a Manner implicature extends to other adjectival constructions in similar ways as the EVAL account did, although I will argue that it does so more naturally. I will begin by explaining how this account can be extended to predict that MP constructions are not evaluative. I will then present an account of the contrast in evaluativity between comparatives and equatives (§5.2.2), and will supplement this prediction with a discussion of the predicted discourse sensitivity of the evaluativity implicature (§5.2.3).

5.2.1 Implicature and MP constructions

It's relatively easy to explain the lack of evaluativity of MP constructions within this framework: evaluativity arises as the result of a markedness competition between antonyms, and independent constraints on MP constructions prohibit negative antonyms from MP constructions entirely. To account for the incompatibility of MPs and negative antonyms, I assumed in §2.1.4 that MPs denote semantic objects of type $\langle\langle d, t\rangle, t\rangle$, as in (29) (from (28) in Chapter 2; Schwarzschild 2005, 2006a, 2012).

(29) Doug is 6ft tall.
    a. $[\![tall]\!] = \lambda x \lambda d.\text{tall}(x, d)$
    b. $[\![tall(Doug)]\!] = \lambda d.\text{tall}(\text{doug}, d)$
    c. $[\![6ft]\!] = \lambda D \in D_{\langle d,t\rangle}.6\text{ft}(D)$
    d. $[\![6ft(tall(Doug))]\!] = 6\text{ft}(\lambda d.\text{tall}(\text{doug}, d))$

The negative-antonym MP construction, according to (29c), is ungrammatical because there are infinitely many degrees to which Doug are short, and MPs like *6ft* can only measure sets of degrees if such a measurement is informative. (From a different perspective, MPs are only defined over finite sets of degrees.)

Due to this restriction, we predict that MP constructions like the one in (29) will never enter into a markedness competition with *Doug is 6ft short*, because such a form is unavailable. Note that this is a distinct prediction from the EVAL account in Rett (2008). Because EVAL encodes evaluativity semantically, in a freely occurring degree modifier, it was predicted to be able to optionally occur in MP constructions. As I discussed in Chapter 3, allowing MPs to have the "gap predicate" interpretation in (29c) in the EVAL account led to the incorrect prediction that MP constructions could have a reading that corresponded to, "Doug is 6ft taller than the relevant standard of tallness." The current proposal, which lacks the prediction that EVAL is in principle available to any degree construction, is an improvement in this respect.[6]

---

[6] In §5.3 I will argue that evaluativity can arise from uninformativity-based Quantity implicatures as well as Manner implicatures. This extension will not however affect this treatment of MP constructions, because (as I will argue) MP constructions are not uninformative like positive constructions are.

There are other reasons to find this approach encouraging: Doetjes (2012) points out that, in Dutch, MPs can sometimes occur with negative antonyms, (30). When they do, they receive the same meaning as the positive-antonym version, but they are notably evaluative (she uses the term "non-neutral").[7]

(30) a. het 20 cm diepe water
         the 20 cm deep water
         'the 20-cm-deep water'

    b. het 20 cm ondiepe water
         the 20 cm shallow water
         'the 20-cm-deep (which is shallow) water'

While we would, as Doetjes points out, need to amend our analysis of MPs to account for this possibility, the fact that these constructions are necessarily evaluative is a clear prediction of the characterization of evaluativity as a Manner implicature. In particular, the data in (30) illustrate that MP constructions are evaluative only when they are marked M-alternatives to semantically equivalent MP constructions.

It is also relatively easy to extend this account to degree demonstrative constructions, which do exhibit a polarity asymmetry with respect to evaluativity, as shown in (17) and (18) from Chapter 3 (repeated below). Imagine again that these demonstratives are uttered in a context in which *A* and *B* are looking at Adam, so his exact height is clear and salient. The contrast between (31) and (32) demonstrates that negative-antonym degree demonstratives, but not positive-antonym ones, are evaluative (i.e. unacceptable in a context in which the evaluativity clearly doesn't hold).

(31) A: Adam's really short.
     B: Doug's (about) that tall too.
     B': Doug's (about) that short too.

(32) A: Adam's really tall.
     B: Doug's (about) that tall too.
     B': #Doug's (about) that short too.

I'll assume that degree demonstratives, like individual demonstratives, pick out a specific degree in context. Let's imagine that Adam is $4'5''$ for the "short" scenario in (31) and $6'5''$ for the "tall" scenario in (32). A relational account of gradable adjectives predicts the semantics in (33) and (34), respectively.

(33) a. ⟦Doug is that tall too⟧ = tall(doug,$4'5''$)
    b. ⟦Doug is that short too⟧ = short(doug,$4'5''$)

---

[7] The translations in (30) are mine, intended to reflect evaluativity where Doetjes reports it to occur. Doetjes argues that the English *70 years young* is idiomatic and different from the Dutch examples, in part because "*young* seems to lose its normal interpretation."

(34) a. ⟦Doug is that tall too⟧ = tall(doug,6′5″)
      b. ⟦Doug is that short too⟧ = short(doug,6′5″)

Recall that these antonyms are associated with reverse strict orderings, so the truth conditions in (33a) and (33b) (and the truth conditions in (34a) and (34b)) are mutually entailing. We thus predict that the marked, *short* sentence will carry an evaluativity implicature, but the unmarked, *tall* sentence will not, resulting in the supplemented meanings in (35) and (36) for the scenario in (31) and (32), respectively.

(35) a. ⟦Doug is that tall too⟧ = tall(doug,4′5″)
      b. ⟦Doug is that short too⟧ = short(doug,4′5″) $\wedge$ 4′5″ $> s_{short}$

(36) a. ⟦Doug is that tall too⟧ = tall(doug,6′5″)
      b. #⟦Doug is that short too⟧ = short(doug,6′5″) $\wedge$ 6′5″ $> s_{short}$

In the next section, I extend this Manner implicature account of evaluativity to the difference in evaluativity between comparative and equative constructions.

5.2.2 *Equatives versus comparatives*

The account here makes the same sort of prediction with respect to the evaluativity contrast between comparative and equatives as the EVAL account did. In particular, it predicts that the equatives demonstrate a polarity asymmetry with respect to evaluativity because the antonymous constructions are otherwise synonymous, and therefore subject to a markedness competition. The comparative, in contrast, does not, because antonymous comparative constructions are not synonymous.

I'll briefly reproduce this argument within the updated framework and then address the observation from Chapter 3 that evaluativity seems to persist in the equative construction despite it receiving an "at least" interpretation.

The compositional semantics assumed in §2.1 produces the following (preliminary) truth conditions for antonymous comparative and equative constructions.

(37) a. ⟦Adam is taller than Doug⟧ = Max(λd.tall(adam, d)) $>$
         Max($\lambda d'$.tall(doug, d'))
      b. ⟦Adam is shorter than Doug⟧ = Max(λd.short(adam, d)) $>$
         Max($\lambda d'$.short(doug, d'))

(38) a. ⟦Adam is as tall as Doug⟧ = Max(λd.tall(adam, d)) $\geq$
         Max($\lambda d'$.tall(doug, d'))
      b. ⟦Adam is as short as Doug⟧ = Max(λd.short(adam, d)) $\geq$
         Max($\lambda d'$.short(doug, d'))

According to the definition in (7), the comparative and the equative count as Q-alternatives because they differ from one another minimally, in only one instance of the replacement of the degree quantifier. As before, the equative is the weaker Q-alternative of the two because it encodes a non-strict ordering.

Imagine a context that supports the Quantity implicature associated with the equative. Loosely speaking, this is a context in which the speaker and hearers are assumed to be cooperative, and there is nothing in the common ground to suggest that the implicature is false. (As we'll see in §5.3, supporting the implicature also requires that the discourse in which the sentence is uttered also has certain properties.) Generally speaking, a neutral or out-of-the-blue context of utterance is one that will support an equative's Quantity implicature.

In these contexts, the meaning of the equative is strengthened to the "exactly" truth conditions in (39).

(39) a. ⟦Adam is as tall as Doug⟧ = $\text{Max}(\lambda d.\text{tall}(\text{adam}, d)) = \text{Max}(\lambda d'.\text{tall}(\text{doug}, d'))$

   b. ⟦Adam is as short as Doug⟧ = $\text{Max}(\lambda d.\text{short}(\text{adam}, d)) = \text{Max}(\lambda d'.\text{short}(\text{doug}, d'))$

Recall Levinson's claim that Quantity implicatures are calculated before Manner implicatures. This predicts that it is the truth conditions in (39) that are relevant for calculating M-alternatives, relative to the definitions in (9) and (10). In other words, any context that supports an equative's Q-strengthening, as in (39), is a context in which an equative counts as an M-alternative to its antonymic counterpart.

It's clear, based on the evidence presented in §3.2.2, that negative adjectives are marked relative to their positive antonyms. In §5.1.1 I adopted the practice of interpreting this lexical markedness contrast by treating negative adjectives as negated versions of their positive antonyms. In addition to predicting that the two are associated with reverse orderings of the same dimension, this also predicts that a construction with a negative antonym is marked relative to one with a positive antonym because the former can be reduced to the latter by a deletion operation in the parse tree. The result is a prediction that (39b) is a more marked M-alternative to (39a).

As a result, we predict that the marked form is associated with the marked meaning, evaluativity, as in (40).

(40) a. ⟦Adam is as tall as Doug⟧ = $\text{Max}(\lambda d.\text{tall}(\text{adam}, d)) = \text{Max}(\lambda d'.\text{tall}(\text{doug}, d'))$

   b. ⟦Adam is as short as Doug⟧ = $\text{Max}(\lambda d.\text{short}(\text{adam}, d)) = \text{Max}(\lambda d'.\text{short}(\text{doug}, d')) \land d > s_{\text{short}}$

I'll return in §5.2.3 to explain why evaluativity seems to be associated with the embedded (rather than the matrix) clause.

One significant shortcoming of the EVAL account was its prediction with respect to "at least" equatives. The data below are repeated from (59) and (60) from Chapter 3. They demonstrate that negative-antonym equatives seem to be evaluative even in contexts in which their Q implicature is not supported (41) or when they are overtly modified by *at least* (42).

(41)   Adam is as short as Doug, in fact he's shorter. $\rightarrow$ Adam/Doug is short.

(42)   a. Adam is at least as short as Doug. $\rightarrow$ Adam/Doug is short.
       b. Adam is exactly as short as Doug. $\rightarrow$ Adam/Doug is short.

The antonymic pairs of these "at least" equatives aren't M-alternatives despite the fact that the M-alternative definition in (9) is relatively weak: it counts ϕ' as an M-alternative to ϕ if ϕ' is entailed by ϕ (not just, as stipulated in the EVAL account, if ϕ and ϕ' are mutually entailing). This is because the positive equative in (43a) is true when Adam is taller than Doug (but (43b) is not), while the negative equative in (43b) is true when Adam is shorter than Doug (but (43a) is not).

(43)   a. Adam is at least as tall as Doug.
       b. Adam is at least as short as Doug.

There are a few possible ways to account for the evaluativity of modified equatives in an implicature-based account. I will present two here. First, there is reason to think that the equative modifiers *at least* and *exactly* modify not the equative morpheme *as* but the generalized quantifier resulting from the combination of *as* and its internal argument (*as Doug (is tall)* in e.g. (41); Rett 2010, 2014a). This is similar to the claim that *at least* in (44) modifies *some students* (as opposed to *some*).

(44)   At least some students passed the test.

There is another potential parallel: in (44), arguably, the scalar implicature associated with *some* is part of the input to the modifier *at least*. This suggests that the implicature is calculated locally rather than globally, making it plausible that the relevant M-alternatives are calculated below the modifier *at least*. I'll discuss local implicatures a little later in this section; there is evidence that Manner implicatures, like scalar implicatures, are calculated locally. This seems like a natural account of the evaluativity of the modified equatives in (42), and could serve to help generalize the account to "at least" equatives in a relatively natural way.

Second, we could explain the evaluativity of modified negative-antonym equatives by arguing that evaluativity is a *generalized* conversational implicature, and so more fundamentally associated with the string *as short as* than other, particularized implicatures. As Atlas and Levinson (1981) say, "Conversational inferences may well have degrees of conventionalization" (p. 5). Evaluativity, as a Manner implicature, is associated more with form than use, which makes it a good and plausible candidate for conventionalization. Because equatives are strengthened to mean "exactly" in the standard case, this would predict that the evaluativity associated with *as short as* in the common case is conventionalized and extended to other cases.

Again, to quote Levinson (2000), "the distinctions are tortuous" (p. 373). Levinson (and Grice and Horn before him) differentiated between conventionalized and generalized conversational implicature because the latter are clearly related to the

Cooperative Principle, while the former bear no clear relationship to it. But the notion of generalized conversational implicature requires a diachronic perspective whose intricacies I cannot commit to here. Nevertheless, I believe that the parallels between evaluativity and (other) Manner implicatures strongly suggests treatment by the R Principle, while certain facts about its semantics suggest that evaluativity, as a Manner implicature, is more conventionalized than your average scalar implicature.

I'll end this section by providing some additional evidence that evaluativity in equatives and degree questions behaves like other Manner implicatures.

In §4.4 I argued that Manner implicatures behave slightly differently than scale-based Quantity implicatures in terms of global/local calculation. I argued that the Manner implicature associated with the periphrastic causative in (46) (repeated below) could either project or be calculated locally, depending on context. In the global interpretation, it is the speaker's belief that the sheriff was caused to die in an atypical way (i.e. was not strictly speaking murdered). In the local interpretation, this implicature is associated with the judge's beliefs.

(45)   The judge believes that Adam caused the sheriff to die.

Additional evidence for the ability of Manner implicatures to be calculated locally is in (46). Imagine a scenario in which a team of hit men are discussing their work orders. They charge $500 for a hit, but charge an extra $250 if they're asked to make the job look like an accident. In this context, the contrast between *kill* and *cause to die* can be calculated locally. In (46b), for instance, the Manner implicature that changes a killing event to an atypical killing event is embedded under negation; the instruction to the fellow hit man is to kill someone, but not to spend the extra time and energy making it look like an accident.

(46)   a. We have a flat rate on hits. But every time you cause someone to die, you have to make sure to charge $250 extra.
        b. This time, don't cause him to die. The customer sounds like a cheapskate.
        c. You caused him to die, but you forgot to charge an extra $250 for it.

The periphrastic construction in (46c) shows that the implicature can even license anaphora (see also Anderbois et al. 2010, 2013).

The same generalizations hold for evaluativity in negative-antonym equatives and degree questions. In (47) the evaluativity associated with the equative can be interpreted locally or globally, depending on the context. Recall that evaluativity in equatives is associated with the internal argument; this will be the subject of the next section.

(47)   a. (Robin's really confused about everyone's heights.) Robin thinks Doug is short, and she believes Adam is as short as Doug.
        b. (Robin thinks Adam is 5'0''. Doug is also 5'0'', but Robin doesn't know that counts as short.) Robin believes Adam is as short as Doug.

In the context in (47a), the evaluativity implicature "Doug is short" is a local implicature, associated with Robin's beliefs. The sentence is true and felicitous in a context in which Doug and Adam are in fact tall, demonstrating that the evaluativity does not have to be interpreted globally. In the context in (47b), the same evaluativity implicature is a global implicature, associated with the speaker's beliefs.

The sentences in (48) also demonstrate that the evaluativity carried by negative-antonym degree questions can be interpreted locally. The embedded degree questions in (48) can easily be substituted with the proposition *that Adam is short*.

(48) a. Everyone who knows how short Adam is also knows he wears platform shoes.
     b. This time, don't tell anyone how short Adam is. He's extremely sensitive about his height.
     c. Don't tell Lindsey how short Adam is, she won't want to date him because of it.

For instance, in (48b), the evaluativity implicature is most naturally interpreted as scoping under the negative command. It is clear that the hearer should not tell others that Adam is short, but it seems as though (48b) is also compatible with the hearer telling others Adam's exact height in a context in which having this height would not qualify him as short.

In parallel with (46c), (48c) suggests that the implicature can even license anaphora. Again, this is consistent with the characterization of evaluativity in equatives as a Manner implicature, given the parallel data in (46).

While the embedded degree questions in (48) can be freely substituted with *that Adam is short*, their positive-antonym counterparts can only receive a non-evaluative interpretation, and therefore cannot be substituted with their corresponding positive construction. (48c) can be uttered in a situation in which Adam is embarrassed that he is short, but (49a) cannot be uttered in a situation in which Adam is embarrassed that he is tall (and is not naturally paraphrased by (49b)).

(49) a. Don't tell anyone how tall Adam is.
     b. Don't tell anyone that Adam is tall.

Recall the data in (50) and (51) from §3.2.2, repeated below. Croft and Cruse (2004) claim that the proportional modifiers affect the two antonyms differently; (50a) is true iff Adam is shorter than Doug and (50b) only if Adam is taller than Doug, whereas both of the sentences in (51) require Adam to be shorter than Doug.

(50) a. Adam is half as tall as Doug.
     b. Adam is twice as tall as Doug.

(51) a. Adam is half as short as Doug.
     b. Adam is twice as short as Doug.

This contrast could potentially be explained by the Manner implicature approach to evaluativity coupled with the assumption that these implicatures can be calculated locally, and thereby are embeddable under a truth-conditional operator, as we've seen in other examples above. In particular, we would predict this asymmetry if the internal argument to *half as tall* and *twice as tall* in (50) were the set of degrees to which Doug is tall, but the internal argument to *half as short* and *twice as short* in (51) were the set of degrees to which Doug is short which count as short, i.e. the degrees of height he is associated with that exceed the "short" scale. (51a) would be true in a situation in which Adam counts as short, but has half as many degrees above the "short" standard as Doug does (and is therefore less short). (51b) would be true in a situation in which Adam counts as short, but has twice as many degrees above the "short" standard as Doug does (and is therefore more short).

It seems like this approach would correctly account for the fact that both constructions in (51) require that Doug be shorter than Adam. However, doing so would require significantly altering our definition of the equative morpheme (as it stands, we predict that equatives cannot be modified, although it is relatively easy to modify the definition appropriately) and proposing a compositional semantics for *twice* and *half*, which would take us too far afield.

To sum up this section: I've analyzed the evaluativity associated with negative antonyms as a Manner implicature, the result of a markedness competition with counterpart constructions formed with positive antonyms. While the evaluativity associated with negative-antonym equatives is traditionally characterized as projective content (e.g. a presupposition, Rett 2007, 2008; Breakstone 2012; Bogal-Allbritten 2010), there's evidence that evaluativity can be calculated locally, counting as input for truth-conditional operators like embedding verbs and negation, and licensing anaphora. This flexibility in the manifestation of evaluativity is especially natural in a treatment of evaluativity as a conversational implicature, given the discussion of other e.g. Manner implicatures in Chapter 4.

In contrast, it is hard to see how the EVAL account could explain these truth-conditional cases of evaluativity, at least in degree quantifier constructions. The EVAL account predicts the following truth conditions for a negative-antonym equative, repeated from §3.2.3.

(52) ⟦Adam is as short as EVAL Doug⟧ =
      $\text{Max}(\lambda d.\text{short}(\text{adam}, d)) = \text{Max}(\lambda d'.\text{short}(\text{doug}, d') \wedge d' > s_{\text{short}})$

The EVAL account characterized evaluativity as a definedness condition (provided that the maximality operator is undefined over empty sets). It's hard to imagine how this account, in which EVAL is semantically encoded, could be used to explain instances of markedness-based evaluativity in which the content doesn't seem to project globally. If the sentence in (52) is undefined in a context, presumably any sentence with (52) embedded in it would also be undefined in that context.

These facts do however call for a theory that allows Manner implicatures to be calculated locally (and, as a result, manipulated by truth-conditional operators). The periphrastic causative data in (45) and (46) motivate such a theory independently of the phenomenon of evaluativity. It's not obvious to me whether these data can be dealt with by recent theories that call for a syntactic treatment of locally calculated implicatures (e.g. Chierchia et al. 2009). There are alternatives; Levinson (2000) has addressed the Manner implicature data explicitly and proposed a reconceptualization of the semantics/pragmatics interface to account for their ability to influence the truth conditions of a sentence. Others, like Simons (2010, 2014), seem to be in a good position to account for the local calculation of all conversational implicatures (not just scalar ones) even more naturally. Once we have a theory of embedded or localized Manner implicature, we can account for the fact that even overtly modified negative-antonym equatives are evaluative (43b) in a way that can affect the truth conditions of the sentence as a whole (51). Alternatively, we could in principle treat the evaluativity of e.g. *at least as short* by appealing to some notion of conventionalized implicature.

Recall that another problem with the account demonstrated in (52) was that it had to stipulate that the evaluativity-based markedness competition was restricted syntactically to the lower clause. I'll revisit this restriction in the next section, showing that it is predicted by an implicature-based account of evaluativity. In doing so I'll spend more time exploring the projection properties of markedness-based evaluativity. In §5.3 I take up an explanation of evaluativity in positive constructions.

5.2.3 The equative argument asymmetry

In this section I will argue that whether or not the evaluative content of a negative-antonym adjectival construction projects depends at least in part on its role in discourse, which is an explicit prediction of van Kuppevelt (1996); Simons et al. (2011).

Original evidence that evaluativity in negative-antonym equatives projects is repeated below (from (87) in §3.1.2). (53) demonstrates that the evaluativity associated here with the *as*-clause projects outside of the antecedent of conditional or above negation, becoming a global presupposition of the sentence as a whole.

(53) a. If Doug is as short as Adam, he will not be able to go on the ride.
      b. It's not the case that Doug is as short as Adam.

The observation is that each of these sentences presuppose that Adam (and only Adam) is short, suggesting that the internal argument of equatives is evaluative, and that this evaluativity projects, but that the external argument isn't.

I'll make two claims in the following order. First, that the evaluativity of negative-antonym equatives and degree questions, analyzed here as a Manner implicature, projects only when the evaluativity is not-at-issue. Second, I'll argue that this constraint on the projection of evaluativity in these constructions accounts for the observed evaluativity asymmetry between the two arguments of the equative, data that were left virtually unexplained in the EVAL account.

Recall that Barker (2002) observed that positive constructions—by virtue of their evaluativity—can have a descriptive or metalinguistic use, depending on context. The descriptive use is the familiar one, in which the speaker uses the positive construction to say something about e.g. Adam's height. The metalinguistic use comes out in contexts in which the addressee knows Adam's height—i.e. both interlocutors are standing in the same room with him—but does not know the salient standard of e.g. tallness.

This metalinguistic context is just where we'd expect evaluativity to be relevant to the Question Under Discussion (QUD) and, therefore, at-issue. And this is in fact what we see. Imagine a context in which *A* and *B* are at a party full of baseball players, including Dick McAuliffe and Al Kaline, but *B* is unfamiliar with the sport, and is expressing curiosity about what it takes to be a successful baseball player.

(54)   A: Take McAuliffe over there. He's as short as Kaline.
       B: Ah, I hadn't realized that counts as short for a baseball player. I would have guessed that counts as tall.

(55)   A: Take McAuliffe over there. He's as tall as Kaline.
       B: #Ah, I hadn't realized that counts as tall for a baseball player. I would have guessed that counts as short.

The intuition is that the proposition expressed by *A* includes—specifically, entails— that McAuliffe and Kaline are short for baseball players. This proposition can be directly addressed in discourse, as B's response shows. (It can also be negated in this context: *That couldn't possibly count as short for a baseball player!*) Because the positive-antonym equative in *A*'s utterance in (55) isn't evaluative, it lacks this metalinguistic use, and so does not carry a similar entailment.

The evaluativity associated with negative-antonym degree questions, too, can be an entailment of the sentence when the evaluativity is relevant to the QUD or is the topic of discussion. In the same scenario as above, the following exchange is felicitous:

(56)   A: *(glancing at McAuliffe)* I never knew how short McAuliffe is.
       B: Wow, that counts as short for a baseball player? They are significantly taller than cricketers.

(57)   A: *(glancing at McAuliffe)* I never knew how tall McAuliffe is.
       B: #Wow, that counts as tall for a baseball player? (They're significantly shorter than cricketers.)

Again, the intuition is that *A*'s statement in (56) entails that McAuliffe is short, and has the effect of informing *B* about the standard of comparison for baseball players. In contrast, the positive-antonym degree question in (57) is not evaluative, and therefore cannot be similarly informative.

According to Roberts (1990), that there are (at least) two ways to address a QUD in discourse: by answering the question, or by restricting the QUD to a subquestion. An example of restriction into a subquestion is in (58).

(58)   A: Who went to the party?
       B: Did Adam say Doug was there?

B's response in (58) restricts the QUD to a question about whether Doug went to the party, which qualifies in Roberts' semantics as a subquestion.

However, when the QUD regards evaluativity, responding with an evaluative degree question actually answers, rather than restricts, the QUD. This is demonstrated in (59), where B's response is sufficient to answer A's question.

(59)   A: I'm a little worried about the actress playing me in the movie. Is she tall or short?
       B: *(to the casting agent)* How short is Susan again?
       A: That's fine, as long as she's short.

This is in contrast with the exchange in (60). Because B's question isn't evaluative, it does not serve to answer the QUD. In contrast to (59), A cannot learn anything from B's question.

(60)   A: I'm a little worried about the actress playing me in the movie. Is she tall or short?
       B: *(to the casting agent)* How tall is Susan again?
       A: #That's fine, as long as she's tall.

This demonstrates that the evaluativity associated with negative-antonym degree questions, when at-issue, can be an entailment of a sentence, functioning as part of an assertion. This is consistent with the predictions in Simons et al. (2011) and, I believe, further evidence in favor of an implicature-based approach to evaluativity. In what follows I will refer to this as the "discourse sensitivity of evaluativity," made explicit in (61).

(61)   **The discourse restriction on evaluativity**
       For an utterance u with an evaluativity implicature ϵ: if ϵ addresses the QUD (is "at issue"), it is an entailment of u; otherwise, ϵ is a presupposition of u.

That evaluativity is sensitive to discourse considerations like topic or QUDs can also explain what I'll refer to as the "equative argument asymmetry." Recall that the same projection tests that suggested that evaluativity in equatives could project (53) also determined that only the internal argument of the equative (the *as* clause) was evaluative.

(62)   a. If Doug is as short as Adam, he will not be able to go on the ride.

   b. It's not the case that Doug is as short as Adam.

In particular, the only proposition projecting outside of the antecedent in (62a) is that Adam is short (but not that Doug is short); ditto for the negation in (62b). It seems as though evaluativity is associated with the external argument (Doug in this case) only via the truth conditions of the equative: if Adam is short and Doug is (at least) as short as Adam, then it follows that Doug is short.

A major shortcoming of the EVAL account was its inability to explain the equative argument asymmetry. In §3.3 I reviewed the attempts to address it, but these all involved restricting the markedness competition surrounding the distribution of EVAL in ways that were syntactically implausible and very hard to execute semantically.

By the syntactic account presented in §2.1, the internal and external arguments of a comparison construction denote a set of degrees. I'll refer to these sets of degrees as the "internal argument value" and "external argument value," respectively.

In this implicature-based account of evaluativity, the equative argument asymmetry falls out quite nicely from a related observation about the discourse sensitivity of comparison constructions, demonstrated in (63).

(63)   A: How tall/short is Doug?

   B: He's as tall/short as Adam.

   B′: #Adam is as tall/short as he is.

What (63) seems to show is that an equative can be used to address a question about an individual x's measure along some dimension iff x is in the external clause of the equative. In other words, the two arguments of the equative seem to be very strictly encoded as comment (the external argument) and topic (the internal argument). (64) shows that comparatives are similarly discourse-sensitive.

(64)   A: How tall/short is Doug?

   B: He's taller/shorter than Adam.

   B′: #Adam is taller/shorter than he is.

Based on (63) and (64), I'll offer the following informal generalization.

(65)   **The discourse sensitivity of comparison constructions**

   A comparison construction with an external argument value x and an internal argument value y is felicitous iff x is relevant to the QUD.

According to (65), the external and internal arguments of an equative differ in their at-issue status: the value encoded in the external clause will be at-issue, and the value encoded in the internal clause not-at-issue.

It's interesting to note that this is consistent with the formalization of Q- and M-alternatives that I presented in §5.1.1, in which (66b)—but not (66c)—was considered to be an M-alternative to (66a). I repeat the definition of M-alternatives and the M Principle in (67) and (68).

(66) a. Adam is taller than Doug.
     b. Adam is shorter than Doug.
     c. Doug is shorter than Adam.

(67) M-ALTERNATIVES
Let ϕ denote a semantic object of type $\langle \omega, t \rangle$. The set of **M-alternatives** for ϕ, written as $A_{Mstr}(\phi)$, is defined as $A_{Mstr}(\phi) := \{\phi' : \llbracket \phi' \rrbracket \subset \llbracket \phi \rrbracket\}$.

(68) THE M PRINCIPLE
Do not use ϕ if there is another sentence $\phi' \in A_{Mstr}(\phi)$ such that both:
a. $\phi' < \phi$, and
b. ϕ' is weakly assertable.

We now know that there are important discourse-related differences between the comparatives in (66). (66a) and (66c) count as potential M-alternatives to one another because they are mutually entailing. But they are not competitors, according to the M Principle, because they are weakly assertable in distinct contexts. This contextual sensitivity of markedness competitions might be more transparent in other systems; see Matsumoto (1995).

The claim that (66a) and (66c) are not generally both assertable in the same context is bolstered by the contrast below, which suggests that the QUD can privilege different antonyms when it doesn't privilege the external or internal argument.[8]

(69) A: Which of your brothers is taller?
     B: Doug is taller than Adam.
     B′: ?Adam is shorter than Doug.

The equative argument asymmetry, demonstrated in (62), can be explained by an interaction of the discourse sensitivity of evaluativity and the (independently observed) discourse sensitivity of comparison constructions. The current proposal predicts that, if a comparison construction is evaluative, then each of its arguments is evaluative, but that the evaluativity behaves differently in each argument. It is projective content in the internal argument because the internal argument is not-at-issue. And it is entailed content in the external argument because the external argument is at-issue.

---

[8] See Clark (1969a,b, 1972); Flores D'Arcais (1970); Higgins (1977) for experimental evidence of the contrast in (69).

But the same theory that predicts a connection between the data in (62) and in (63) also predicts that a manipulation of the QUD can affect the position and truth-conditionality of the evaluativity associated with a negative-antonym equative. And this appears to be the case.

Imagine that *A* and *B* are at a party in Argentina, but *A* is new to the country and curious about its inhabitants.

(70)   A: I don't really know what counts as tall or short in Argentina.
       B: Well you're as short as most tourists are. (Argentinians are *d*-tall on average . . .)

B's response in (70) sounds a little unnatural without any further explanation, but it is possible, I think, to interpret it as addressing the QUD. Namely, if *B*'s utterance is a felicitous response to the QUD ("What counts as tall and short in Argentina?"), it is so because (a) it encodes evaluativity in the external clause; and (b) that evaluativity, because it is relevant to the QUD, is entailed (rather than presupposed) by the equative. *B*'s response in (70) informs *A* about the standards of tallness and shortness in Argentina by determining them with respect to her height (and *A* comes out short in the comparison). In effect, it means, "You're shorter than the average Argentinian." Contrast this with the much more unnatural exchange in (71):

(71)   A: I don't really know what counts as tall or short in Argentina.
       B: #Well you're as tall as most tourists are. (Argentinians are *d*-tall on average . . .)

B's response in (71) doesn't seem to address the QUD at all, and so it seems like a violation of the Relevance maxim. This is because positive-antonym equatives aren't evaluative, and so there's nothing in the external clause or anywhere else in the equative that can address *A*'s curiosity about Argentinian heights.

The goal of this section was to explore consequences of the claim that evaluativity in equatives and degree questions is a Manner implicature. I argued that, while evaluativity is generally projected content in equatives, it can in some contexts be entailed by an equative. I've also argued that this discourse sensitivity of evaluativity can be coupled with independent observations about the discourse sensitivity of the internal and external arguments in comparison constructions to explain why evaluativity often (in out-of-the-blue contexts) only projects from the internal argument of evaluative equatives.

In the next section I will take up the issue of evaluativity in positive constructions, where evaluativity is not sensitive to antonymy. I will argue that evaluativity, in these constructions, is an uninformativity-based Quantity implicature, rather than a Manner implicature.

But I'll end this section by flagging a potential confound in tests for evaluativity in context. In a discourse-initial context, illustrated in (72), the account here predicts that only the B_4 response in (72) is evaluative. However, in a discourse-initial context, all of these responses are felicitous and informative responses to the question. And they all seem to suggest that Doug is tall or short, depending on the antonym used.[9]

(72) A: Is Doug tall or short?
        B_1: He's taller than Adam.
        B_2: He's shorter than Adam.
        B_3: He's as tall as Adam.
        B_4: He's as short as Adam.

This is arguably not because each construction is evaluative (and because, as a result, the implication is strengthened to an entailment in this context). Instead, these sentences seem evaluative by virtue of the fact that they introduce Adam as relevant to the QUD and, consequently, as the relevant standard of comparison. If Adam represents the contextual standard for tallness or shortness, then in the absence of additional information about the context (or Adam's relevance to it), B's responses are evaluative because they explicitly relate Doug to the relevant standard (represented by Adam). If this is right, the comparative construction (and the positive-antonym equative) are evaluative in this context by virtue of the truth-conditional content encoded in the degree quantifier and its arguments, not by some added evaluative meaning.

Based on the results of a series of experiments examining evaluativity in discourse-initial contexts such as these, Brasoveanu and Rett (2014) support this conclusion: the meaning of an otherwise non-evaluative degree construction can, in discourse-initial contexts, mimic evaluativity by virtue of the hearer's assumptions about the relationship between the two arguments, the relevance of the standard of comparison, and what counts as a salient standard for the purposes of evaluativity. I've tried to minimize these effects in the data reported here, but they seem to be very real discourse considerations of evaluativity and deserve careful treatment.

5.3 Evaluativity in positive constructions

Famously, positive constructions are always evaluative, regardless of the polarity of the antonym.

(73) a. Adam is tall.
        b. Adam is short.

The EVAL account—and the proposal in Breakstone (2012)—treated positive constructions as obligatorily evaluative because their non-evaluative versions were semantically vacuous. In particular, the truth conditions in (74) are trivially true

---

[9] Sam Cumming (p.c.) points out that the intuition that the other responses are evaluative requires a particular intonation, loosely described as one that implies the finality of the answer.

because they assert what they presuppose (given the positive extension presupposition): that there is some degree to which Adam is tall and short, respectively.

(74) a. ⟦Adam is tall⟧ = $\lambda w \exists d[\text{tall}(w)(\text{adam}, d)]$ (non-evaluative)
      b. ⟦Adam is short⟧ = $\lambda w \exists d[\text{short}(w)(\text{adam}, d)]$ (non-evaluative)

The EVAL account proposed that any degree construction could in principle contain a null EVAL, and so positive constructions were analyzed as in principle ambiguous between an evaluative and a non-evaluative interpretation. The non-evaluative interpretations never surfaced because they were completely uninformative.

In contrast, the present account does not predict that the positive constructions in (73) are each ambiguous between an evaluative and a non-evaluative interpretation. It analyzes both antonyms as relations between individuals and degrees (whose domain is restricted to individuals that instantiate the predicate to some degree). This predicts that the *only* semantic meanings associated with positive constructions are the vacuously true truth conditions in (74). The predicted result is thus one in which positive constructions are "degree tautologies": constructions whose scalar or degree semantics is trivially true. In this section I argue that evaluativity is the (only) natural consequence of this meaning being strengthened in context via a Quantity implicature.

5.3.1 *Tautologies and the maxim of Quantity*

An extension of Grice's Quantity maxim (or Horn's Q Principle) suggests that positive constructions take on a non-conventional, evaluative meaning because they are semantically trivial. Grice's discussion of tautologies is repeated below (1975: 52):

> Extreme examples of a flouting of the first maxim of Quantity are provided by utterances of patent tautologies like *Women are women* and *War is war*. I would wish to maintain that at the level of what is said, in my favored sense, such remarks are totally noninformative and so, at that level, cannot but infringe the first maxim of Quantity in any conversational context. They are, of course, informative at the level of what is implicated, and the hearer's identification of their informative content at this level is dependent on his ability to explain the speaker's selection of this *particular* patent tautology.   (original emphasis)

I have already, in the context of Manner implicatures, explained why the added, implicated content in some negative-antonym degree constructions is evaluativity (as opposed to some other meaning). This explanation comes from considerations of what it means for a gradable predicate to be informative relative to its antonym (§5.1.2; Bolinger 1972). Consequently, a prediction of this account is that the truth-conditional meaning of both of the positive constructions in (74) is supplemented with an evaluativity component (and, furthermore, one that is an entailment of the sentence).

The contrast with questions helps enforce this point. Degree questions like those in (13) (repeated below) are like positive constructions in that the degree argument of their adjective is existentially bound in their (pre-implicature) semantic meaning.

(75)   a. $[\![\text{How tall is Adam?}]\!] = \lambda p \exists d[p(w^@) \wedge p = \lambda w.\text{tall}(w)(\text{adam}, d)]$
      b. $[\![\text{How short is Adam?}]\!] = \lambda p \exists d[p(w^@) \wedge p = \lambda w.\text{short}(w)(\text{adam}, d)]$

But the meaning of these questions differ in a crucial way from the predicted semantic meaning of positive constructions in (74); they are not trivial. These questions partition the space of possible answers into many different propositions, corresponding to the various degrees Adam could be tall or short, respectively. Because this is significant semantically, the two degree questions aren't subject to the Q Principle in the way tautologies are. This leaves them susceptible to the M Principle, which results in their contrast in evaluativity (and the supplemented meanings in (76), §5.1.1).

(76)   a. $[\![\text{How tall is Adam?}]\!] = \lambda p \exists d[p(w^@) \wedge p = \lambda w.\text{tall}(w)(\text{adam}, d)]$
      b. $[\![\text{How short is Adam?}]\!] = \lambda p \exists d[p(w^@) \wedge p = \lambda w.\text{short}(w)(\text{adam}, d) \wedge d >$
        $s_{\text{short}}]$

Contrast this with the *yes/no* questions in (77) and their corresponding semantic (i.e. pre-implicature) meaning.

(77)   a. $[\![\text{Is Adam tall?}]\!] = \lambda p[p(w^@) \wedge p = \lambda w \exists d[\text{tall}(w)(\text{adam}, d)]$
      b. $[\![\text{Is Adam short?}]\!] = \lambda p[p(w^@) \wedge p = \lambda w \exists d[\text{short}(w)(\text{adam}, d)]$

As it stands, given our analysis of gradable adjectives and a Hamblin/Karttunen-style approach to questions, the questions in (77) are just as semantically trivial as their positive-construction counterparts: each both presuppose that Adam has a height—because they contain gradable adjectives, which carry a positive extension presupposition—and also ask whether Adam has a height (a degree on the "tall" and "short" scale, respectively). This makes them just as trivial and uninformative (or non-information-seeking) as positive constructions, which predicts that their meanings will both be supplemented by an uninformativity-based Quantity implicature, as in (78).

(78)   a. $[\![\text{Is Adam tall?}]\!] = \lambda p[p(w^@) \wedge p = \lambda w \exists d[\text{tall}(w)(\text{adam}, d) \wedge d > s_{\text{tall}}]$
      b. $[\![\text{Is Adam short?}]\!] = \lambda p[p(w^@) \wedge p = \lambda w \exists d[\text{short}(w)(\text{adam}, d) \wedge d > s_{\text{short}}]$

These meanings correctly predict that the *yes/no* questions will partition the space of possible worlds into those in which Adam is significantly tall/short (a *yes* answer) and those in which he is not (a *no* answer).

Importantly, the use of an uninformativity-based Quantity implicature to supplement trivial semantic meaning changes the meaning of the positive construction (and the *yes/no* questions in (77)) so that they no longer enter into a markedness-based competition. Manner scales require one scalemate to be at least as informative as another, and these forms no longer are. The *tall* sentence requires that Adam's height exceed (on the 'tall' scale) the salient 'tall' standard, while the *short* sentence requires that Adam's height exceed (on the 'short' scale) the salient 'short' standard.

This Quantity-implicature-based approach to evaluativity in positive constructions can be seen as similar in some respect to theories in which evaluativity in positive constructions is treated as degree quantifier domain restriction (Kennedy 2009; Francez and Koontz-Garboden forthcoming; Grano and Kennedy 2012; Schwarzschild 2010, 2012; Bogal-Allbritten 2013). There are some intriguing parallels between evaluative constructions and constructions with individual quantifiers that exhibit quantifier domain restriction, as suggested by (79).

(79)   John remembered every student's name.

(79) can only be interpreted sensibly with an implicit restriction on the domain of the quantifier; a reading that corresponds to something like "in his class." This is in part because it seems implausible that John could remember the name of every student that currently or has ever existed. To account for this reading, Stanley and Szabó (2000) and Stanley (2002) propose that the QP comes with a pair of null contextual variables to restrict its domain: an individual x (in this example, it would pick out John's class) and a relation R relating students to x (in this example, the relation "is in").

A quantifier domain restriction approach to evaluativity in the positive construction would extend this explanation to the domain of the existential degree quantifier assumed to be at play in the positive construction. This is, it should be said, despite the fact that quantifier domain restriction in the individual domain is generally only a property of universal quantifiers.

Many of those who treat evaluativity in positive constructions as instances of quantifier domain restriction have argued that implicature-based approaches are too general to be correct (Szabó 2001; Stanley and Szabó 2000; Stanley 2002; King and Stanley 2005, responding to "unarticulated constituent" theorists like Recanati 2002). As I've argued in §5.1.2, there is a reasonably clear explanation of why the strengthening of degree constructions amounts to evaluativity, and there's evidence that it is a relatively general phenomenon. Evaluativity is a Manner implicature because atypicality, where gradability is concerned and where antonyms are relevant, amounts to being above a contextual average. And evaluativity is an uninformativity-based Quantity implicature because restricting degrees to those above a contextual standard is significantly more informative than restricting it some other way.

This appropriately predicts that the evaluative meaning carries over to constructions, like the negative-antonym equative, whose meaning is strengthened for considerations other than informativity. In contrast, a quantifier domain restriction approach to evaluativity in positive constructions is less general than the phenomenon of evaluativity calls for because it provides no explanation of why, out of all the comparison constructions, only the domains of existential quantifiers in negative equatives are routinely restricted. In this respect, a domain restriction approach to evaluativity in positive constructions is restricted in its empirical scope in just the same way the POS account is.

Interestingly, as pointed out by Schwarzschild and others, comparatives with no overt *than* clause also seem to receive something like an evaluative interpretation, as shown in (80).

(80) a. The older gentleman can be seated now.
     b. Heavier people prefer this type of shoe.

Their lack of an argument corresponds to an evaluative reading, rather than a weak or vacuous interpretation. But there is a notable difference in politeness between these constructions and their positive construction counterparts. Arguably, the comparatives sound more polite because they are more indirect (Brown and Levinson 1978). This suggests an account in which both positive constructions and comparatives with no overt *than* clause take on an evaluative interpretation for Quantity-related reasons, and the comparative forms (because they're already evaluative) additionally take on a polite interpretation for Manner-related reasons.

The semantics of positive constructions predicted by the simple compositional semantics of this system results in trivial meanings for both positive- and negative-antonym positive constructions. They are, effectively, degree tautologies. We can thus explain their evaluativity as an uninformativity-based Quantity implicature, following Grice's suggested treatment of tautologies. This correctly predicts a contrast between positive constructions and *how* questions in terms of their polarity sensitivity; it also correctly predicts the evaluativity of *yes/no* questions containing unmodified adjectives. Finally, it has the benefit of providing a unified treatment of evaluativity, namely one in which evaluativity arises as an implicature when it is needed to supplement semantic meaning or to explain the use of marked forms.

5.3.2 *The semantic properties of uninformativity-based Quantity implicatures*

In this section, I'll return to some previous observations about the behavior of uninformativity-based Quantity implicatures and will provide some evidence that evaluativity in positive constructions behaves just as we might expect given the analysis in the previous section.

In §4.2.1, I suggested that uninformativity-based Quantity implicatures differ from (some) scale-based Quantity implicatures in part because they are not cancellable or defeasible, as illustrated in (81).

(81) a. War is war ... #in fact, violence is avoidable in war.
     b. Bankers are bankers ... #in fact, many bankers are lovely.
     c. Boys will be boys ... #in fact, they often behave unpredictably.

The difference in cancellability between scale-based and uninformativity-based Quantity implicatures could plausibly have to do with a difference in the degree to which they are conventionalized or generalized; I unfortunately do not have much to say by way of an explanation.

But what is useful here in defense of the current proposal is that this general observation about the uncancellability of uninformativity-based Quantity implicatures also holds for evaluativity in the positive construction, as in (82).

(82) a. Adam is tall . . . #in fact, he's of average height.
    b. Adam is a tall man . . . #in fact, he's of average height.
    c. Adam is short . . . #in fact, he's of average height.

It also seems as though the evaluativity implicature in positive constructions is generally calculated locally. It can be manipulated by truth-conditional operators like negation, as in (83).

(83) a. Adam isn't tall.
    b. If Adam were tall, he would make the basketball team.

The sentence in (83a) remains true despite Adam having a height, but it is false if his height exceeds the relevant contextual standard. In (83b), the truth of the consequent is contingent on Adam's being significantly tall, not his having a height.

This seems to be true for the strengthened interpretation of tautologies, as well, although the examples are less natural.

(84) a. It's not always the case that war is war. The involvement of drones has complicated things immensely.
    b. If bankers are bankers, there's little hope in Wall Street reform.

In the absence of any necessary conditions for conversational implicatures, I take these parallels to be as encouraging evidence that evaluativity is an implicature as we could possibly hope for. There is one other way in which evaluativity in positive constructions could conform with our expectations for implicature: if it is discourse-sensitive, behaving like a presupposition or entailment depending on whether or not it is at-issue.

Van Kuppevelt (1996) explicitly demonstrated that scale-based Quantity implicatures are discourse-sensitive (see §4.3). But the situation is significantly different for uninformativity-based Quantity implicatures. In the case of scalar implicatures, a sentence's compositional meaning is strengthened from one informative meaning to a yet more informative meaning (e.g. from involving "at least three" to "exactly three"). But in the case of uninformativity-based Quantity implicatures, a sentence's compositional meaning is strengthened from a trivial meaning to a non-trivial meaning. If the implicature responsible for the strengthening is not-at-issue, it is hard to imagine what would license the construction.

And, in fact, it's hard to imagine a felicitous use of a tautology or positive construction in a context in which its supplemented meaning is not-at-issue. The discourse in (85) is an attempt to construct such a context. Imagine *A* and *B* work at a soap factory that for years has manufactured soap that is extremely smelly and vibrant in color.

The soap scientists have however just invented two new varieties, one colorless and the other odorless; although the colorless one is significantly less smelly than their old soaps, and the odorless one is significantly more subdued in color. *A* and *B* are having a hard time keeping the new packaging straight, however, and keep getting the new soap mixed up.

(85) A: I can't tell these apart. Is this the odorless one?
      B: No, that one's smelly.

(85) suggests that a positive construction can be an acceptable response to a question of whether a bar of soap has a non-zero degree of odor. And, in this scenario, *B*'s response seems plausibly non-evaluative; the colorless soap doesn't count as smelly in the context of the soap factory.

This context could in principle be changed to test more canonical relative adjectives, like our trusty pair *tall* and *short*, but would require an even more implausible scenario of two-dimensionality, etc. I am optimistic however that such sentences would behave the same way. While I believe that a Quantity-implicature approach to evaluativity in positive constructions has several things going for it—including a parallel with Manner implicatures in other constructions and clearly parallel behavior with other uninformativity-based Quantity implicatures—it is easy to admit that this proposal would be strengthened by a better understanding of how to test for conversational implicatures (and how to test for differences between types of conversational implicature).

To sum up this section: while I've analyzed evaluativity in equatives and degree questions as a Manner implicature, I argue here that evaluativity in positive constructions is instead a particular subspecies of Quantity implicature. I've defended this approach as the best of both worlds: it allows for a unified, independently motivated treatment of evaluativity (as an implicature) while accounting for the difference in the two types of constructions in terms of their sensitivity to antonymy. Specifically, the account predicts that evaluativity will be a component of any adjectival construction with a viable M-alternative (predicting the evaluativity of negative-antonym equatives and degree questions) or in any uninformative adjectival construction.

The theory that evaluativity arises in positive constructions as the result of an uninformativity-based Quantity implicature predicts that evaluativity is connected to the positive construction in a particular, intrinsic way, in parallel with the non-trivial interpretations of sentences like *War is war*. I've argued that it correctly predicts that evaluativity is a non-cancellable semantic component of positive constructions, and that it can be calculated locally (and thus serve as input to truth-conditional operators). It remains unclear whether the evaluativity in positive constructions (or uninformativity-based Quantity implicatures in general) demonstrates the same discourse sensitivity observed in scale-based Quantity implicatures (van Kuppevelt 1996) or Manner implicatures (§4.3 and Simons et al. 2011).

In Chapter 6, I will provide additional support for this approach to evaluativity by arguing that it makes at least two specific predictions outside of the core data addressed here, regarding markedness and semantic triviality, and that these predictions are borne out. But first I'll end this chapter by discussing how an implicature-based approach to evaluativity can help address unexpected differences between relative antonym pairs, and also differences between relative adjectives and other classes, like absolute and extreme adjectives.

5.4 Evaluativity and other adjective classes

In §2.1.3, I distinguished between relative adjectives (RAs) like *tall* and absolute adjectives (AAs) like *full* based on several different tests (for a nice overview, see Burnett 2012). One difference between RAs and AAs is their compatibility with certain modifiers, as demonstrated below.

(86)   Relative adjectives
    a. ??Adam is completely tall/short.
    b. ??The pond is 100% deep/shallow.
    c. ??Max is fully eager/uneager to help.

(87)   Absolute adjectives
    a. The figure was completely visible/invisible.
    b. The room was 100% full/empty.
    c. The flower was fully open/closed.

Another reliable test of the distinction comes from their different behavior in definite descriptions (Kennedy 2007; Syrett et al. 2009).

(88)   a. Pass me the tall one.
    b. Pass me the empty one.

The definite description in (88a)—which involves a relative adjective—will pick out the taller of the two glasses regardless of whether either glass qualifies as tall. (Or, possibly, a definite with an RA can fix the standard of comparison discourse-initially, while a definite with an AA cannot, as argued in Brasoveanu and Rett 2014.) In contrast the AA definite in (88b) will have a referent if and only if there is exactly one completely empty glass. It will fail to refer in contexts in which more than one glass is completely empty, or in which neither glass is completely empty, even if one is clearly more empty than the other.

Following work by Yoon (1996) and Rotstein and Winter (2004), Kennedy and McNally (2005) account for the contrast between relative and absolute adjectives, as well as the contrast between total and partial antonym pairs (as in (89) and (90)), in which the antonyms appear to lexicalize different endpoints, as demonstrated (in part) by their distribution with these same degree modifiers:

(89) Lower-bound (partial) adjectives are not modifiable
    a. The pipe is completely ??famous/unknown.
    b. The room became 100% ??loud/quiet.
    c. The pipe is fully ??bent/straight.

(90) Upper-bound (total) adjectives are modifiable
    a. The treatment is completely safe/??dangerous.
    b. This product is 100% pure/??impure.
    c. We are fully certain/??uncertain about the results.

I include in (91) a partial list of each type of adjective class, taken from the appendix in Rett (2008).

(91) Members of the adjective classes

RELATIVE		TOTAL/PARTIAL		ABSOLUTE	
positive	*negative*	*total*	*partial*	*positive*	*negative*
fast	slow	clever	dull	transparent	opaque
good	bad	deep	shallow	open	closed
heavy	light	kind	cruel	complete	incomplete
high	low	polite	rude	perfect	imperfect
large	small	pretty	plain	possible	impossible
old	young	clean	dirty	true	false
tall	short	dry	wet	visible	invisible

To account for the distribution of adjectival modifiers like the ones in (86) and (87), Kennedy and Levin (2008) argue that relative adjectives and absolute adjectives (and total/partial adjectives) differ in terms of the structure of the scales they are associated with. They claim that RAs are associated with scales that have no intrinsic upper or lower bound ("open scales"); AAs are associated with scales that have intrinsic upper and lower bounds ("closed scales"); partial adjectives are associated with scales that have an intrinsic lower bound; and total adjectives are associated with scales that have an intrinsic upper bound (both "partially closed scales").

The intuition behind this claim is that there is a context-invariant point at which something can be maximally clean, but there is not a context-invariant point at which something can be maximally tall. If we define modifiers like *completely* in terms of these bounds, we can account for their ability to modify AAs but not RAs. This additionally explains the asymmetry in partial and total adjectival pairs, illustrated in (89) and (90).

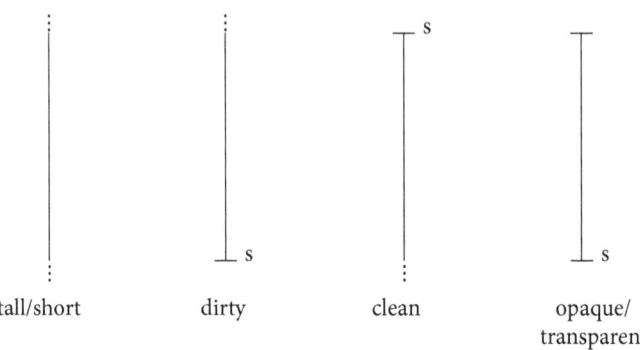

FIGURE 5.3. Adjective classes and scale bounds

Kennedy and McNally's theory is illustrated in Figure 5.3, where the horizontal lines represent lexicalized bounds on a scale, and *s* marks the bound used for an adjective class's standard.

Of course, as we saw, adjectival constructions involving relative adjectives like *tall* and *short* can nevertheless make use of a standard. Kennedy and McNally (2005) argue that, for the purposes of evaluativity, the difference between relative and absolute (and total and partial) adjectives is that the former use contextually valued standards in their evaluative interpretations, whereas the latter co-opt their lexically specified bounds.

To account for this difference, (Kennedy 2007: 36) proposes that evaluativity standards are restricted by a principle of **Interpretive Economy**.

(92)   **Kennedy's (2007) Principle of Interpretive Economy**
Maximize the contribution of the conventional meanings of elements of a sentence to the computation of its truth conditions.

Informally, this means something like: "It's more economical to value a standard with a lexicalized bound than with context." A further extension of (92) privileges an absolute adjective's lower bound over its upper bound.

Kennedy (2007) wasn't clear about the status of the Principle of Interpretive Economy. For our purposes, it can viewed as a generalization about what counts as salient for the purpose of a pragmatic variable: whenever a scale comes with a bound, that bound (or the lowest bound) is the most salient.

The theory of evaluativity in the previous few sections focused exclusively on relative adjectives. The other classes of adjectives—absolute, total, and partial—behave differently than relative adjectives with respect to evaluativity (see also Toledo and Sassoon 2011). In §5.4.1, I'll discuss how the present account extends to absolute, total, and partial adjectives; in §5.4.2 I'll return to address the relative adjectives that Sassoon (2011) and Breakstone (2012) argued do not pattern like *tall* and *short*.

5.4.1 *Absolute adjectives*

Absolute (AA), total (TA), and partial (PA) adjectives don't display the same patterns of evaluativity as (standard) relative adjectives. In Rett (2008), I characterized the pattern as follows:

(93)   Evaluativity and scale structure

	COMPARATIVE		EQUATIVE	
	positive	*negative*	*positive*	*negative*
RAs	no	no	no	yes
T/PAs	no	yes	no	yes
AAs	yes	yes	yes	yes

I came to these conclusions by examining the behavior of each class of adjectives in comparison constructions, using the Bierwisch Test for evaluativity. I will caution, however, that some of these judgments are not particularly strong; see Lassiter and Goodman (2013) for some experimental considerations.

(94)   RELATIVE ADJECTIVES
   a. Adam is taller than Doug. $\nrightarrow$ Doug is tall.
   b. Adam is shorter than Doug. $\nrightarrow$ Doug is short.
   c. Adam is as tall as Doug. $\nrightarrow$ Doug is tall.
   d. Adam is as short as Doug. $\rightarrow$ Doug is short.

(95)   TOTAL/PARTIAL ADJECTIVES
   a. This shirt is cleaner than these jeans. $\nrightarrow$ These jeans are clean.
   b. This shirt is dirtier than these jeans. $\rightarrow$ These jeans are dirty.
   c. This shirt is as clean as these jeans. $\nrightarrow$ These jeans are clean.
   d. This shirt is as dirty as these jeans. $\rightarrow$ These jeans are dirty.

(96)   ABSOLUTE ADJECTIVES
   a. The front window is more opaque than the back window. $\rightarrow$ The back window is opaque.
   b. The front window is more transparent than the back window. $\rightarrow$ The back window is transparent.
   c. The front window is as opaque as the back window. $\rightarrow$ The back window is opaque.
   d. The front window is as transparent as the back window. $\rightarrow$ The back window is transparent.

Brasoveanu and Rett (2014) report experimental results that confirm these intuitions, modulo the considerations of discourse salience discussed in §5.2.3. Toledo and Sassoon (2011) examine the distribution of evaluativity across adjective classes using the definite description test in (88); I will return to their conclusions shortly.

Given Kennedy's Principle of Interpretive Economy in (92), the differences in evaluativity between RAs on the one hand and AAs and T/PAs on the other hand fall out naturally from independent observations about the differences in the standards invoked by each type of adjective. Partial (e.g. *dirty*) and absolute (e.g. *opaque*) adjectives repurpose their lower bounds as evaluative standards. Because the positive extension presupposition requires that any individual predicated of a gradable adjective must instantiate that predicate to some degree, and because the standards for partial and absolute adjectives are their lower bounds, any individual in the extension of these adjectives has a measure that exceeds the salient standard of comparison.

As a result, all of the partial adjective constructions in (95) and the AA constructions in (96) are evaluative for any individual that exhibits the predicate to some degree. Kennedy's Principle of Interpretive Economy predicts that these constructions are evaluative not by virtue of the fact that they contain POS, EVAL, or trigger an evaluativity implicature, but because being on the scale entails exceeding the standard of comparison in every context.

The situation is slightly different for total adjectives like *clean*, whose intrinsic bound is the top (rather than the bottom) of the scale. For *clean*, it's no longer true that any individual on the scale is above the standard. Instead, any individual on the scale is below the standard. The result is that the total adjective constructions in (95) are never evaluative; being on the scale is negatively correlated with exceeding the standard in every context.

From this perspective, RAs behave the way they do because they differ from other types of adjectives in being context-sensitive. And, according to the account presented here, this context-sensitivity is the result of semantic strengthening via conversational implicature. This is a natural extension of the accounts in Kennedy and McNally (2005) and Rett (2008); a recent version can be found in Lassiter and Goodman (2013).

Recently, Toledo and Sassoon (2011) have argued that relative and absolute adjectives additionally differ in the type of comparison classes represented by their evaluative standards. To account for this difference, they propose a particular adaptation of Kennedy's (2007) approach. I'll briefly review it here.

Toledo and Sassoon (2011) examine differences between relative and absolute adjectives based on their different performance in the definite description test illustrated in (88). They argue that relative adjectives' standards of comparison are determined relative to their comparison class, as discussed in §2.2.1, while the other adjective classes use standards of comparison that are determined relative to possible world counterparts of the individual that the adjective is being predicated of. They term these "extensional category comparison classes" and "counterpart comparison classes," respectively. Their empirical claims (from p. 146) are illustrated below. They claim that while we can infer from the sentences in (98) and (99) something about "the way a given individual can be, or normally is," we cannot infer the same from the sentences in (97).

(97) **relative adjectives**, e.g. *tall/short*: an extensional category comparison class
    a. x is tall/short $\not\rightarrow$ x is as tall/short as x can be
    b. x is tall/short $\not\rightarrow$ x is not as tall/short as x can be

(98) **absolute adjectives**, e.g. *full/empty*: a counterpart comparison class
    a. x is full $\rightarrow$ x is as full as x can be (x can't be fuller)
    b. x is empty $\rightarrow$ x is as empty as x can be (x can't be emptier)

(99) **total/partial adjectives**, e.g. *dirty/clean*: a counterpart comparison class
    a. x is dirty $\rightarrow$ x can be cleaner (less dirty)
    b. x is clean $\rightarrow$ x can't be cleaner (less dirty)

To account for this difference, Toledo and Sassoon propose a more nuanced picture of the difference between relative adjectives and absolute/total/partial adjectives (p. 143):

We propose that the standard of membership in the interpretation of the positive form of an adjective is determined based on three factors:

- The comparison class evoked in the interpretation of that adjective, which determines the degrees on its lexically encoded scale that are relevant for assigning truth conditions;
- An economy principle (following Kennedy 2007) which dictates that an interpretation relative to a maximum or a minimum endpoint within a comparison class takes precedence over one relative to an arbitrary midpoint;
- A grammaticalization principle according to which the type of standard that is usually selected for an adjective is encoded as a default convention.

It's important to note that Toledo and Sassoon (2011) presuppose, like other advocates of the POS account, that only positive constructions are evaluative. Presumably, given the data reviewed in §3.1, these restrictions on the standards invoked by particular adjective classes extends to any construction in which these adjectives are associated with an evaluative interpretation (contrary to their wording above).

This perspective is illustrated in the following descriptions of evaluativity in a relative and absolute positive construction, respectively.

(100) This student is tall.   *relative*
    a. **comparison class**: extensional, classes of other students
    b. **grammaticalization principle**: standard is generally an average
    c. **economy principle**: use average in the absence of maxima or minima

(101) This cup is full.   *absolute*
    a. **comparison class**: intensional, comprised of counterparts of the cup
    b. **grammaticalization principle**: standard is generally a maximal one
    c. **economy principle**: where possible, use maxima or minima as endpoints

To implement this difference, Toledo and Sassoon restrict POS as follows (p. 145) for a contextually valued function f to degrees and contextually valued function C to comparison classes:

(102)   a. For a partial A_P (namely, an adjective whose argument's comparison class is typically lower closed), $POS(A_P, w) = \lambda x \in D_x, \exists y \in C(A_P, x, w), f(A_P, w)(x) > f(A_P, w)(y)$; e.g. *The table is dirty* is true iff the table is covered with more dirt than one of its contextually salient counterparts (so the table's degree exceeds the minimum for that table).

   b. For a total A_T (namely, an adjective whose argument's comparison class is typically upper closed), $POS(A_T, w) = \lambda x \in D_x. \forall y \in C(A_T, x, w), f(A_T, w)(x) \geq f(A_T, w)(y)$; e.g. *The cup is full* is true iff the cup is at least as full or fuller than any of its salient counterparts (so the cup's degree is the maximum for that cup).

   c. For a relative A_R, $POS(A_R, w) = \lambda x \in D_x. f(A_R, w)(x) > s(C(A_R, x, w))$; e.g. *The child is tall* is true iff the height of the child is above some midpoint standard, $s(C(\text{tall}, x, w))$, within a comparison class ranging over different individuals (the child's classmates, boys of his age, boys in general, etc.).

This is a brute-force account of the difference illustrated in (100) and (101), and one that relies on a POS approach in which evaluativity is semantically encoded (in a null operator). It proposes that there are three different POS morphemes—one each for partial, total, and relative adjectives—which encode different restrictions on the relevant comparison class and whose distribution is presumably governed by some process of semantic selection.

As I've argued here, there are lots of reasons to prefer an implicature-based approach to evaluativity over a compositional semantic one. Importing Kennedy's Principle of Interpretive Economy into the implicature-based approach I'm proposing here seems relatively straightforward; the principle, as Kennedy worded it, seems naturally Gricean.

It is however less clear how to incorporate into the implicature-based approach Toledo and Sassoon's observations about the difference between relative and absolute adjectives in terms of the type of comparison class invoked. Ideally, the account presented here would be supplemented with some pragmatic account of why extensional category comparison classes are most natural or salient for constructions formed with relative adjectives, while counterpart comparison classes are most natural or salient for constructions formed with absolute adjectives. I will have to leave this goal to future research.

Before I move on to discuss the extension of the implicature-based account of evaluativity to relative adjectives other than *tall* and *short*, I'll briefly mention one other class of adjectives: extreme adjectives (Paradis 2001; Bogal-Allbritten 2011;

Morzycki 2012). These adjectives are like AAs in that every construction they occur in is evaluative. (103) is a partial list of extreme adjectives; (104) illustrates the distribution of evaluativity.

(103) Extreme adjectives

positive	*negative*
happy	sad
beautiful	ugly
fat	skinny
great	terrible
brilliant	stupid

(104) EXTREME ADJECTIVES
   a. Adam is more brilliant than Doug. $\rightarrow$ Doug is brilliant.
   b. Adam is stupider than Doug. $\rightarrow$ Doug is stupid.
   c. Adam is as brilliant as Doug. $\rightarrow$ Doug is brilliant.
   d. Adam is as stupid as Doug. $\rightarrow$ Doug is stupid.

I will follow Morzycki (2012) in considering extreme adjectives to be like AAs in that they are restricted in such a way that all individuals in their extensions are individuals who exceed their standard of comparison. Morzycki (2012) provides further evidence for the claim that these adjectives form a natural class based on the distribution of what he calls (pp. 569–70) "extreme degree modifiers," words like *downright* and *full-on* that seem to only be able to modify extreme adjectives; cf. (105).

(105)   a. downright destitute/??solvent
        b. full-on crazy/??sane

To sum up: not all antonym pairs demonstrate the same evaluativity pattern as *tall* and *short* do. In the case of absolute, total/partial, and extreme adjectives, the difference doesn't seem to have to do with a difference in the presence or absence of an evaluativity implicature, but rather with differences in the semantic consequences of non-strengthened interpretations. We can explain why all AA, extreme, and partial adjective constructions are evaluative by independent observations about their scale structure, independently determined by other phenomena (e.g. the distribution of certain modifiers). This can also explain why no total adjective construction is evaluative. The evaluativity patterns exhibited by total, partial, and absolute adjectives are thus consistent with the implicature-based approach developed in this section, despite the fact that the evaluativity of constructions containing these non-relative adjectives isn't attributable to implicature.

The different scale structures associated with these adjectives cannot, however, account for differences in patterns of evaluativity within relative adjective constructions. In the next section, I suggest that—to the extent RAs behave differently in terms of evaluativity—this might be a result of different degrees of conventionalization.

5.4.2 *Other relative adjectives*

The generalizations about the distribution of evaluativity in equatives and degree questions reported in §3.1 hold only for relative adjectives. But, as observed in Breakstone (2012) and Sassoon (2011), these generalizations don't hold as we might expect for all relative adjectives.

Breakstone and Sassoon offered *warm* and *cold* as an example of an RA pair that behave differently than *tall* and *short*. Before them, Lehrer (1985) undertook a very detailed investigation of the distribution of evaluativity across antonym pairs. I'll present her descriptive conclusions and then return to Breakstone's and Sassoon's claims.

Lehrer (1985) gives a descriptive account of markedness in adjectives. She treats evaluativity—which she refers to as "committedness"—as a prime indication of markedness. (I adopt the same conclusion, but we might disagree on the direction of causality.[10]) She says (p. 421): "Neutralization [= non-evaluativity] of one member of the pair in questions is the commonest of the properties [of antonymy]."

She does however identify a number of antonym pairs that do not display this distribution of evaluativity, "pairs of antonyms in which neither member is neutral in questions" (p. 402), or in which both members seem to yield evaluative degree questions. She dubs them "doubly marked" antonym pairs (see also Ljung 1974).

(106)   Lehrer's (1985) list of doubly evaluative antonym pairs

abstract/concrete	ferocious/meek	innocent/guilty
austere/lush	feminine/masculine	lush/barren
beautiful/ugly	graceful/awkward	peaceful/violent
delicate/rugged	graceful/clumsy	reassuring/frightening
dominating/submissive	harsh/mild	reassuring/threatening
dry/sweet	hot/cold	positive/negative
dry/wet	impulsive/restrained	pungent/bland
fat/thin		

Her tests for evaluativity (pp. 403–4) are familiar, but her interpretation of the data is complicated. She argues that there is a strict subset of the antonym pairs in (106) which are evaluative in degree questions but not in comparatives, for instance. And the table mixes different adjective classes together: *dry/wet* are total/partial, and *beautiful/ugly* are clearly extreme adjectives.

To account for these differences in evaluativity, Lehrer (1985) follows Cruse (1976) in assuming that adjectives can differ in terms of how much of a dimension's scale they

---

[10] Lehrer says: "There is, in spite of these counterexamples, a strong correlation between markedness in questions and committedness [= evaluativity]. Cruse suggests that the two phenomena should correlate because they are different aspects of the same property—the ability of a word to name the whole antonym scale or only part of it." (1985: 404–5)

cover. She suggests that the difference between *long/short* and *hot/cold* is that "*Hot* and *cold* name different parts of the scale, whereas *long* can name the whole scale," as illustrated in (107).

(107)   Antonym scales, Lehrer (1985)

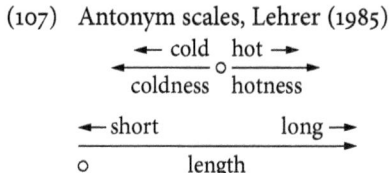

She also proposes that a dimension of measurement can be associated with more than one antonym pair, as illustrated in (108), where |M| signifies the midpoint of the scale.

(108)   Shared antonym scales, Lehrer (1985)

hot   warm |M| cool   cold

Similarly, we have

ferocious   aggressive |M| timid   meek

And maybe

fat   plump |M| thin

However, Lehrer admits that this explanation can't extend to all of the adjective pairs in (106). And it is hard to imagine how her perspective on these differences in evaluativity could extend to the Kennedy and Levin (2008) framework, in which some but not all of these differences are lexicalized.

Breakstone (2012) and Sassoon (2011) focus on the antonym pairs *warm/cold* (or *hot/cold*), *fat/skinny*, *rich/poor*, and *heavy/light*. They argue that these are RA antonym pairs—and thus in the scope of the EVAL account—that are nevertheless both evaluative in degree questions. Sassoon's test is repeated in (109) from §3.4.3.

(109)   a. ?This ice cream is as warm as that one.
        b. ?How warm is the ice cream?
        c. ?How cold is the fire?

I expressed some doubts about the accounts in Breakstone (2012) and Sassoon (2011) of these differences in evaluativity in §3.4.3. One worry is the question of whether or not it's correct to categorize these adjectives as relative adjectives. While I don't find *100% warm* to be acceptable, it seems to be quite natural to modify *warm* with *completely*, as in *This won't get you completely warm but it will help*, which is one of Kennedy and McNally's (2001) tests for absolute or total adjectives. It's also not clear to me how *warm* fares in Syrett et al.'s (2009) definite description test. In other words, it's not clear to me that I can point to a table with two glasses of lemonade on it—one of which is icy and the other one of which is merely extremely cold—and refer to *the warm one*.

I have similar worries for the other antonym pairs they discuss. Perhaps the classes of relative and absolute adjectives are not as categorical as Kennedy and McNally (2005) assume; perhaps an adjective's membership in these classes can change in context, as we might expect given Kennedy's (2007) Principle of Interpretive Economy.

But perhaps, in light of these worries, another way of phrasing Breakstone's and Sassoon's complaint is: if the class of relative adjectives is hard to determine, how can the EVAL account, or any account of evaluativity that relies on a strong relative/absolute distinction, claim to be able to predict which constructions or utterances are evaluative?

Regardless of the particular data discussed in Breakstone (2012) and Sassoon (2011), I am very willing to admit that only a strict subset of relative adjective antonym pairs behave identically to *tall* and *short* in terms of evaluativity. The ones that do, based on my intuitions, include *long/short, old/young, wide/narrow, good/bad, large/small, fast/slow,* and *thick/thin.* While it is by no means an exceptionless claim, these adjectives, as Sassoon (2011) argues, tend to be measure adjectives in the sense of Kennedy and Svenonius (2006): they tend to be those pairs for which the positive antonym can be modified by a measure phrase.

I will summarize the situation as I see it. The implicature-based account of evaluativity presented in Chapter 5, like the EVAL account in Rett (2007, 2008), makes different predictions for absolute adjectives than it does for relative adjectives, based on independent claims about differences in scale structure in Kennedy and McNally (2005) and Kennedy (2007). But while it seems to be successful in its predictions for clear instances of each class of adjectives, there are a number of adjectives that seem to be part of either (or neither) class, and it's not clear how to account for their evaluativity (or lack thereof).

Instead of arguing that there is a third class of adjectives, sharing properties with both relative and absolute adjectives, I will tentatively suggest that the relevant problem here concerns M-alternatives. In particular: *tall* and *short* are clear antonyms in English, while pairs like *warm* and *cold* are not. The problem is not with a markedness-based theory of evaluativity, nor with the classification of these adjectives as relative (as opposed to absolute) adjectives. Rather, the differences in evaluativity they exhibit have to do with differences in the lexical inventory of English that forms the basis for the calculation of M-alternatives. (Which is the truer antonym of *cold, hot* or *warm*? Where does *cool* fit in? Why doesn't *tall* have a tempered positive version, like *hot* does in *warm*?)

Recall Lehrer's (1985) suggestion (following Cruse 1976) that adjectives associated with a particular dimension could nevertheless differ in where their standards fall on the scale. She argues (p. 423) that this requires a notion of conventionalization along the following lines: "A lexical entry for each word with an antonym would include a cross-reference to that antonym and would state whether and when neutralization of the opposition occurs, just in those cases where the possibility of neutralization does not follow from general principles. In addition, the lexical entry for each term would state which part of the scale was covered by the term." There are two important points here: first, that adjectives can and perhaps should be conventionally or lexically associated with their antonym (as opposed to merely contextually associated); and second, that the extent to which an adjective is conventionally associated with its antonym can vary across adjectives.

There is evidence for Lehrer's claim, even outside of the category of adjectives, and its role in implicature calculation. Geurts (2011) reports that there can be cross-linguistic differences in terms of what words count as Q-alternatives. He cites Matsumoto (1995) for observing a difference in implicature between the English sentence in (110a) and the Japanese translation in (110b):

(110) a. Michio is Takashi's brother.
       b. Kochira wa Takashi-kun no kyoodai no Michio-kun desu.
          this   TOP Takashi-Mr GEN brother GEN Michio-Mr COP

The Japanese version carries the implicature that the speaker does not know the relative age of Michio and Takashi. And this seems to be a direct result of the fact that Japanese has a more complex system of sibling terms, as in (111).

(111) a. *kyoodai* 'brother'
       b. *ani* 'older brother'
       c. *otooto* 'younger brother'

The idea that a language's lexical inventory could result in cross-linguistic differences in Q-alternatives and, consequently, the distribution of Quantity implicatures across languages seems fairly uncontroversial. I'll suggest here that similar differences in lexical inventories of antonym pairs can result in cross-linguistic differences in M-alternatives, with the result that languages can in theory differ in terms of which antonyms are evaluative in degree questions and comparison constructions. In the case of gradable adjectives, there's reason to think that some antonym scales could have more than two members, resulting in less stable judgments with respect to evaluativity.

There is additional reason to think that apparently synonymous adjectives can differ in terms of scale structure or some related property across languages. Schwarzschild (2005) and Murphy (2006) observe that the class of measure adjectives—those adjectives that can be modified by MPs—differ somewhat across languages. (112) (originally from Zamparelli 2000) and (113) (originally from Corver 1990) are instances of MP constructions in other languages that are illicit in English.

(112) pesante quasi   due tonnellate   *Italian*
       heavy   almost two tons
       'weighs almost two tons' (lit. *is two-tons heavy)

(113)   is 2 boeken rijk   *Dutch*
        is 2 books   rich
        'owns two books' (lit. *is two-books rich)

I am unable to offer a clear suggestion about which antonym pairs need to be treated differently from *tall* and *short*; I do not have clear intuitions about, for instance, the evaluativity of degree questions formed from the antonyms *hot* and *cold*. I suspect that speakers' judgments about these adjectives are in fact unstable. (An informal survey of native speakers indicated that they were split completely down the middle about whether or not the famously skinny model Twiggy could be chubbier one day than she was the day before, a test of whether the antonym *chubby*—intuitively somewhere between *fat* and *skinny* on the weight dimension—is evaluative in comparatives.)

But I would like to argue that an implicature-based approach to evaluativity—in which the distribution of evaluativity relies on the ability of speakers to calculate and coordinate on M-alternatives—leaves a suitable amount of wiggle room to account for these empirical issues. It strengthens the parallel between evaluativity and scale-based Quantity implicatures, like that illustrated in (110): in both cases, relevant alternatives are calculated in part from contextual information and in part from lexical information. And it is arguably preferable to an analysis, like the proposals in Breakstone (2012) and Sassoon (2011), which ties evaluativity differences to metaphysical differences, which (unlike lexical information such as what counts as an antonym) do not vary across languages. A similar argument has been made for the cross-linguistic differences in the class of measure adjectives demonstrated above (Schwarzschild 2005) and in the class of mass nouns (Schwarzschild 2011).

There is independent reason to think that Manner implicatures associated with adjectival constructions behave differently across languages. In Swedish, litotes receive a systematically different interpretation than they do in English, as (114) and (115) demonstrate.

(114)   Det var inte illa.
        That was not   bad
        'That was good.'

(115)   Det var inte helt   fel.
        That was not   completely wrong
        'That was well done.'

The English gloss of the litotes in (114) receives a very different interpretation in English: they receive a "gap reading" (Horn 1991a; see also §4.2.2), which is relatively weak, meaning something like "neither good nor bad". But the Swedish utterance receives what Horn calls the "exceptional reading," meaning something like "better than expected."[11]

If the interpretations of litotes do in fact differ across languages as well as across contexts (as Erasmus and Horn 1991a have already demonstrated), it does not seem desirable to explain the interpretations of these litotes in terms of differences in Swedish speakers' conversational cooperativity, or in the contexts in which they are uttered. It instead seems plausible that the Swedish versions of the antonyms *good/bad* and *right/wrong* differ subtly in their relationship to one another relative to the English antonym pairs, and in the extent to which one lexicalizes or restricts a certain type of standard, along the lines of the proposal in Cruse (1976) and Lehrer (1985). If this is right, we have every reason to expect similar differences in how relative adjective antonym pairs in English relate to one another. And an account that ties differences in evaluativity to differences in the calculation of M-alternatives for a given adjective in a particular construction in a particular context seems to offer the right level of flexibility for these judgments.

5.5 Discussion

The theory proposed in this section has its roots in the EVAL account in Rett (2007, 2008) which took as its focus the observations that (a) evaluativity isn't restricted to positive constructions and (b) its presence outside of positive constructions is conditioned by considerations of markedness.

I have adopted many of the assumptions of that account, namely that the contrast between *tall* and *short* is one of markedness, and that the difference in evaluativity between negative-antonym comparative constructions (e.g. *Adam is shorter than Doug*) and negative-antonym equative constructions (e.g. *Adam is as short as Doug*) is related to their contrast in strictness of ordering (i.e. $>$ versus $\geq$).

Instead of encoding evaluativity in a null operator, however, I've proposed that it is a conversational implicature. Important to this argument is the large class of phenomena in which related implicatures seem to accompany marked forms (e.g. periphrastic causatives and litotes; McCawley 1978; Horn 1984; Levinson 2000). If we need to postulate something like the R Principle (or Grice's Manner maxim) to account for these data, and if evaluativity can be addressed in the same way, it seems preferable to an account of evaluativity that requires construction-specific, null operators.

This implicature-based approach to evaluativity provides two different explanations for evaluativity in two different types of constructions. In positive constructions,

---

[11] Data from Ingvar Lofstedt, p.c., a Swedish/English bilingual. He offers the following commentary on (114): "I give a talk at an international conference, and two people (an American and a Swede) give me feedback afterwards. The American says, 'That was not bad.' This comment sounds patronizing and arrogant to me. But if the Swede says (114), I would be very grateful; it is a generous expression of praise, even though it is word-for-word the same phrase as what the American said."

whose compositional semantic meanings are trivially true, evaluativity arises as the result of the Q Principle (or Grice's Quantity maxim), just as it seems to for truisms like *War is war*.

In equatives, degree questions, and degree demonstratives—any construction in which only the negative-antonym version is evaluative—evaluativity arises as the result of the Marked Meaning Principle (Horn's 1984 Principle of Least Effort), which exhorts interlocutors to associate marked forms with marked meanings (and unmarked forms with unmarked meanings).

In §5.1.2 I offered an explanation of why an uninformativity-based Quantity implicature and a Manner implicature result, in the case of adjectival constructions, in an evaluative interpretation (instead of some other interpretation). I've argued that these degree constructions are strengthened in terms of the strictly-ordered degree scales they refer to. And I've argued that there are principled reasons why atypicality in terms of gradable predicates amounts to a requirement that an individual exceed a (relatively high) standard. Based on a significant amount of evidence in Bolinger (1972), I've argued that this is a general phenomenon: semantically underinformative degree expressions are routinely interpreted as intensified relative to their compositional semantic meaning.

I have argued that this implicature-based approach to evaluativity can account for a number of things that the EVAL account cannot. In particular, it allows for a flexibility in terms of the at-issue status of evaluativity that the EVAL account does not. This prediction is based on evidence that implicatures are sensitive to properties of discourse (van Kuppevelt 1996; Simons et al. 2011), and appears to be borne out differently for the Manner implicatures associated with e.g. equative constructions than it is for the Quantity implicature associated with positive constructions.

I've also argued that the discourse-sensitivity of implicatures can predict the asymmetrical evaluativity of the internal argument of equatives. The explanation draws on an independent observation that the internal argument of a comparison construction is almost never at-issue. We consequently predict that evaluativity would be projected content in these clauses.

In the last section, I extended the characterization of evaluativity as an implicature to adjectives other than *tall* and *short*. The predictions of the account are straightforward for absolute adjectives like *open/closed*, total/partial adjectives like *clean/dirty*, and extreme adjectives like *beautiful/ugly*. The constructions containing these adjectives are either always or never evaluative in ways that are directly attributable to their scale structure (Kennedy and Levin 2008).

I draw from responses to the EVAL account (like Breakstone 2012; Sassoon 2011) the conclusion that there are some adjectives that behave at least in part like relative adjectives but that do not exhibit the same or as clear-cut evaluativity patterns as *tall/short*. It seems clear that there are uses of the degree question *How warm is it?*, for instance, that are at least in some contexts undeniably evaluative.

Instead of arguing that these adjectives form a separate class, and altering the theory of evaluativity accordingly, I have instead suggested that these antonym pairs relate to each other in a less straightforward way than other antonym pairs. They are therefore less clearly M-alternatives to one another, depending on context and other considerations. The present proposal—in which the evaluativity of degree questions, degree demonstratives, and equatives is the result of the calculation of antonymic M-alternatives that may be conventionalized to varying degrees—might be unsatisfying in its restrictiveness but is, in my mind, a welcome perspective on what appear to be very subtle and contextually sensitive judgments of evaluativity.

Chapter 6 examines ways in which this theory can be extended to other phenomena related to evaluativity, which I believe provides extra support for the proposal. But I will end this chapter by briefly reviewing ways in which an implicature-based approach to evaluativity is preferable over its alternatives, especially those discussed in Chapters 2 and 3 which encode it semantically.

Unlike POS accounts, an implicature-based approach to evaluativity can account for evaluativity outside of positive constructions (namely, in equatives, degree questions, and degree demonstratives). Unlike the EVAL theory, it can account for the evaluativity of negative-antonym equatives that receive an "at least" interpretation; the tendency of evaluativity to be associated with the internal (rather than external) clause of the equative; and the fact that the evaluativity associated with e.g. equatives can at times be truth-conditional (or function like an entailment rather than presupposition of the sentence).

But its main advantage over the POS and EVAL accounts is that it doesn't require the postulation of a null semantic operator. It predicts that positive constructions mean what they do because they have to, and speakers take advantage of this fact. This perspective on evaluativity can be extended back to Bartsch and Vennemann (1972), who say (p. 172):

The function of syntax is not simply to verbalize semantic representation but to do it "well"; i.e., to provide shortcuts which allow the speaker to express complex meanings in short and simple surficial structures. Thus . . . [(116a)] is better than [(116b)], where "better" here stands for "expressing the same semantic representation with fewer words and a simpler surface phrase structure."

(116)   a. John is tall.
        b. John's height is greater than the average of the heights of boys.

A very common complaint against the POS and EVAL accounts is that they each predict, at least in theory, that a natural language could in principle have an overt version of the null evaluativity morphemes. I argued in Chapter 2 that this doesn't seem to be the case.

While the lack of overt evaluative morphemes across languages might be seen as a failure of the POS and EVAL accounts, it could easily be seen as support of an implicature-based approach to evaluativity. Horn (1972) and Gazdar and Pullum (1976) argue that Grice's account of implicature (and their adaptations of it) carries along with it predictions about lexicalization. In particular, they claim that implicatures of the sort Grice predicts could not be lexicalized, precisely because they could be expressed instead (and more economically) as an implicature.

There is, I think, reason to be skeptical of this very general prediction; recent work by e.g. Chierchia et al. (2009) arguing that Quantity implicatures are encoded in a covert *only* highlights the relationship between (local) scalar implicature and the semantic import of words like *only*. But Levinson (1983) argues compellingly that this is just the sort of place we would expect to see a contrast between particularized and generalized implicature (p. 163):

> Conversational implicature can be shown to provide systematic constraints on what is a *possible lexical item* in a natural language . . . The basic constraint imposed is roughly as follows:

> (117)   If the use of a lexical item *w* carries a generalized conversation implicature *I*, then *ceteris paribus* there will be no lexical item *x* that directly encodes *I*.

The original motivation for a constraint like (117) comes from McCawley's (1978) observation about the relationship between color terms like *pink* and *pale red*. But it extends quite naturally to evaluativity. In a theory in which evaluativity is encoded in a generalized Manner implicature—as is the case here, for at least some instances of evaluativity—we can appropriately account for what has historically been a complication for semantic theories of evaluativity: the fact that there is no evidence that languages lexicalize evaluativity.

6

Extensions of the evaluativity implicature

"I don't think women are better than men. But I do think that men are worse than women."

Louis C.K.

Characterizing evaluativity as a conversational implicature allows us to account for its distribution across adjectival contstructions without construction-specific stipulations or null morphemes (like POS or EVAL). In this chapter, I'll argue that it has the added benefit of making welcome predictions outside of the canonical evaluativity data. In particular: if evaluativity is the property of marked adjectival constructions, we'd expect to see it correlated with marked strategies other than those involving negative antonyms. I will argue in §6.1 that this is in fact what we see. And if evaluativity is the property of semantically trivial adjectival constructions, we'd expect to see it pop up in semantically trivial constructions other than the positive construction. I will argue in §6.2 that this, too, is the right prediction.

In this account, I assumed that evaluativity is the product of marked gradable predicates. If this is right, then we would also predict to see something like evaluativity associated with lexical categories other than adjectives. I've already reviewed a few proposals that the concept of evaluativity is useful in the treatment of some verbal constructions; I'll return to these in §6.2.1, and in §6.3 I'll argue that the account can be extended to account for apparent evaluativity in some nominal constructions.

6.1 Markedness beyond antonymy

It's clear that comparison constructions can be formed with positive or negative antonyms; this results in a markedness-based contrast in evaluativity for equatives (the less informative comparison construction) but not for comparatives (the more informative comparison construction).

Yet the formulation of the R Principle in §5.1.1 that takes into account structural complexity (see also Katzir 2007) predicts that two comparison constructions that differ in ways other than their antonyms can nevertheless qualify as M-alternatives. In this section, I'll present two different empirical observations that support this prediction: first, that periphrastic comparatives are evaluative, regardless of antonym type (§6.1.1). And second, that equatives with measure phrase standards—which are marked relative to MP constructions—are also evaluative regardless of antonym type (§6.1.2).

6.1.1 Comparative periphrasis

There are morphological restrictions in English on the types of adjectives that can combine with the synthetic comparative marker *-er*. Where *-er* is prohibited morphologically, the analytic *more* can be used, as shown in (1).

(1) a. *The new virus strain is contagiouser than the old one.
     b. The new virus strain is more contagious than the old one.

For adjectives that can combine morphologically with the synthetic *-er*, this analytic stategy becomes an optional strategy, as shown in (2).

(2) a. Adam is taller than Doug.   *synthetic*
     b. Adam is more tall than Doug.   *analytic*

Furthermore, the two strategies illustrated in (2) seem to differ in terms of evaluativity. As I reported in Rett (2008), the analytic version in (2b) is evaluative; it seems to presuppose that Doug is tall. This intuition is confirmed by the projection tests in (3), in which the projection of evaluativity in the antecedent of the analytic comparative in (3b) is incompatible with the consequent (that Adam would count as short).

(3) a. If Adam is taller/more tall than Doug, he will likely make the basketball team.
     b. If Adam is taller/#more tall than Doug, he would likely still count as short.

The implicature-based approach proposed in the previous chapter can account for this difference in evaluativity given an explanation about the difference between the comparatives in (2) in terms of markedness. Following Bresnan (1973), Corver (1997), and Embick (2007), I assume that *more* lexically decomposes into the synthetic marker *-er* and the quantity adjective *much* (Corver refers to this as "*much*-support"). In many theories (see in particular Rett 2006, 2008, 2014b; Solt 2010, 2014), this means that the two constructions are synonymous, but that the analytic comparative in (2b) is more marked than the synthetic (2a) by virtue of the fact that it contains an additional morpheme.

And in fact, the definitions of M-alternatives and the M Principle from §5.1.1 characterize the two as M-alternatives of one another, and of the analytic (2b) as the more marked alternative to the synthetic (2a).

(4) M-ALTERNATIVES

Let ϕ denote a semantic object of type $\langle \omega, t \rangle$. The set of **M-alternatives** for ϕ, written as $A_{Mstr}(\phi)$, is defined as $A_{Mstr}(\phi) := \{\phi' : [\![\phi']\!] \subset [\![\phi]\!]\}$.

(5) THE M PRINCIPLE

Do not use ϕ if there is another sentence $\phi' \in A_{Mstr}(\phi)$ such that both:

a. $\phi' < \phi$, and

b. ϕ' is weakly assertable.

As a result, according to (5) and the Marked Meaning Principle, the theory correctly predicts that the analytic comparative in (2b) is evaluative due to its relationship to the synthetic comparative in (2a).

There is evidence that this periphrastic evaluativity is cross-linguistically robust. As I pointed out in Rett (2008), Russian displays the same contrast with respect to its synthetic (6a) and analytic (6b) comparatives (Matushansky 2002; Pancheva 2005, 2006; Krasikova 2009; (6) is from Matushansky 2002).

(6) a. Germann   byl sil'nee čem   ego protivnik.
       Germann-NOM was stronger what-INSTR his adversary-NOM

    b. Germann   byl rostom bol'še čem   ego protivnik.
       Germann-NOM was more   strong what-INSTR his adversary-NOM
       'Germann was stronger than his adversary.'

As with English, the analytic (6b) is evaluative, while the synthetic (6a) is not. Krasikova (2009) confirms this judgment by showing that only the synthetic is compatible with a continuation like *but he is not strong* (p. 277).

Bogal-Allbritten (2010) argues that the same generalization holds for Navajo. The data in (7) contrast in terms of the comparative morphology. (7a) involves the synthetic comparative marker (glossed CA for "comparative aspect") attached to the adjective, resulting in the comparative adjective *'áníłnééz*. (7b) involves the analytic comparative strategy involving the adverbial *'át'éego* and absolute aspect marking ("AA") on the adjective (*nineez*), with the result that (7b) is more marked than (7a).

(7) a. Shimá   shideezhí   yilááh   'áníłnééz, 'áko ndi doo
       my-mother my-younger.sister 3'O-BEYOND CA-3s-tall but   NEG
       t'áá 'áłah yéigo nineez   da.
       both   very AA-3s-tall NEG
       'My mother is taller than my younger sister, but they are both not very tall.'

    b. Shimá   shideezhí   yilááh   'át'éego   nineez, # 'áko
       my-mother my-younger.sister 3'O-BEYOND 3s-be-ADV AA-3s-tall   but
       ndi doo t'áá 'áłah yéigo nineez   da.
       NEG both   very AA-3s-tall NEG

'My mother is taller than my younger sister, #but they are both not very tall.'
paraphrase offered by speaker: 'They're both very tall, but my mother is even
taller.'

Bogal-Allbritten (2010) says of this contrast:

When the degree construction contains an AA. . .-marked adjectival verb that could have been
CA-marked, the contextual norm is entailed, as in [(7b)]. By contrast, the CA-marked verb used
in the same adjectival construction carries no such entailment [(7a)].

This evaluativity contrast in comparison strategies is a direct result of any account
in which evaluativity is tied to marked constructions, so the prediction is shared by
an implicature proposal and the EVAL account.

As mentioned in Rett (2008), some speakers of English report a contrast in evaluativity between clausal and phrasal comparatives, as in (8) (see Pancheva 2006, for a
discussion of the difference).

(8) a. Adam is taller than Doug.   *phrasal*
     b. Adam is taller than Doug is.   *clausal*

The same is true of Bulgarian, where clausal comparatives contain optional rela-
tivizing material, as in (9).[1]

(9) a. Marija e po-visoka ot   Ivan.
        Maria is -*er*-tall   from Ivan
        'Maria is taller than Ivan.'   *phrasal*
     b. Marija e po-visoka ot   kolkoto   e Ivan.
        Maria is -*er*-tall   from how-much is Ivan
        'Maria is taller than (what) Ivan is.'   *clausal*

While the phrasal synthetic comparative in (9a) is non-evaluative, the clausal synthetic
comparative in (9b) is evaluative.

In some Balkan languages, the degree *wh*-phrase can occur with an optional
quantity adjective (for discussion see Rett 2006). In these cases, we see a contrast
in evaluativity as well. The Macedonian positive-antonym degree question in (10a)
is non-evaluative, just like its English counterpart, but the "periphrastic" version in
(10b) is evaluative.[2]

(10) a. Kolku e   visoka?
        how   is-3SG tall-FsG
        'How tall is she?'

     b. Kolku mnogu e   visoka?
        how   much is-3SG tall-FsG
        'How tall is she?'

---

[1] Data from Pancheva (2006) and Roumyana Pancheva (p.c.).
[2] Thanks to Slavica Kochovska (p.c.) for this data.

We would predict that this contrast in evaluativity extends to comparative constructions in those Balkan languages that form comparison constructions with *wh*-clauses.

I will end this section by highlighting the fact that these were very straightforward predictions of a relatively simple characterization of markedness and the assumption that the marked interpretation of a degree construction is evaluativity. These data were all mentioned in Rett (2008) in regard to the EVAL account, but the theory couldn't deal with them naturally, given that it did not (arguably, could not) provide a detailed account of the markedness competition. A theory, like the EVAL one, in which evaluativity is semantically encoded in a particular subconstituent of a degree construction is one that cannot be generalized to data like the ones above in which a difference in markedness can occur at any point in the sentence (e.g. periphrasis of the comparative marker or periphrasis of the standard marker).

These data are however very natural for a Manner implicature account that predicts that the use of any marked form will correspond to an evaluative interpretation. It also predicts that, while the (synthetic) comparative and the equative are related in the traditional way on a scale of informativity, as in Figure 6.1 (repeated from §2.1.5), the synthetic comparative is itself related to a number of different comparative strategies on a manner scale, as in Figure 6.2.

The idea is that the synthetic clausal and the analytic comparative forms are both marked relative to the synthetic phrasal, and so we expect each to be evaluative (by virtue of its markedness competition with the synthetic phrasal comparative). I have not marked the difference between analytic phrasal and clausal in Figure 6.2 because the difference is irrelevant. The analytic clausal might be more marked still than the analytic phrasal, relative to the synthetic phrasal, but that additional level of markedness is not relevant for the purposes of the evaluativity implicature. This implicature theory of evaluativity predicts that the only two constructions considered by the interlocutors for the purpose of Manner implicatures is the form uttered and its least marked synonymous counterpart.

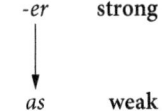

FIGURE 6.1. *A Quantity scale for comparatives and equatives*

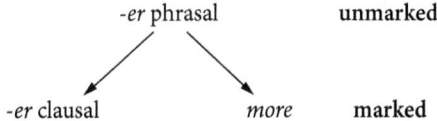

FIGURE 6.2. *A Manner scale for comparatives*

The next section reviews a second source of evidence that the markedness competition for the purposes of evaluativity is just as general as an implicature-based account would predict.

6.1.2 *Measure phrase equatives*

In English, measure phrases (MPs) like *6ft* or *400 years* can serve as standards in (or internal arguments of) comparison constructions, as in (11).

(11)   a. Trees can be older than 400 years.
        b. Trees can be as old as 400 years.

In Rett (2010, 2014a) I've termed these "measure phrase comparatives" and "measure phrase equatives (MPEs)," respectively.

MPEs are unlike clausal equatives of the sort we've been discussing in at least two significant ways. First, they most naturally receive an "at most," as opposed to an "exactly" or an "at least" interpretation. Second, they tend to be evaluative, regardless of whether they're formed with positive or negative antonyms.

The first point is illustrated in (12) (from Rett 2014a).

(12)   (Over the course of the day,) The children dove as deep as 20m.
        a. ... For instance, Michael dove 15m.   "at most"
        b. #... For instance, Michael dove 25m.   "at least"

The second point is evident in that positive-antonym MPEs, unlike their clausal counterparts, entail the corresponding positive construction, as demonstrated in (13).

(13)   a. Tennis balls are as heavy as golf balls. ↛ Golf balls are heavy.
        b. Tennis balls are as heavy as 60g. → 60g is heavy (for a tennis ball).

Rett (2014a) offers additional evidence that MPEs are evaluative: they can have a metalinguistic interpretation, as Barker (2002) would predict. Imagine a context in which an American is asking an Australian about the weather patterns there.

(14)   Australian: It gets really hot in Australia. For instance, it was as hot as 35° today in Melbourne!
        American: Oh, so 35° is hot in Celsius. 35° is cold in Fahrenheit!

MPEs are formed with the same degree quantifier *as* as clausal equatives are. Presumably this morpheme contributes the same meaning to the two constructions. What conditions the difference in meaning, and what conditions the difference in evaluativity?

In Rett (2014a) I attribute these two idiosyncratic properties of MPEs to their competition with MP constructions. In particular, I assume that MPEs are on a Q scale with MP comparatives and are on an M scale with MP constructions, as suggested in

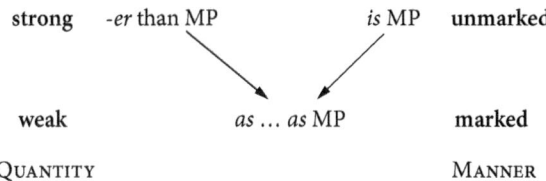

FIGURE 6.3. *The scales for measure phrase equatives*

(15) and represented in Figure 6.3 (in contrast to the one relevant scale for clausal equatives and comparatives shown in Figure 6.1).[3]

(15) *Trees can be as old as 400 years* . . .
    a. . . . is less informative than *Trees can be older than 400 years*
    b. . . . is more marked than *Trees can be 400 years old*

I will not explain the "at most" interpretation here, but I will emphasize the significance of the evaluativity of MPEs. To account for it I assume, as above, that the "at least" semantics encoded in the equative morpheme is strengthened to an "exactly" interpretation given its stronger scalemate, e.g. the MP comparative in (15a). In these contexts, the MPE is synonymous with—but more marked than—its MP construction counterpart. As a result, a speaker's use of an MPE in a context that supports a Quantity implicature triggers a Manner implicature that results in evaluativity.

This is an important point: an account of evaluativity in which it is encoded in a semantic operator like EVAL yet is restricted to the embedded clause of comparatives would have no obvious reason to privilege a positive-antonym equative with an MP standard over one with a DP phrasal or clausal standard. The relevant markedness competition needs to be more global, in the way outlined in §5.1.1. I know of no other treatment of evaluativity that correctly predicts an evaluativity contrast between (13a) and (13b).

This section provides, I think, strong evidence that one of the predictions of the implicature-based account of evaluativity in Chapter 5 is borne out; namely, that the Marked Meaning Principle isn't restricted to considerations of antonymy. But the current proposal identifies a second source of evaluativity: uninformativity-based Quantity implicature, which I argued is responsible for the evaluativity of positive constructions. This aspect of the theory suggests that any semantically trivial construction containing a gradable predicate will be evaluative (regardless of antonymy). In the next section, I'll provide evidence that this is in fact the case.

---

[3] In some cases, as in the MPE in (13), the less marked construction involves a verb (e.g. *Tennis balls weigh 60g*) or, alternatively, no predicate at all (e.g. *Tennis balls are 60g*).

6.2 Uninformativity beyond positive constructions

Positive constructions are evaluative because, otherwise, they would be meaningless; they would assert what they presuppose, namely that the individual denoted by the subject instantiates the gradable predicate to some degree, as demonstrated by the compositional semantics in (16).

(16) a. $[\![\text{Adam is tall}]\!] = \exists d[\text{tall}(\text{adam}, d)]$
      b. $[\![\text{Adam is short}]\!] = \exists d[\text{short}(\text{adam}, d)]$

In §5.3 I referred to positive constructions as "degree tautologies," highlighting their connection with Grice's examples like *War is war*.

The account proposed in Chapter 5 suggests that evaluativity could arise as an uninformativity-based Quantity implicature in other adjectival constructions that are otherwise un- or underinformative. In this section, I'll suggest that at least two distinct evaluative phenomena could be analyzed in just this way.

6.2.1 Verbal evaluativity

In §2.3 I reviewed two distinct proposals for extending POS from adjectival constructions to verbal constructions: the treatment in Piñón (2005) of "adverbs of completion," exemplified in (17); and the treatment in Kennedy and Levin (2008) of the telic variability of degree achievements, exemplified in (18).

(17) a. The glass is completely empty. $\rightarrow$ The glass is empty.
      b. The glass is partly empty. $\nrightarrow$ The glass is empty.

(18) a. The soup cooled for an hour.   *atelic*
      b. The soup cooled in an hour.   *telic*

Both proposals involved two extensions of adjectival POS: first, a verbal variant with with a different argument structure than adjectival POS; and second, a counterpart of verbal POS (DEG for Piñón, μ_v for Kennedy and Levin) that did not contribute evaluativity. This first extension accounted for the presence of evaluativity in verbal constructions in the first place, the second accounted for the fact that these constructions seemed to be optionally evaluative.

In Chapter 3 I argued that EVAL was an improvement on POS at least in that it predicted a wider distribution of evaluativity, in part because EVAL divorced the evaluative component of POS from its quantificational contribution. I will briefly suggest in this section that an implicature-based approach to evaluativity is similarly able to account for data like these. I will however focus only on the degree achievement data; my suspicion is that the "adverbs of completion" data discussed by Piñón (2005) can benefit from recent innovations in theories of scale structure the semantics of absolute adjectives (Kennedy and McNally 2005 and §5.4.1).

Degree achievements are like the gradable adjectives they derive from in that they are associated with a degree argument in addition to their individual and event arguments, as suggested in (19) (see Rett 2013, for a discussion of the nature of this degree argument). This is almost certainly a simplified semantics for degree achievements, but it's sufficient to illustrate the implicature proposal here.

The truth conditions in (19a) can be read as "*x* cooled during *e* to degree *d*." Following Kennedy and Levin (2008), this degree might need to be restricted to only degrees of change.

(19)   a.   ⟦to cool⟧ = $\lambda d \lambda x \lambda e.\text{cool}(x, e, d)$

       b.   ⟦The soup cooled this morning⟧ = $\exists d[\text{cool}(\iota x[\text{soup}(x)], e, d) \wedge \text{this-morning}(e)]$

The semantics for *cool* in (19a) result in the truth conditions in (19b) for the sentence *The soup cooled this morning*, assuming that *this morning* can modify the event argument of the verb. (This is not a critical assumption; *this morning* could alternatively value the argument, or restrict a time argument associated with the event.) This predicts that the sentence is true iff the soup experienced some degree of change along the "cool" scale that morning.

My goal here is to highlight some similarities and differences between the "positive verbal construction" in (19b) and the positive (adjectival) constructions I analyzed in Chapter 5 as degree tautologies. There is some sense in which (19b) is uninformative; it does not specify how much the soup cooled, and is true even if the soup cooled a very small amount (modulo issues of granularity). It is however not completely uninformative: it doesn't assert what it presupposes, and it's not true in every world. In contexts in which it's not clear whether the soup changed temperature at all, the sentence in (19b) is informative; on the other hand, in contexts in which it's clear or presupposed that the soup cooled (not, e.g., gotten warmer), (19b) is relatively uninformative.

This is a natural consequence of the assumption that some locutions, like tautologies, are always uninformative, while the (un)informativity of other constructions varies from context to context, depending in part on the Question Under Discussion. In other words: a sentence doesn't have to be a tautology to be uninformative in a context. If uninformative utterances can carry conversational implicatures, and if uninformativity varies across contexts, then we predict that non-tautalogical constructions can carry uninformativity-based Quantity implicatures, in certain contexts.

And this seems to be the case, at least for conversational implicatures generally; consider the exchange in (20).

(20)   A: Who won the race?

       B: A fast person.

The sentence (presumably B's response, on some level) *A fast person won the race* isn't a tautology; it's possible for slow people (or slow tortoises) to win races. But a natural interpretation of B's response is one in which it carries a conversational implicature; namely, one that indicates that (s)he doesn't care to answer the question, or doesn't know the answer to the question. The exchange seems natural in a context in which B was also a competitor in the race, and is bitter about losing to a rival. This is, arguably, an uninformativity-based Quantity implicature (a product of the submaxim "Make your contribution as informative as required"), triggered by a non-tautological utterance in a context in which it's clear that the speaker was expected to be more informative.

It should be clear that this utterance, even in response to the same question, doesn't always carry this implicature; in a context in which there is a race between slow and fast people, the same exchange seems informative, and B's utterance doesn't seem to carry an uninformativity-based implicature.

I will argue here that the optional evaluativity in degree achievement constructions like *The soup cooled* is a natural consequence of an account of evaluativity as an uninformativity-based Quantity implicature, coupled with the discourse-sensitivity of implicature. I'll first illustrate that the evaluativity associated with unmodified degree achievement constructions is context-sensitive in the way the implicature associated with B's response in (20) is. I'll then suggest how this can be extended to the modified (a)telic constructions in (18).

Imagine that a group of chemists have discovered a new gas, *XYZ*, and are testing its chemical properties. To do so, they put a bowl of soup, at $110°$F, in a chamber filled with *XYZ*. In this context, the exchange in (21) is natural, and B's response is not evaluative.

(21)   A: What happened with the soup?
          B: It cooled!

In particular, it is consistent with (but does not require that) the soup cool a significant amount. It's acceptable, for instance, in a context in which *XYZ* caused a $1°$ drop in the soup's temperature (assuming $1°$ is a small amount of change in the context).

Consider instead a context in which the scientists have entered a competition for energy-efficient cooling systems. Contestants are only allowed to use a particular amount of energy, but in order to win the competition, their system must cool a bowl of soup from $110°$ to $90°$ in the time allotted (say, 5 minutes). All of the competing systems are cooling systems, but some are more effective than others. The scientists on the *XYZ* team are waiting for the results when B comes back from the testing station and the exchange in (21) takes place.

In this context, B's response is evaluative; it is used to signify that the soup cooled at least to $90°$ (assuming that $90°$ is the salient standard of coolness in this context). We know that it is evaluative because, intuitively, B's response would count as false or at least disingenuous as a report that their system failed the test because it cooled the soup, but only by, say, 1°.

A quick summary: uninformativity-based Quantity implicatures arise whenever an utterance is uninformative—a potential property of all sentences (not just tautologies)—depending on context. This was verified by the discussion of (20) for a Quantity implicature. The discussion of (21) suggests that the generalization extends to degree constructions as well, and therefore to evaluativity. Specifically: degree achievement constructions, unlike positive constructions, are not tautologous. But the extent to which they are informative seems to vary from context to context, and (as predicted) in a way that conditions their evaluativity.

That evaluativity is optional in degree achievement constructions but not in positive constructions is thus a symptom of the ability of the former to be informative in some contexts. That evaluativity is optional in degree achievement constructions but not in e.g. negative-antonym equatives reflects the ability of Quantity implicatures, but not Manner implicatures, to be context-sensitive. This is a nice result that does not rely on the postulation of two null operators in free variation (one which encodes evaluativity and another that does not).

The result can be extended to the telicity tests in (18) with two additional assumptions. First, that uninformativity-based Quantity implicatures can be calculated locally, as suggested in §5.3.2 for the positive construction. And second, that the atelic *for an hour* and the telic *in an hour* differ in their selectional requirements: the former is only compatible with non-evaluative constructions, the latter only with evaluative constructions.

We have independent evidence that *for-* and *to-*phrases place requirements on the (a)telicity of their arguments, explaining the contrast in (22).

(22) a. Adam crossed the street in two minutes/*for two minutes.
      b. Adam slept for two minutes/*in two minutes.

These additional assumptions about *for-* and *to-*phrases are therefore relatively uncontroversial, especially given the well-documented relationship between verbal evaluativity and telicity (see, for instance, Hay et al. 1999; Kennedy and Levin 2008). But a formal implementation of this approach requires a detailed account of local conversational implicature. Following the discussion in Chapter 5, I will stop short of providing one so that I can remain agnostic on whether local implicatures are syntactically or pragmatically conditioned.

In conclusion, the characterization of evaluativity as an uninformativity-based Quantity implicature, provided some compositional mechanism for computing implicatures locally, and given the natural connection between telicity and evaluativity, directly predicts the phenomenon of verbal evaluativity. First, it predicts that evaluativity is a potential implicature of any construction with a gradable predicate (not just adjectival constructions). Second, it predicts that evaluativity is a potential implicature of any construction, provided a context in which that construction counts as uninformative in the right sort of way. This, along with the claim that positive constructions are always uninformative, while degree achievements are only uninformative in some contexts, explains the difference between adjectival and verbal constructions in terms of the optionality of evaluativity. And third, given independently motivated accounts of *for-* and *to*-phrases—and given evidence that evaluativity implicatures can be calculated locally—it predicts that certain modifiers, including *completely*, correlate in a predictable way with evaluativity (Piñón 2005).

In the next section I'll extend this concept of optional uninformativity-based Quantity implicatures to a particular adjectival construction that seems to be optionally evaluative: two-parameter comparatives.

6.2.2 *Two-parameter comparatives*

I have so far discussed comparison constructions that have only one parameter (i.e. adjective). In both the clausal and phrasal comparatives in (23), the internal argument is implicitly formed from the same parameter (here, tallness) as the external argument (Bresnan 1973).

(23)   a. Adam is taller than Doug.   *clausal*
       b. No man is taller than himself.   *phrasal*

Comparatives can, however, be formed with two parameters. This type of construction is usually divided into two subtypes: indirect comparatives and comparisons of deviation (CODs), each with distinct properties. I will review the ways in which these two subtypes of two-parameter comparatives differ and then suggest that their differences can be explained by appealing to the same treatment of optional evaluativity used in the previous section.

A comparative with two parameters is either an indirect comparative or a comparison of deviation (Bale 2007, 2008).[4] They are exemplified in (24).

(24)   a. Adam is taller than he is wide.   *indirect comparative*
       b. Adam is more tall than he is wide.   *comparison of deviation*

There are three primary differences between the two sub types of two-parameter comparatives, widely assumed to be related: **morphology, dimension of measurement,** and **evaluativity.** Indirect comparatives are compatible with synthetic

---

[4] Bresnan (1973), McCawley (1988) call some CODs "metalinguistic comparatives," as in (i).

i. a. It is more hot than humid.
    b. John is more sad than tired.

The term comes from the intuition that these comparatives describe how the predicates are most appropriately used. McCawley (1988) suggests that they are elliptical for e.g., "It is more appropriate to call it hot than humid." Following Embick (2007), I will not differentiate between CODs and metalinguistic comparatives; both are evaluative and both strongly prefer analytic morphology.

morphology, compare degrees on two distinct scales, and are not evaluative. This first property is shown in (24a). The second property is evident in the interpretation of (24a): it is true iff Adam's height (i.e. his tallness) is greater than his radius (i.e. his wideness), a likely scenario.

That indirect comparatives are not evaluative is underscored by the example in (25) (from Bale 2008):

(25)   Unfortunately, Mario is more intelligent than I am beautiful.

indirect comparative

In a context in which it's clear that Mario is stupid, this indirect comparative could be used by the speaker to describe his unflattering appearance. This is compatible with the claim that indirect comparatives are not evaluative, i.e. do not entail the corresponding positive construction formed from either parameter adjective.

In contrast are **comparisons of deviation** (Bartsch and Vennemann 1972; Kennedy 1999). Some examples are in (26).

(26)   a. Adam is more tall than he is wide.
       b. Adam is more intelligent than he is devious.
       c. That dinner was more expensive than it was tasty.
       d. The pool was deeper than Tim was tall.

Comparisons of deviation differ from indirect comparatives in the three properties listed above. They tend to be unnatural with analytic comparative morphology (Embick 2007). And in contrast to indirect comparatives, CODs compare degrees to which an individual's measure deviates from the relevant standards (i.e., differential degrees), instead of directly comparing the measures. This can be seen by contrasting the interpretations of the two constructions in (24). While (24a) describes most individuals (individuals whose height is greater than their diameter), (24b) has a distinct meaning. It presupposes that Adam is both tall and wide, and states that the extent to which he is significantly tall exceeds the extent to which he is significantly wide.

Thus, CODs are evaluative, also in contrast to indirect comparatives. To illustrate this contrast, Bale (2008) provides the minimal pair in (27).

(27)   a. I'm prettier than I am intelligent, although unfortunately I'm quite ugly.

indirect comparative

       b. ?I'm more pretty than intelligent, although unfortunately I'm quite ugly.

comparison of deviation

As I said, these three differences between indirect comparatives and CODs are generally taken to be related; in other words, it's common to assume a correlation between CODs' analytic morphology, evaluativity, and comparison of deviation interpretation.

The differences between these two types of two-parameter comparatives are especially mysterious in light of Kennedy's (1999) examples of cross-polar anomaly, illustrated in (28).

(28) a. #Larry is more tired than Michael is clever.
     b. #My copy of *The Brothers Karamazov* is heavier than my copy of *The Idiot* is old.

Kennedy labels these comparatives (from his p. 16) as unacceptable, and proposes the restriction in (29) to explain why (p. 36):

(29) **Kennedy's (1999) incommensurability restriction**
"A comparative construction is semantically well-formed only if the compared adjectives have the same dimensional parameter."

The restriction in (29) raises questions about the differences amongst two-parameter comparatives: When are they acceptable? What makes an acceptable construction an indirect comparative versus a comparison of deviation (or vice versa)?

In what follows, I will adopt the standard perspective that the difference between an anomalous two-parameter comparative (e.g. (28)) and a comparison of deviation (e.g. (26)) is that the latter undergoes a repair strategy. I will add to this account an informal proposal that the difference between the two subtypes of two-parameter comparatives (and cross-polar anomaly) is at least in part a matter of the context of evaluation.

Kennedy's (1999) treatment of CODs treats them as involving a sort of repair strategy. It presupposes, based on (29), that direct comparison of the arguments in two-parameter comparatives is semantically unviable. It includes the proposal that degrees of e.g. tallness and wideness can, when these properties are both evaluative, be coerced into degrees of deviation from the parameters' respective standards. If we assume that degrees of deviation have in common the same dimension of measurement, specifically deviation from a standard, we can explain why CODs are acceptable, why they compare degrees of deviation, and consequently why they are evaluative (see also Bale 2007, 2008).

My specific, implicature-based implementation of this approach is, informally, as follows. In a context that does not force an evaluative interpretation of the two-parameter comparative in (30) (in which it's not already part of the common ground that Adam is tall and wide), it has the indirect interpretation in (30a), which goes against the incommensurability restriction in (29). The result is an unacceptable utterance.

(30) ⟦Adam is taller than he is wide⟧ =
     a. $\mathrm{Max}(\lambda d.\mathrm{tall}(\mathrm{adam}, d)) > \mathrm{Max}(\lambda d'.\mathrm{wide}(\mathrm{adam}, d'))$ *non-evaluative*
     b. $\mathrm{Max}(\lambda d.\mathrm{tall}(\mathrm{a}, d) \wedge d > s_{\mathrm{tall}}) > \mathrm{Max}(\lambda d'.\mathrm{wide}(\mathrm{a}, d') \wedge d' > s_{\mathrm{wide}})$
                                                            evaluative

In a context in which the two-parameter comparative in (30) receives an evaluative interpretation—specifically, if it is part of the common ground that Adam is tall and wide—it can receive a comparison of deviation interpretation, as in (30b), and thereby does not violate the incommensurability restriction. The result is an acceptable utterance (albeit one with a distinct interpretation from (30a)).

In this approach, the third property relevant for the difference between indirect comparatives and CODs—that the latter necessarily involve analytic comparative morphology—comes from the independent observation in §6.1.1 that analytic comparatives that have acceptable synthetic counterparts are evaluative as the result of a Manner implicature. That is, if a two-property comparative (formed with relative adjectives) has synthetic comparative morphology, it is necessarily non-evaluative; but if it has analytic morphology, it may or may not be evaluative. And the COD interpretation can only come about in a context that supports an evaluative interpretation of the comparative, as a repair strategy.

In other words, in §5.3 I argued that positive constructions are evaluative because they are degree tautologies, and therefore are meaningless unless they carry an evaluativity implicature. Given (29), we can say a similar thing about the COD in (30): because they combine adjectives that are associated with different dimensions, CODs are meaningless unless they are evaluative. From this perspective, the evaluativity of CODs comes about as an uninformativity-based Quantity implicature that behaves like a repair strategy.

This is only a gesture at an account of the obligatory evaluativity of CODs; a full account would include, at least, an explanation of how and why two-parameter comparatives can come to be acceptable despite not having an evaluative (or COD) interpretation, as indirect comparatives do. There is already work that can address these issues (see Bale 2008, and references therein).

But I hope to have illustrated that the evaluativity (and, consequently, the interpretation) of CODs can be accounted for along the same lines of other uninformativity-based evaluativity implicatures: a construction with a gradable predicate (of any lexical category) is evaluative in a context c if it is otherwise uninformative in c. This uses the Gricean program to model Kennedy's and others' intuition that CODs arise as a sort of repair strategy, albeit a context-sensitive one.

And in fact there is evidence that an account of CODs needs to treat their evaluativity as context-sensitive. In her review of Kennedy (1999), Hendriks (1999) argues that, in order for a two-parameter comparative to receive a COD interpretation, there must be a causal relation between the two clauses. In particular (p. 13), "the acceptability of [(31)] might be caused by certain pragmatic factors which somehow license a mapping between two distinct scales."

(31) Fortunately, the ficus was shorter than the ceiling was low, so we were able to get it into the room.

(31) is an example of a two-parameter comparative with synthetic morphology, so it could in theory be either an indirect comparative or a comparison of deviation. According to Hendriks, whether it receives an indirect comparative or a COD interpretation has to do with discourse considerations like the coherence relation between the two clauses (as in Kehler 2001). This underscores the need to tie the evaluativity of two-parameter comparatives at least in part to the context and discourse of utterance.

There is one other interesting consideration for the extension of the implicature-based account of evaluativity to two-parameter comparatives. I suggested above that two-parameter comparatives can receive COD interpretations (instead of counting as unacceptable cross-polar anomalies) if they are uttered in a context that supports their being strengthened with an evaluativity Quantity implicature. If evaluativity can also arise as the result of a Manner implicature, we would predict that markedness could play a role in whether a two-parameter comparative is anomalous or a COD. And this seems to be the case. Büring (2008) reports that cross-polar anomalies are improved when the first adjective is a negative antonym, as in (32).

(32)   a. *Unfortunately, the house is higher than the ladder is short.
        b. Unfortunately, the ladder was shorter than the house was high.

The data Büring reports on are ultimately more complicated than the pair in (32) suggests; as in the rest of this section, I do not intend to provide a full analysis of the extension of the account in Chapter 5 to these data, but only suggest what such an extension might look like. I nevertheless hope to have shown that evaluativity plays a crucial role in some comparative constructions. In particular, I hope to have shown how we can think of two-parameter comparatives as optionally evaluative, depending on context, with their evaluativity correlating in different ways with their deviation interpretations and their morphology.

If this is right, then these data provide additional support for an account of evaluativity in which it's tied in some cases to uninformativity in degree constructions and, in other cases, to markedness. The general nature of the approach makes for a natural extension to evaluativity outside of adjectival constructions, and the context-sensitivity of the proposal makes for a natural extension to apparently optional evaluativity, two phenomena which were treated in tandem in the accounts in Piñón (2005) and Kennedy and Levin (2008) (as reviewed in §2.3). I'll end this chapter by discussing one final phenomenon that falls under this umbrella: DPs that seem to have an evaluative interpretation.

6.3 Evaluative DPs

An implicature-based approach to evaluativity can also be extended to account for what appears to be evaluativity in phrases and constructions that don't involve (overt) degree morphology or gradable predicates. I'll argue here that, along the lines of the analysis in the previous section, the relative uninformativity of some DPs—I'll discuss indefinites and *wh*-phrases in particular—results in some contexts in evaluativity. I'll show that this is unpredicted by other accounts of evaluativity but is a natural consequence of the implicature-based approach advocated here.

Recall that Grice (1975: 56) discusses indefinites in terms of uninformativity-based Quantity implicatures:

> Anyone who uses a sentence of the form *X is meeting a woman this evening* would normally implicate that the person to be met was someone other than *X*'s wife, mother, sister, or perhaps even close platonic friend. Similarly, if I were to say *X went into a house yesterday and found a tortoise inside the front door*, my hearer would normally be surprised if some time later I revealed that the house was *X*'s own. I could produce similar linguistic phenomena involving the expressions *a garden, a car, a college*, and so on. Sometimes, however, there would normally be no such implicature ('I have been sitting in a car all morning'), and sometimes a reverse implicature ('I broke a finger yesterday').

Grice thus proposes an account of indefinites in which they carry an uninformativity-based Quantity implicature (the result of a violation of the first clause of his Quantity maxim, "Make your contribution as informative as required"). Informally, this treats the hearer as assuming the speaker would have described the individual more specifically (using e.g. a possessive) if the speaker was related to the individual in a more specific way.

According to the account in Chapter 5, indefinites could carry Quantity implicatures other than this "not closely related" one, depending on the context. In particular, the use of an indefinite should in principle carry an evaluativity implicature in contexts in which a degree of measurement is a more salient or more specific property of the individual than its relation to the speaker. And this is in fact what we see, as exemplified in (33).

(33) a. Doug owns a number of shoes.
      b. The family controls some amount of oil.
      c. Now [that's]$_F$ a car.
      d. You've got some nerve.

Geurts (2011: 182–3) observes this phenomenon as well; he extends it to bare plurals. He says: "In (34), *money* means something like 'considerable means,'" giving (34) as an example.

(34) Buying a house is easy if you've got money.

Geurts draws this same parallel between tautology and this use of indefinites, calling the phenomenon in (34) an instance of "semantic narrowing" due to an uninformativity-based Quantity implicature. He observes (p. 183) that it happens "quite smoothly, because world knowledge alone suffices to bias the hearer towards a specific interpretation."

I have not researched the full extent to which this phenomenon is universal, but Gillon (2010) has recently observed what seems to be a similar phenomenon in Innu-aimun (an Algonquian language spoken in Eastern Canada). She argues that plural forms of mass nouns in Innu-Aimun are ambiguous between a reading equivalent to the English translation, as well as an evaluative reading, as in (35).

(35)   a. pimî
          oil
          'oil'

       b. pimî-a
          oil-INAN.PL
          'amounts of oil' or 'lots of oil'

This seems related to the ability of the English *amount of oil* to receive an evaluative interpretation in, e.g., *The family invests quite heavily in coal but it also owns an amount of oil*.

Unmodified DPs seem to be able to take on an evaluative meaning in exclamatives, as well. As I argue in Rett (2011), all exclamatives are evaluative, and they also all denote degree properties. As a result, they coerce evaluative degree interpretations in the absence of overt degree morphology. In Rett (2011), I referred to the degree arguments of phrases without overt degree morphology as "freebie degrees". In this section, I attempt to explain their availability based on an implicature account of evaluativity.

The exclamatives in (36) illustrate that exclamatives receive degree interpretations, and that they are evaluative. For instance, (36a) can only receive an interpretation in which the speaker is exclaiming about the degree to which the desserts are delicious, in contrast to an individual interpretation in which the speaker is exclaiming about the individual members of the set or plurality of delicious desserts John baked. (It's worthwhile noting that the latter, individual interpretation is the only one available to questions headed by *what*; cf. Zanuttini and Portner 2003.)

(36)   a. (Wow,) What delicious desserts John baked!
       b. (Wow,) What a good guy!
       c. (Oh,) The beautiful things she's seen!

That exclamatives are evaluative is illustrated by (36b); the exclamative is, intuitively, only felicitous if the individual in question counts as significantly good. (This, too, is in contrast with the degree question *How good is that guy?*, as discussed in detail in §3.1.)

The data in (37) show that these DP-headed exclamatives can receive the same evaluative degree interpretations in the absence of the overt gradable predicates *delicious, good,* or *beautiful.*

(37) a. (Wow,) What desserts John baked!
      b. (Wow,) What a guy!
      c. (Oh,) The things she's seen!

Discourse-initially, (37a) seems to receive a reading in which the speaker is expressing that (s)he had not expected the high degree to which the desserts John baked are delicious or impressive; but there are contexts in which the same exclamation can carry a negative connotation. The same goes for (37b); discourse-initially, it most naturally receives a positive interpretation (the speaker had not expected that John be good to such a high degree), but it can also receive a negative interpretation (in a context in which the speaker witnesses John steal money out of his friend's wallet). Arguably, these constructions would be relatively uninformative in the absence of their evaluativity.

We have seen that a variety of different DPs—singular indefinites, bare plurals, *wh*-phrases, and definites (in (37c))—can receive an evaluative interpretation in various contexts. I'll have more to say in a second about what sort of contexts these tend to be. But for now I'll just stress that the dimension of measurement involved in the evaluative component is extremely context-sensitive.[5]

That evaluative DPs are completely dependent on context for their dimension of measurement (and, consequently, their truth conditions) is expected, given a theory in which these DPs aren't intrinsically gradable; i.e., they do not, in contrast to gradable adjectives, lexicalize a degree argument (and are not, consequently, associated with a dimension of measurement).

In Rett (2011), I posited a null operator M-OP to associate these DPs with a degree argument in the semantics. In this section, I suggest that the evaluativity is the result of an uninformativity-based Quantity implicature, one of several possible ways in which the meaning of a DP can be strengthened or narrowed in context. Depending on one's formal implementation of uninformativity-based Quantity implicatures, this characterization of evaluative DPs might obviate the need for a null measurement operator like M-OP, at least in these contexts.

But what are the contexts that result in evaluative interpretations of DPs? The indefinite *a woman* cannot, for instance, receive an evaluative interpretation in Grice's

---

[5] This is reminiscent of the observation in Potts (2007), Schroeder (2008), Constant et al. (2009), and McCready (2010, 2012) that epithets can receive either a positive or negative interpretation. (i) is repeated from (27) in §5.1.2.

i. a. Fucking Mike Tyson won another fight. He's wonderful.
    b. Fucking Mike Tyson got arrested again for domestic violence. #He's wonderful.

X is meeting a woman this evening. (In other words, that sentence is not naturally interpreted as meaning "*X* is meeting an amazing woman this evening.")

To address this question, I'll briefly mention another context in which DPs seem to be evaluative. Morzycki (2009) observes that nominals can receive a degree interpretation when modified by certain adjectives; he characterizes this interpretation as one in which "the nominal predicate is claimed to hold to a high degree" (p. 176).

(38) a. George is an enormous idiot.
      b. Three huge goat cheese enthusiasts were arguing in the corner.

He shows that this type of reading is available across languages; that it is only available in attributive constructions (cf. *George is an idiot, and he is enormous*); and that it is only available with "adjectives that predicate bigness" (p. 179) instead of smallness (cf. *George is a tiny idiot*). (He dubs this "The Bigness Generalization.")

Bolinger (1972) offers the same generalization using the following minimal pair (p. 92):

(39) a. He has considerable money.
      b. *He has trivial money.

Morzycki proposes an analysis of nouns in which they, like gradable adjectives, lexicalize a degree argument. His analysis treats both as denoting measure functions; in the case of *idiot*, as denoting (p. 185) "a measure function from individuals to their degree of idiocy."

(40) $[\![\text{idiot}]\!] = \lambda x \iota d[x \text{ is } d\text{-idiotic}]$

His analysis of the data in (38) parallels those of Piñón (2005) and Kennedy and Levin (2008) for verbal evaluativity; he uses MEAS to typeshift the meaning of the noun and applies POS to the modifying adjectives, resulting in the constituency in (41).

(41) $[[_{\text{DegP}}$ POS big] MEAS idiot]

The result of the theory is a semantics for sentences like (38a) that means, roughly, "the size of the extent to which George is an idiot is enormous."

Morzycki (2009) shows that, in certain contexts, nominals are associated with degree arguments. But he stops short of positing a POS for nouns because his evidence only suggests that DPs can be evaluative when they're modified by adjectives. As we've seen, the distribution of evaluative DPs is much wider than this.

Grice predicted that some DPs can be uninformative in some contexts, in which case they are supplemented with an uninformativity-based Quantity implicature. He provided an example in which the meaning of an indefinite is strengthened with information about the relationship between the denoted individual and the speaker. But there is no reason to think that that is the only way in which the meaning of uninformative DPs can be strengthened. In the case of constructions with overt degree morphology—those involving gradable adjectives or certain verbs—the most natural Quantity implicature available for strengthening the meaning is evaluativity on the scale of dimension encoded by the degree predicate, as argued in §5.1.2. But because these DPs don't lexicalize or restrict a dimension of measurement, evaluativity is only one of many possible Quantity implicatures available for strengthening the meaning.

How the meanings of these DPs are strengthened depends at least in part on the QUD. In particular, that a DP which is uninformative in a particular context is strengthened via a (Quantity-based) evaluativity implicature if, as in the exclamatives in (36), indefinite constructions in (33), and "bigness" contexts in (38), the construction requires it (or if the evaluative degree property pertains to the QUD; see also Kratzer 1999; Potts 2007; Morzycki 2009).

This theory is relatively easy to extend to the indefinites in (33). I'll discuss the examples that don't involve focus, repeated in (42), and will return to those that do.

(42)   a. Doug owns a number of shoes.
       b. The family controls some amount of oil.

(42a) is arguably trivially true in just the same way that positive constructions are trivially true. I'll adopt the simplified semantics for *a number of x* in (43a), resulting in the truth conditions for (42a) in (43b) (using Predicate Modification and Existential Closure).

(43)   a. $[\![$a number of$]\!] = \lambda P \lambda x \exists d[P(x) \wedge \#(x) = d]$
       b. $[\![$Doug owns a number of shoes$]\!]$
          $= \exists x[\text{owns}(\text{doug}, x) \wedge \exists d[\text{shoes}(x) \wedge \#(x) = d]]$

The truth conditions in (43b) can be paraphrased as "Doug owns some shoes and they are associated with some quantity." These truth conditions, like the compositional semantics of positive constructions, assert what they presuppose; it is a logical consequence of Doug's owning shoes that the shoes he owns are associated with some quantity. The result is a DP analog of the positive construction, effectively a degree tautology.

It seems reasonable to assume that there's something about the meaning of *a number* that, in contrast to Grice's example *a woman*, makes most salient for the purposes of semantic strengthening a scale of quantity (instead of a relationship to the speaker, as *a woman* might). It also seems reasonable to think that this Quantity implicature is generalized or conventionalized to some degree in indefinites like *a number* or *some amount*. Perhaps *a lot*—which seems to only have an intensifier reading—is an example of an indefinite in which this meaning has been fully lexicalized.

This hypothesis is explicitly defended by Bolinger (1972: chapters 3–4), who notes the contrast in (44) (p. 82) as evidence of a contrast in the status of evaluativity associated with the different indefinites.

(44) a. What a lot!
      b. *What a number!
      c. What a spread!
      d. *What a dimension!

This implicature-based perspective of evaluative DPs is clearly relevant to their evaluative use in exclamations, which are generally characterized as expressions of the speaker's surprise or attitude that the at-issue proposition is noteworthy (see also Merin and Nikolaeva 2008). (Elliott 1974: 242, characterizes them as reactions to "abnormal or unexpected situations.") If exclamations are licensed only when their semantic content counts as noteworthy, we can conclude that exclamations are constructions in which standard DP denotations tend to be underinformative and also in which the most salient strengthening of a DP tends to be one in which its degree is significant.[6]

Bolinger (1972: 93) discusses the evaluativity of indefinites like *a looker*. He notes that they receive their evaluative interpretation in exclamations, like (45a), but also with "emphasis," as in (45b). (I preserve his method of indicating emphasis.)

(45) a. She's a looker, believe me!
      b. She's a looker, beliéve yóu mé.

It seems as though focal stress is sufficient to bring out the evaluative interpretation of at least some DPs, as illustrated in (46).

(46) That's not a pizza. [This]$_F$ is a pizza!

(46) highlights the role of informativity in evaluative DPs and the extent to which this is context-sensitive. In a more run-of-the-mill context, the sentence *This is a pizza* will be interpreted as true iff the demonstrative in fact picks out pizza, and the negated indefinite *That's not a pizza* as true iff the demonstrative picks out a non-pizza.

The account proposed here is that this is the result of uninformativity-based Gricean reasoning: the hearer assumes that the speaker is obeying the first principle of Grice's (1975) Quantity maxim, "Make your contribution as informative as required" (or Horn's 1984 Q Principle, "Make your contribution sufficient"). He also assumes that the speaker is being truthful, etc. As a result, he interprets the utterance with a lower-bounding or strengthening implicature, paraphrasable as something like "a significantly big/impressive/delicious/authentic pizza."

Focal stress seems to be an important (although possibly not crucial) aspect of the evaluative DPs in (33c) and (46). As with exclamatives, this is consistent with a

---

[6] I argue in Rett (2011) that exclamatives force a degree interpretation. If this analysis is right, then evaluativity is the only Quantity implicature available to the exclamatives in (37). There are however other, non-degree-based accounts of exclamatives which allow in principle for other implicatures; see Zanuttini and Portner (2003) for *wh*-exclamatives like (37a) and (37b) and Portner and Zanuttini (2005) for nominal exclamatives like (37c).

characterization of focus as semantically strengthening an utterance. Rooth (1996) offers a related implicature-based theory of the meaning of indefinites in sentences like the ones in (46).

The evaluativity strengthening of DPs also seems to be brought out by the 'bigness' predicates examined in Morzycki (2009). In other words: if exclamatives and focus constructions use intonation or prosody to signal that a DP's meaning is significant or note-worthy, adjectives like *considerable* or *enormous* seem to do it lexically. There is one interpretation of (47) in which it asserts that George is an idiot and enormous (for an idiot); but when the adjective is interpreted as a modifier, it requires that the DP receive a note-worthy interpretation.

(47)   George is an enormous idiot.

As Morzycki (2009) states (p. 180): "If in fact a degree reading comes for free whenever a novel adjective of bigness is coined, it suggests strongly that the availability of degree readings is not an accidental lexical property of these adjectives, but rather an essential part of the job description for adjectives of bigness." Morzycki's Bigness Generalization is therefore reducible to Bolinger's (1972) intensification generalization: if adjectives can trigger uninformativity-based Quantity implicatures that strengthen the meaning of a DP in a scalar sense, and if there is a general, universal tendency for scales to be strengthened via intensification, then we predict that modifiers that predicate bigness can bring out this implicature, while "smallness" predicates do not. I should, however, point out that this approach is silent on Morzycki's Predicative Restriction (the observation that these evaluative interpretations are only available when the DPs are modified by attributive rather than predicative adjectives).

The implicature-based account of evaluativity in Chapter 5 predicts that evaluativity could be a property of any construction in any context, so long as (a) the construction counts as uninformative in that context; and (b) that context makes most salient the scalar extent of the relevant property. This predicts—correctly, I think—that verbs can receive evaluative interpretations even when they're not overtly modified. Sassoon (2011: 543) observes, citing Bierwisch (1989): "*[I]t weighs* conveys *It weighs a lot*, rather than *It weighs something* perhaps due to the triviality of the latter ...".

Notice that verbs, too, can receive an "evaluative" or intensified interpretation in exclamatives. While the declarative sentence *He cooks* is typically interpreted to mean that he cooks habitually, the inversion exclamative in (48a) is most naturally interpreted to mean he cooks incessantly. (A related contrast holds for *He can cook* and (48b), which is most naturally interpreted as expressing surprise that he cooks as well as he does.)

(48)   a. Boy, does he cook!
        b. Man, can he cook!

We can also reproduce Bolinger's (1972) focal stress data for verbs, as in (49):

(49)   He [cooks]$_F$, believe you me!

However, both Bolinger (1972) and Morzycki (2009) note apparent lexical restrictions on the ability of nouns and verbs to receive evaluative interpretations, or to be associated with scales at all. Bolinger offers the somewhat minimal pair in (50) (p. 160); *hesitate*, but not *wait*, can receive a degree interpretation (see also Rett 2013).

(50)   a.   Why do you hesitate so?
       b.   #Why do you wait so?

Morzycki (2009) dubs the relevant subclass "gradable nouns"; he offers the contrast in (51), cf. (38b) (p. 190).

(51)   a.   complete idiot/dork/fascist
       b.   #complete smoker/goat cheese enthusiast/fan of curling

I unfortunately have nothing to say about the differences between verbs and nouns that can and cannot receive scalar (and therefore evaluative) interpretations. But I do hope to have shown that the phenomenon of evaluativity strengthening is relatively general, and certainly exists outside of constructions with gradable adjectives.

6.4 Discussion

The goal of this chapter has been to provide additional empirical support for the implicature-based proposal in Chapter 5 outside of the core data presented and discussed in §3.1. I argued that a characterization of evaluativity as an Manner implicature and as an uninformativity-based Quantity implicature makes two significant predictions: first, that evaluativity is the property of marked constructions that don't involve negative antonyms (an extension of evaluativity as a Manner implicature); and second, that evaluativity can be a property of other uninformative degree constructions (an extension of evaluativity as an uninformativity-based Quantity implicature).

There are several ways in which an adjectival or degree construction can be marked; in §6.1.1 I reviewed several different types of periphrastic comparison strategies, several of which occur in English. I argued that the account in Chapter 5 can easily explain the contrast in evaluativity between (52a) and (52b) because the latter is more marked than the former.

(52)   a.   Adam is taller than Doug.
       b.   Adam is more tall than Doug.

I also provided some evidence that this prediction is supported in other languages, as well, including languages (like Navajo) in which comparatives are optionally formed with additional aspect marking, and languages (like Bulgarian) in which the standard marker (*than* in English) is optional.

In contrast to the EVAL account, an implicature-based approach to evaluativity that includes a robust characterization of M-alternatives can account for these differences in meaning between constructions whose differences in markedness are varied and relatively hard to pin down. The involvement of M-alternatives also allows for a certain amount of speaker variation. This could explain why some (but not all) speakers of English find a difference in evaluativity between (53a) and (53b): it's possible that the clausal comparative counts as an M-alternative to the phrasal one in only some dialects.

(53) a. Adam is taller than Doug.   *phrasal*
      b. Adam is taller than Doug is.   *clausal*

I have also reviewed the usefulness of an implicature-based approach to evaluativity for an account of equatives whose standard is an MP, as in *Trees can be as old as 400 years*. I argued, based on Rett (2014a), that these MPEs count as Q-alternatives to their comparative counterparts (e.g. *Trees can be older than 400 years*) but also as M-alternatives to their MP construction counterparts (e.g. *Trees can be 400 years old*). Among other things, this accounts for the intuition that MPEs are generally evaluative, regardless of the polarity of the antonym.

The consequence for the overall proposal in Chapter 5 is this: the characterization of evaluativity as a Manner implicature predicts that evaluativity will arise across degree constructions and as the result of a number of different kinds of markedness. The discussion here shows that this is in fact the case: certain comparison constructions are evaluative, regardless of the antonym involved, apparently because they involve some kind of periphrasis.

The second prediction involves informativity. I argued that positive constructions are evaluative because they are degree tautologies, resulting in a Quantity implicature. In §6.2 I extended this prediction to other kinds of uninformative degree constructions. Assuming that non-tautological utterances can vary in the extent to which they count as informative from context to context, the account in Chapter 5 predicts that (some) degree constructions will become evaluative in contexts in which their literal or compositional content ('what is said') is uninformative. I have argued that this seems to be the case for instances of evaluativity in the verbal domain, in particular for degree achievement constructions like *The soup cooled*, which are evaluative depending on context or on whether they are overtly modified by a word or phrase that requires (non-)evaluativity.

In §6.2.2 I extended this proposal to two-parameter comparatives like *This meal was more expensive than it was tasty*, which receive a COD interpretation when they are evaluative. Borrowing aspects of the accounts in Kennedy (1999) and Rett (2008), I argued that evaluativity in these constructions can be seen as something like a repair strategy, necessary for changing otherwise illicit truth conditions into informative ones. In this approach, the repair strategy is a (locally calculated) Gricean one, rather than compositionally determined or represented.

In §6.3 I extended the notion of evaluativity as a Quantity implicature to DPs, using data from Bolinger (1972) and an observation from Geurts (2011). The evaluative interpretation of DPs like *a number of shoes* provides support for the prediction that evaluativity is a natural way of strengthening the interpretation of all kinds of degree constructions, not just those involving adjectives. An implicature-based account of evaluativity allows for a single unified explanation of these data, preventing us from, for instance, positing (and constraining the distribution of) several null morphemes for different types of constructions with different types of argument structures.

This chapter has been by far the most exploratory; I have not provided explanations of what a speaker's set of M-alternatives looks like in a language with multiple comparison strategies, nor how evaluativity implicatures are calculated locally. I haven't provided an account of why some two-parameter comparatives are strengthened to CODs, which do not need to be strengthened in order to be acceptable (i.e. indirect comparatives), and which are unacceptable (i.e. cross-polar anomalies). And I haven't provided an account of why some DPs can be gradable (and, therefore, receive evaluative interpretations) while others cannot. I do however hope to have gone some way in illustrating the empirical breadth of an implicature-based approach to evaluativity, and that the predictions made by such an account are, as far as I've explored them, correct.

The remaining chapter offers a summary of everything discussed here.

7

Conclusion

The simplest construction an adjective can occur in—the positive construction—has created a historical rift among theorists proposing semantic accounts of gradable adjectives. Roughly two approaches to the data in (1)—and their differences in evaluativity—are represented in the literature.

(1) a. Adam is tall.   *positive construction*; evaluative
     b. Adam is 6ft tall.   *MP construction*; non-evaluative
     c. Adam is taller than Doug.   *comparative*; non-evaluative

One type of approach defines gradable adjectives in terms of their simplest use, in terms of their meaning in positive constructions like (1a). These theories build evaluativity into the semantics of gradable adjectives and are tasked with explaining its absence in other constructions.

Klein (1980, 1982) is perhaps the best-known advocate of this approach. He focuses primarily on the contrast between positive constructions like (1a) and comparatives like (1c), and attributes the absence of evaluativity in the latter to the presence of an overt standard, introduced by the *than* clause. In doing so, he famously rejects theories that characterize gradable adjectives in terms of degrees. Such an approach, arguably, runs into trouble with a compositional semantic account of MP constructions like (1b) and also creates significant problems for the treatment of antonyms (see Kennedy 1999 for an excellent review of the problems that arise in a degree-free semantics of adjectival constructions).[1] It also fails to account for the evaluativity of (some) equative constructions, exemplified in (2).

(2) Adam is as short as Doug.

The other type of approach defines gradable adjectives in terms of their use in the more complicated constructions like (1b) and (1c). It associates gradable adjectives

---

[1] Recently, a number of degree-free logics have been proposed, in the spirit of Klein's work, to treat the semantics of adjectival constructions, especially as it concerns vagueness. Neeleman et al. (2004), Doetjes et al. (2011), and Burnett (2012) represent to my mind the best of these "neo-Kleinian" approaches, but they do not, in their current form, address all of Kennedy's concerns.

with degrees—characterizing them either as relations between individuals and degrees (type $\langle e, \langle d, t \rangle \rangle$, as in (3)) or as measure functions (type $\langle e, d \rangle$)—but not with particularly high or evaluative degrees.

(3) $[\![\text{tall}]\!] = \lambda x \lambda d.\text{tall}(x, d)$

In these theories, the evaluative component of positive constructions like (1a) comes about as the result of a null operator in the syntax.

This operator was originally dubbed "POS" because, given the data in (1), its distribution was restricted to (and obligatory in) positive constructions. POS was proposed for measure function accounts of adjectives (Bartsch and Vennemann 1972; Kennedy 1999) and for relational accounts of adjectives (Cresswell 1976; von Stechow 1984). POS theories therefore treat the difference in evaluativity in (1a) and the pair in (1b) and (1c) as a morphological one: the former contains a null morpheme that contributes evaluativity, while the latter two do not (and cannot, for type reasons). Specifically, POS is thus designed so that it can only occur in the absence of degree modification (as in (1b)) or quantification (as in (1c)). When it occurs, it restricts the degree associated with the adjective to only those that exceed a contextual standard, and either saturates (in the measure function approach) or existentially binds (in the relational approach) the degree. These accounts were reviewed in Chapter 2.

Another version of this type of approach was proposed in Rett (2007, 2008) to adjust for the relatively broad distribution of evaluativity, for instance in negative-antonym equatives like (2). This account, which characterizes gradable adjectives as relations between individuals and degrees, separates the two functions of POS: it encodes evaluativity in a null degree modifier, and relies on existential closure to bind the degree argument in positive constructions. The account is then responsible for explaining restrictions on the distribution of EVAL: why it is obligatory in positive constructions and negative-antonym equatives like (2) but optional in MP constructions like (1b) and comparatives like (1c).

The proposal draws on contrasts between comparatives and equatives in terms of their strictness of ordering, and contrasts between antonyms in terms of markedness. But it relies on a markedness-based semantic competition that is relatively unmotivated and incapable of explaining certain empirical facts; for instance, why only the embedded clause in (2) seems to presuppose evaluativity. This account was reviewed in Chapter 3.

Both types of approaches have in common the assumption that the evaluative component of (1a) is part of the compositional semantics, in Grice's (1975) terminology, of what is said. This assumption is understandable; the evaluative component of positive constructions can serve as the input to truth-conditional operators like negation (4a) and is not cancellable (4b).

(4)   a. Adam isn't tall.
      b. Adam is tall . . . #in fact, he's of average height.

But this assumption—and the corresponding null morphemes used to implement it—has made a compositional semantics of gradable adjectives and adjectival constructions appear untenable, at least to some. Klein (1980: 3) rebuked accounts that relied on a null semantic operator to account for the differences illustrated in (1). ("As far as I can tell, there is no independent justification for introducing POS; it is merely a device for fixing up the semantics.") But Klein's arguably more compositional approach to the semantics of the positive construction have proven difficult to extend to adjectival constructions broadly, and I am unaware of any attempts within a degree-free semantics to account for evaluativity outside of positive constructions (e.g. in negative-antonym equatives).

The goal of this book has been to argue that evaluativity is better thought of as an implicature, rather than part of what is said. This argument has relied largely on empirical parallels between evaluativity and other types of implicature: uninformativity-based Quantity implicatures and Manner implicatures. These data, and the original theories that characterize them as implicatures, were reviewed in Chapter 4.

I have assumed a fairly standard relational account of gradable adjectives, illustrated in (3) and outlined in §2.1. I've also assumed that the positive construction denotes a proposition due to an application of existential closure which binds the degree argument of the gradable adjective (Heim 1982; Diesing 1992), resulting in (5).

(5) $[\![$Adam is tall$]\!] = \exists d[\text{tall}(\text{adam}, d)]$

In §5.3, I argued that this analysis appropriately characterizes positive constructions as "degree tautologies": uninformative because they assert what they presuppose, namely that Adam has some degree of tallness. I drew a parallel between positive constructions and tautologies like *War is war* and *Boys will be boys*, analyzed in Grice (1975) as carrying Quantity implicatures (triggered by the first principle of the Quantity maxim, "Make your contribution as informative as required").

If the evaluativity of positive constructions is the result of an uninformativity-based Quantity implicature, we expect it to behave like other uninformativity-based Quantity implicatures. I argued that they have in common their inability to be cancelled (6a) and their ability to be targeted by negation (6b).

(6)   a. War is war . . . #in fact, violence is unavoidable in war.
      b. It's not always the case that war is war. The involvement of drones has complicated things immensely.

In §5.2 I argued that the relational account of adjectives in (3), combined with standard semantic accounts of comparative and equative morphemes as degree quantifiers, had another consequence for theories of implicature. The semantics predicts that equatives—but not comparatives—formed with different antonyms are mutually entailing. This is demonstrated in (7) and (8).

(7) a. ⟦Adam is taller than Doug⟧ =
         $\text{Max}(\lambda d.\text{tall}(\text{adam}, d)) > \text{Max}(\lambda d'.\text{tall}(\text{doug}, d'))$
     b. ⟦Adam is shorter than Doug⟧ =
         $\text{Max}(\lambda d.\text{short}(\text{adam}, d)) > \text{Max}(\lambda d'.\text{short}(\text{doug}, d'))$

(8) a. ⟦Adam is as tall as Doug⟧=
         $\text{Max}(\lambda d.\text{tall}(\text{adam}, d)) \geq \text{Max}(\lambda d'.\text{tall}(\text{doug}, d'))$
     b. ⟦Adam is as short as Doug⟧ =
         $\text{Max}(\lambda d.\text{short}(\text{adam}, d)) \geq \text{Max}(\lambda d'.\text{short}(\text{doug}, d'))$

The "exactly" interpretation of the equatives represented in (8) arises as the result of a scale-based Quantity implicature strengthening; I'll return to this assumption soon.

There are many reasons to think that negative antonyms (e.g. *short*) are marked relative to their positive-antonym counterparts (e.g. *tall*; Lehrer 1985; Cruse 1986; Heim 2007; Rett 2008). If this assumption is correct, we expect the negative-antonym equative in (8b) to carry a Manner implicature as a result of its relationship to the unmarked positive-antonym equative in (8a).

There are several different kinds of empirical parallels; one is periphrastic causatives, discussed in McCawley (1978), Horn (1984), Levinson (2000), and illustrated in (9).

(9) a. He killed the sheriff.
     b. He caused the sheriff to die.

These accounts assume that the verb *to kill* and its periphrastic counterpart *to cause to die* have the same compositional semantic meaning; in other words, they both contribute identical meaning to what is said.

They claim that the additional meaning carried by the periphrastic causative comes about as the result of a Manner implicature, calculated relative to the third principle of Grice's Manner maxim ("Be brief, avoid unnecessary prolixity"). The Manner implicature strengthens the proposition in (9a) by restricting it to only atypical instances of killing. The prediction is that (9a) means something like, "He caused the sheriff to die in an atypical way."

If this is right, and if the two equatives in (8) contrast in markedness in the same way as the causatives in (9), we predict the negative-antonym equative in (8b) to mean something like, "Adam is as short as Doug in an atypical way." (And we predict a similar asymmetry for degree questions like *How short is Adam?*.) I argue this in detail in §5.2.2.

The core proposal, presented in Chapter 5, is thus one in which evaluativity arises in some adjectival constructions as the result of a conversational implicature. In constructions that are evaluative regardless of the antonym, evaluativity arises as the result of an uninformativity-based Quantity implicature, the result of the adjectival

construction being underinformative. In constructions in which evaluativity is associated only with negative antonyms, evaluativity arises as the result of a Manner
implicature, the result of using a marked antonym when its unmarked counterpart
would have sufficed.

In my discussion of implicatures and my account of evaluativity as an implicature,
I've relied especially on the Principle of Least Effort proposed in Horn (1984) and the
formal definitions of Q- and M-alternatives based on Katzir (2007) (this is detailed in
§5.1.1).

What is the connection between atypical instantiations of degree predicates and
evaluativity? In §5.1.2 I present evidence, largely from Bolinger (1972), of a universal
tendency for "neutral" degree constructions like *I was calm as calm* to carry on
evaluative meaning. A priori, an "atypical" instantiation of a gradable predicate like
tall is any individual whose tallness is not average (an individual not in the extension
gap between the antonyms *tall* and *short*). This could be someone who is taller
than average, or someone shorter than average. But these two possibilities must be
split up between the antonyms; the result is that atypical uses of each antonym are
associated with the most informative atypical extension, namely the evaluative one.
In other words, being atypically tall amounts to being taller than average, whereas
being atypically short means being shorter than average.

I have also relied on observations about the interaction of projective content like
presupposition and implicature with discourse properties like topic and at-issueness
explored in, for instance, van Kuppevelt (1996). I've used these concepts to account
for the observations that evaluativity is generally neither cancellable nor defeasible
(10), and the differences between positive and comparison constructions in the truth-
conditional status of evaluativity (§5.3).

(10) a. Adam is tall ... #in fact, he is quite short.   *positive construction*
      b. Adam is as short as Doug ... #in fact, Adam is quite short.   *equative*

These evaluativity implicatures are non-cancellable for different reasons. In (10a),
the evaluativity arises as the result of an uninformativity-based Quantity implicature,
and so is obligatory because the utterance would be meaningless without it. In (10b),
the evaluativity arises as the result of a Manner implicature, and so is non-cancellable
because it is tied to the form, rather than the meaning, of the utterance (Hirschberg
1991; Levinson 2000).

The difference in the truth-conditional status of evaluativity in these two types of
constructions is illustrated in (11) and (12). Evaluativity is an assertion in the positive
construction, so the discourse in (11) is felicitous. In contrast, it is a presupposition in
equatives, so the discourse in (12) is infelicitous.

(11) A: Is Adam tall or short?
      B: Adam is tall.   *positive construction*

(12)   A: Is Adam tall or short?
       B: #Doug is as short as Adam.   *equative*

Given independent observations about the discourse sensitivity of truth-conditionality (van Kuppevelt 1996; Roberts 1990; Simons et al. 2011), I've argued that evaluativity is truth-conditional in positive constructions because it almost always addresses the Question Under Discussion (QUD) in positive constructions. In contrast, evaluativity is non-truth-conditional in equatives because it almost never addresses the QUD in equatives. To support this explanation, I've provided examples in which the truth-conditional status of these two types of construction varies accordingly with the QUD. These considerations allowed, among other things, for an account of evaluativity in negative-antonym equatives like (2) in which it projects only from the embedded *as*-clause (§5.2.3).

I've proposed that we consider evaluativity to be a conversational implicature in contrast to previous accounts in which it is encoded in a null operator. This debate could be seen as mimicking a parallel discussion in the scalar implicature literature, where it's been recently proposed that scalar implicatures are triggered by a null operator similar to *only* (e.g. Chierchia et al. 2009). This perspective raises an important question about the significance of my proposal: if evaluativity is a conversational implicature, and if there's (some) reason to think that (other types of) conversational implicature are triggered syntactically, then what do we gain by reconceptualizing evaluativity as an implicature instead of encoded by a null morpheme like POS?

I will present a weak and a strong response to this question, although I'm more inclined to endorse the strong response.

The weak response is that there has, as of yet, been no proposal of a POS or EVAL in which it mimics conversational implicature. I believe the arguments here suggest, at the bare minimum, that we reconceptualize e.g. EVAL as a trigger for Quantity or Manner implicatures, depending on the context. This is an improvement over POS accounts because it correctly predicts the evaluativity of negative-antonym equatives and degree questions. It is an improvement over the EVAL account because it is capable of a fully general explanation of the phenomena as well as an account of the apparent discourse-sensitive properties of evaluativity, leading to (for instance) an asymmetry in evaluativity between the matrix and embedded clauses in the equative.

So, to those inclined to view all types of conversational implicature as syntactically encoded or effected—perhaps because this makes it easier to explain their ability to be calculated locally and thus act as input to truth-conditional operators—it's possible to frame the proposal in Chapter 5 as a suggestion to retool an operator like EVAL into something like the null operator proposed in Chierchia et al. (2009). This will, at the very least, contribute an explanation for the existence of evaluativity that is (in my opinion) absent from the POS and EVAL accounts.

While such an approach would simplify the compositional semantics of evaluativity—explaining, for instance, how the result of a conversational implicature could be targeted by negation and other sentential operators—it is not as compelling as it could be. Unlike the silent *only* or *O* operator proposed in Chierchia et al. (2009) for scalar implicature, the proposal in Chapter 5 casts evaluativity as the result of two distinct implicatures in two distinct contexts: an uninformativity-based Quantity implicature in positive constructions, and a markedness-based Manner implicature in equatives and degree questions. If conversational implicature is triggered by a null operator, it's hard to imagine a single operator that effects both types of strengthening. And because there's no clear overt counterpart of this hypothetical evaluativity-triggering covert operator, the justification for this move is less clear.

Which brings me to the stronger response to the question above: the proposal in Chapter 5 suggests that evaluativity *shouldn't* be encoded in a null morpheme, for a number of reasons. First, this approach explains the presence of evaluativity because it treats it as the result of the larger phenomenon of individuals reasoning about the linguistic behavior of their interlocutors. It's not clear, given certain details in the weak response above, that we could achieve this level of explanation with a null morpheme.

Second, this approach succeeds in a significant way that the POS and EVAL accounts failed: instead of predicting that (some) languages (could) have overt counterparts of POS or EVAL, it arguably predicts that languages generally will *not* have an overt evaluativity-inducing morpheme, which seems to be more in line with the empirical facts. This prediction comes in part from Horn's (1972) reasoning about the relationship between conversational implicature and the lexicon (see also Gazdar 1979; Levinson 1983): if a conversational implicature arises without being explicitly encoded, languages will generally not encode the implicature lexically. This putative extension of Grice's theory is to my mind the best explanation of the lack of overt POS or EVAL morphemes cross-linguistically that is available at the moment.

Third, an account in which evaluativity is the result of a conversational implicature instead of a particular morpheme I think correctly predicts that evaluativity is not intrinsically tied to a particular construction or sequence of words but is instead much more context-sensitive, as I argued in §5.2.3 for Manner implicature evaluativity and in §5.3.2 for Quantity implicature evaluativity. In §5.4.2 I argued that the context sensitivity of evaluativity could explain differences across contexts, speakers, and languages in terms of which relative adjectives exhibit canonical *tall/short* patterns of evaluativity, or if they behave slightly differently.

Chapter 6 is devoted to highlighting other predictions of a conversational implicature approach to evaluativity. In addition to the core data discussed in Chapter 5, the analysis predicts that evaluativity could be a Manner implicature associated with different types of markedness in adjectival constructions. In §6.1 I show that evaluativity can be a property of different periphrastic strategies of comparatives across languages, and also a property of positive-antonym equatives with MP standards.

It also predicts that evaluativity could be an uninformativity-based Quantity implicature associated with constructions other than the positive construction. In §6.2
I argue that we can account for evaluativity in Comparisons of Deviation and some
verbal constructions this way. In §6.3 I argue that we can account for the (optional)
evaluativity of DPs like *a number of* or *some guy* this way (see also Bolinger 1972).
In contrast, it seems like the syntactic and semantic diversity of these constructions
would present a significant challenge for a theory in which evaluativity is encoded in
a null morpheme, and in which the distribution of this morpheme is constrained in a
particular way at a particular level.

An implicature-based approach to evaluativity also addresses long-standing worries
about the semantics of gradable adjectives. I've advocated a degree-semantic treatment
of gradable adjectives in which the positive construction has a trivial compositional
semantics. This allows for a straightforward treatment of other adjectival constructions (like the comparative) and for a treatment of the context sensitivity of these
constructions that does not threaten the compositionality of the formal semantics of
adjectival constructions (contra Klein 1980, 1982).

There are, however, several ways in which this picture of evaluativity must be
supplemented. I have argued that evaluativity implicatures can be calculated locally—
and thus can be negated, etc.—based on parallels from other uninformativity-based
Quantity implicatures and Manner implicatures. But I have not proposed a formal
account of how this could work, or how it could be constrained. I have argued
that evaluativity implicatures are discourse-sensitive, and I have not proposed a
formal system predicting how this could be so. For my explanation of evaluativity
in equatives, I have also relied on Levinson's (2000) argument that (scale-based)
Quantity implicatures are "prior to" Manner implicatures. I have offered no suggestion
regarding the nature of this priority or how it might be implemented formally.

I have also argued that Grice's three types of implicature—conventional, generalized
and particularized—are best understood as representing different points on a continuous spectrum: some conversational implicatures can be more conventionalized than
others in a way that is not necessarily binary. I have used this, in §5.4.2, to explain
the apparent variation in evaluativity patterns within the class of relative adjectives:
some adjectives, like *short* in English, may be more conventionally associated with
their M-alternative and therefore an evaluativity implicature than others. It is not
clear how useful this innovation is, from a synchronic perspective; it is also not clear
what if anything conventionalization correlates with (frequency, perhaps?) or how to
independently test for it.

There is also a significant amount of cross-linguistic research into evaluativity that
still needs to be done. In my criticism of the POS and EVAL accounts I have relied on
the empirical claim that languages do not encode evaluativity in overt morphemes
or lexemes. Ideally this negative claim would have a broader base of evidence in
terms of the diversity of languages as well as the diversity of constructions. (As I've

argued, evaluativity isn't just a property of positive constructions. Evidence for an overt evaluativity marker would show that it occurs everywhere evaluativity does, not just in positive constructions.)

This proposal has addressed a number of issues in the semantics of adjectives and adjectival constructions. But, in doing so, it's raised other issues about the semantic import of conversational implicature and the nature of the semantics/pragmatics interface. I've argued that, while evaluativity often appears to be part of what is said, it is better thought of as part of what is implicated. I defended this claim in part by appealing to independent observations that conversational implicature can be locally calculated. While there is a significant amount of controversy surrounding the formal treatment of local implicature, these discussions have as far as I know focused entirely on scalar implicature. If this proposal is right, the issue of how to treat local implicature can be based on a much broader empirical base, which has the potential to significantly affect formal theory and more general theories of the semantics/pragmatics interface.

I have also taken for granted the nature of conversational implicature; in particular, I've assumed that these implicatures have in common a root in rationality about linguistic behavior (and that they differ in at least this respect from conventional implicature). There is however recent work in the philosophical literature that suggests this assumption is at best oversimplified (e.g. Lepore and Stone forthcoming). Ideally the addition of the phenomenon of evaluativity into the discussion of implicature will be a helpful contribution to this debate as well.

References

Anderbois, S., Brasoveanu, A., and Henderson, R. (2010). Crossing the appositive/at-issue meaning boundary. In Nan Li and David Lutz (eds), *Proceedings of SALT 20*, 328–46. Ithaca, NY: CLC Publications.

Anderbois, S., Brasoveanu, A., and Henderson, R. (2013). At-issue proposals and appositive impositions in discourse. *Journal of Semantics*, Advance Access, 1–46, doi: 10.1093/jos/fft014.

Aristotle (1963). *Aristotelis Categoriae et Liber de Interpretatione*. Oxford: Oxford University Press.

Asher, N. and Txurruka, I. (2007). A discourse-based approach to natural language disjunction (revisited). In M. Aunargue, K. Korta, and J. Lazzarabal (eds), *Language, Representation and Reasoning*. Leioa: University of the Basque Country Press.

Atlas, J. and Levinson, S. (1981). It-clefts, informativeness, and logical form: Radical pragmatics. In P. Cole (ed.), *Radical Pragmatics*, 1–61. New York: Academic Press.

Bach, K. (1994). Conversational implicature. *Mind and Language*, 9: 124–62.

Bale, A. (2007). *The Universal Scale and the Semantics of Comparison*. PhD thesis, McGill University.

Bale, A. (2008). A universal scale of comparison. *Linguistics and Philosophy*, 31(1): 1–55.

Barker, C. (2002). The dynamics of vagueness. *Linguistics and Philosophy*, 25: 1–36.

Bartsch, R. and Vennemann, T. (1972). The grammar of relative adjectives and comparison. *Linguistische Berichte*, 20: 19–32.

Beavers, J. (2011). On affectedness. *Natural Language and Linguistic Theory*, 29: 335–70.

Beck, S. (2012). Lucinda driving too fast again. *Journal of Semantics*, 29: 1–63.

Beck, S., Krasikova, S., Fleischer, D., Gergel, R., Hofstetter, S., Savelsberg, C., Vanderels, J., and Villalta, E. (2009). Crosslinguistic variation in comparison constructions. In J. van Craenenbroeck and J. Rooryck (eds), *Linguistic Variation Yearbook 9*, 1–66. Amsterdam: John Benjamins.

Beck, S. and Rullmann, H. (1999). A flexible approach to exhaustivity in questions. *Natural Language Semantics*, 7: 249–98.

Bhatt, R. and Pancheva, R. (2004). Late merger of degree clauses. *Linguistic Inquiry*, 35: 1–45.

Bierwisch, M. (1989). The semantics of gradation. In M. Bierwisch and E. Lang (eds), *Dimensional Adjectives: Grammatical Structure and Conceptual Interpretation*, 71–237. Berlin: Springer-Verlag.

Biezma, M. (2013). Only one *at least*: Refining the role of discourse in building alternatives. In Kobey Shwayder (ed.), *University of Pennsylvania Working Papers in Linguistics*, vol. 19(1), 12–19. University of Pennsylvania: Penn Linguistics Club.

Blutner, R. (2000). Some aspects of optimality in natural language interpretation. *Journal of Semantics*, 17: 189–216.

Bobaljik, J. (2012). *Universals in Comparative Morphology: Suppletion, Superlatives, and the Structure of Words*. Cambridge, MA: MIT Press.

Bochnak, M. R. (2011). Quantity and gradability across categories. In N. Li and D. Lutz (eds), *Proceedings of SALT 20*, 251–68. Ithaca, NY: CLC Publications.

Bochnak, M. R. (2013). Two sources of scalarity within the verb phrase. In B. Arsenijevic, B. Gehrke, and R. Marn (eds), *Studies in the Composition and Decomposition of Event Predicates*, 99–123. Berlin: Springer-Verlag.

Bochnak, M. R. (forthcoming). The Degree Semantics parameter and cross-linguistic variation. *Semantics and Pragmatics*.

Bogal-Allbritten, E. (2010). Positively uninformative. In *The Proceedings of the MIT Workshop on Comparatives*. Cambridge, MA: MIT Press.

Bogal-Allbritten, E. (2011). Processing evidence for the scales of negative evaluative adjectives. Ms, University of Massachusetts, Amherst.

Bogal-Allbritten, E. (2013). Decomposing notions of adjectival transitivity in Navajo. *Natural Language Semantics*, 21(3): 277–314.

Bogusławski, A. (1975). Measures are measures: In defence of the diversity of comparatives and positives. *Linguistiche Berichte*, 36: 1–9.

Bolinger, D. (1972). *Degree Words*. Paris: Mouton.

Brasoveanu, A. and Rett, J. (2014). Evaluativity in context: An experimental study. Ms, UCSC and UCLA.

Breakstone, M. (2012). Inherent evaluativity. In A. Aguilar, A. Chernilovskaya, and R. Nouwen (eds), *Proceedings of Sinn und Bedeutung 16*, 113–26. Cambridge, MITWPL.

Breheny, R. (2008). A new look at the semantics and pragmatics of numerically quantified noun phrases. *Journal of Semantics*, 25: 93–139.

Bresnan, J. (1973). Syntax of comparative clause construction in English. *Linguistic Inquiry*, 4: 275–344.

Brown, P. and Levinson, S. (1978). Universals in language usage: Politeness phenomena. In E. Goody (ed.), *Questions and Politeness: Strategies in Social Interaction*, 56–310. Cambridge: Cambridge University Press.

Brown, P. and Levinson, S. (1987). *Politeness: Some Universals in Language Use*. Cambridge: Cambridge University Press.

Büring, D. (2008). Cross-polar nomalies. In M. Gibson and T. Friedman (eds), *Proceedings of SALT 17*, 37–52. Ithaca, NY: CLC Publications.

Burnett, H. (2012). *The Grammar of Tolerance: On Vagueness, Context-Sensitivity, and the Origin of Scale Structure*. PhD thesis, UCLA.

Campbell, R. (1981). Language acquisition, psychological dualism, and the definition of pragmatics. In H. Parret, M. Sbisà, and J. Verschueren (eds), *Possibilities and Limitations of Pragmatics*, 93–104. Amsterdam: John Benjamins.

Carlson, L. (1983). *Dialogue Games: An Approach to Discourse Analysis*. Dordrecht: Reidel.

Champollion, L. (2010). *Parts of a Whole: Distributivity as a Bridge between Aspect and Measurement*. PhD thesis, University of Pennsylvania.

Chierchia, G. (1998). Plurality of mass nouns and the notion of "semantic parameter". In S. Rothschild (ed.), *Events and Grammar*, 53–103. Dordrecht: Kluwer.

Chierchia, G. (2004). Scalar implicatures, polarity phenomena and the syntax/pragmatic interface. In A. Beletti (ed.), *Structures and Beyond*, 39–103. Oxford: Oxford University Press.

Chierchia, G. (2010). Mass nouns, vagueness and semantic variation. *Synthese*, 174: 99–149.

Chierchia, G., Fox, D., and Spector, B. (2009). The grammatical voice of scalar implicatures and the relationship between semantics and pragmatics. In P. Portner et al. (eds), *Handbook of Semantics*. Berlin and New York: Mouton de Gruyter.

Chierchia, G. and McConnell-Ginet, S. (1990). *Meaning and Grammar*. Cambridge, MA: MIT Press.

Chomsky, N. (1965). *Aspects of the Theory of Syntax*. Cambridge, MA: MIT Press.

Chomsky, N. (1977). On *wh*-movement. In P. Culicover, T. Wasow, and A. Akmajian (eds), *Formal Syntax*, 71–132. New York: Academic Press.

Chomsky, N. (1981). *Lectures on Government and Binding*. Dordrecht: Foris.

Chung, S. and Ladusaw, B. (2004). *Restriction and Saturation*. Cambridge, MA: MIT Press.

Clark, H. (1969a). Influence of language on solving three-term series problems. *Journal of Experimental Psychology*, 82: 205–15.

Clark, H. (1969b). Linguistic processes in deductive reasoning. *Psychological Review*, 76: 387–404.

Clark, H. (1972). Difficulties people have answering the question, "Where is it?". *Journal of Verbal Learning and Verbal Behavior*, 11: 265–77.

Clark, H. and Clark, V. (1977). *Psychology and Language: An Introduction to Psycholinguistics*. New York: Harcourt, Brace and Jovanovich.

Cobreros, P., Égré, P., Ripley, D., and van Rooij, R. (2012). Tolerant, classical, strict. *Journal of Philosophical Logic*, 41: 347–85.

Cohen, A. and Krifka, M. (2011). Superlative quantifiers as modifiers of meta-speech acts. In B. Partee, M. Glanzberg, and J. Skilters (eds), *The Baltic International Yearbook of Cognition, Logic and Communication*, vol. 6: *Formal Semantics and Pragmatics*, 1–56. Manhattan, KS: New Prairie Press.

Constant, N., Davis, C., Potts, C., and Schwarz, F. (2009). The pragmatics of expressive content: Evidence from large corpora. *Sprache und Datenverarbeitung*, 1–2: 5–21.

Coppock, E. and Brochhagen, T. (2013). Raising and resolving issues with scalar modifiers. *Semantics & Pragmatics*, 2: 1–57.

Corver, N. (1990). *The Syntax of Left Branch Extractions*. PhD thesis, Tilburg University.

Corver, N. (1997). *Much*-support as a last resort. *Linguistic Inquiry*, 28: 119–64.

Cresswell, M. J. (1976). The semantics of degree. In B. Partee (ed.), *Montague Grammar*, 261–92. New York: Academic Press.

Croft, W. and Cruse, D. A. (2004). *Cognitive Linguistics*. Cambridge: Cambridge University Press.

Cruse, D. A. (1976). Three classes of antonyms in English. *Lingua*, 38: 281–92.

Cruse, D. A. (1986). *Lexical Semantics*. Cambridge: Cambridge University Press.

Cusic, D. D. (1981). *Verbal Plurality and Aspect*. PhD thesis, Stanford University.

Diesing, M. (1992). *Indefinites*. Cambridge, MA: MIT Press.

Doetjes, J. (1997). *Quantifiers and Selection*. PhD thesis, Leiden University.

Doetjes, J. (2012). On the (in)compatibility of non-neutral adjectives and measure phrases. In A. Guevara, A. Chernilovskaya, and R. Nouwen (eds), *Proceedings of Sinn und Bedeutung 16*, 197–210. Cambridge, MA: MITWPL.

Doetjes, J., Constantinescu, C., and Souckova, K. (2011). A neo-Kleinian approach to comparatives. In S. Ito and E. Cormany (eds), *Proceedings of SALT 19*, 124–41. Ithaca: CLC Publications.

Dowty, D. R. (1979). *Word Meaning and Montague Grammar*. Dodrecht: Reidel.

Elliott, D. (1974). Towards a grammar of exclamations. *Foundations of Language*, 11: 231–46.

Embick, D. (2007). Blocking effects and analytic/synthetic alternations. *Natural Language and Linguistic Theory*, 25: 1–37.

Farkas, D. and Bruce, K. (2010). On reacting to assertions and polar questions. *Journal of Semantics*, 27: 81–118.

Fillmore, C. (1965). Entailment rules in a semantic theory. *Pola Reports*, 10: 60–82.

von Fintel, K. (2004). Would you believe it? The King of France is back! In A. Bezuidenhout and M. Reimer (eds), *Descriptions and Beyond*, 314–41. Oxford: Oxford University Press.

Fleisher, N. (2011). Attributive adjectives, infinitival relatives, and the semantics of inappropriateness. *Journal of Linguistics*, 47: 341–80.

Flores D'Arcais, G. B. (1970). Linguistic structure and focus of comparison in processing of comparative sentences. In G. B. Flores D'Arcais and W. J. M. Levelt (eds), *Advances in Psycholinguistics*, 307–21. Amsterdam and New York: North-Holland.

Fodor, J. (1970). Three reasons for not deriving "kill" from "cause to die". *Linguistic Inquiry*, 1: 429–38.

Fox, D. (2003). The interpretation of scalar items: Semantics or pragmatics, or both? Talk given at University of Texas at Austin.

Fox, D. (2006). Free choice disjunction and the theory of scalar implicatures. Ms, MIT.

Francez, I. and Koontz-Garboden, A. (forthcoming). Semantic variation and the grammar of property concepts. *Language*.

Frege, G. (1884). *Foundations of Arithmetic*, trans. J. L. Austin. Evanston, IL: Northwestern University Press, 1980.

Frege, G. (1919). Negation. In P. Geach and M. Black (eds), *Translations from the Philosophical Writings of Gottlob Frege*, 117–35. Oxford: Blackwell, 1952.

Fretheim, T. (1992). The effect of intonation on a type of scalar implicature. *Journal of Pragmatics*, 18: 1–30.

Fults, S. (2011). Vagueness and scales. In P. Egré and N. Klinedinst (eds), *Vagueness and Language Use*. Houndmills, Basingstoke: Palgrave Macmillan.

Gajewski, J. and Sharvit, Y. (2012). In defense of the grammatical approach to local implicatures. *Natural Language Semantics*, 20: 31–57.

Gawron, J. M. (1995). Comparatives, superlatives and resolution. *Linguistics and Philosophy*, 18: 333–80.

Gazdar, G. (1979). *Pragmatics: Implicature, Presupposition, and Logical Form*. New York: Academic Press.

Gazdar, G. and Pullum, G. (1976). Truth-functional connectives in natural language. In S. S. Mufwene, C. A. Walker, and S. B. Steever (eds), *Papers from the 12th Regional Meeting of the Chicago Linguistics Society*, 220–34. Chicago, IL: CLS.

Geach, P. (1972). *Logic Matters*. Berkeley: University of California, 1990.

George, B. (2011). *Question Embedding and the Semantics of Answers*. PhD thesis, UCLA.

Geurts, B. (2011). *Quantity Implicatures*. Cambridge: Cambridge University Press.

Gillon, C. (2010). The mass/count distinction in Innu-aimun: Implications for the meaning of plurality. In B. Rogers and A. Szakay (eds), *Proceedings of the 15th Workshop on Structure and Constituency in the Languages of the Americas*, 12–29. Vancouver: University of British Columbia Working Papers in Linguistics.

Graff, D. (2000). Shifting sands: An interest-relative theory of vagueness. *Philosophical Topics*, 20: 45–81.

Grano, T. (2012). Mandarin *hen* and universal markedness in gradable adjectives. *Natural Language and Linguistic Theory*, 30: 513–65.

Grano, T. and Kennedy, C. (2012). Mandarin transitive comparatives and the grammar of measurement. *Journal of East Asian Linguistics*, 21: 219–66.

Grice, P. (1967). Logic and conversation. Unpublished lectures; Lecture 3 reprinted in Peter Cole (ed.), *Syntax and Semantics*, vol. 9: *Pragmatics*. New York: Academic Press, 1978.

Grice, P. (1975). Logic and conversation. In P. Cole and J. Morgan (eds), *Syntax and Semantics*, vol. 3: *Speech Acts*. New York: Academic Press.

Grice, P. (1989). *Studies in the Way of Words*. Cambridge, MA: Harvard University Press.

Groenendijk, J. and Stokhof, M. (1989). Type-shifting rules and the semantics of interrogatives. In G. Chierchia, B. Partee, and R. Turner (eds), *Properties, Types and Meanings*, vol. 2: *Semantic Issues*, 21–68. Dordrecht: Kluwer.

Grosu, A. and Landman, F. (1998). Strange relatives of the third kind. *Natural Language Semantics*, 6: 125–70.

Hackl, M. (2000). *Comparative Determiners*. PhD thesis, MIT, Cambridge, MA.

Hale, K. (1971). A note on a Walbiri tradition of antonymy. In D. Steinberg and L. Jakobovits (eds), *Semantics: An Interdisciplinary Reader*, 472–82: Cambridge: Cambridge University Press.

Harnish, R. (1976). Logical form and implicature. In T. Bever, J. Katz, and D. Langendoen (eds), *An Integrated Theory of Linguistic Ability*, 313–91. New York: Crowell.

Haspelmath, M. and Buchholz, O. (1998). Equative and similative constructions in the languages of Europe. In J. van der Auwera (ed.), *Adverbial Constructions in the Languages of Europe*, 277–334. Berlin: Mouton de Gruyter.

Hay, J., Kennedy, C., and Levin, B. (1999). Scalar structure underlies telicity in "Degree Achievements". In T. Matthews and D. Strolovitch (eds), *Proceedings of SALT 9*, 127–44. Ithaca, NY: CLC Publications.

Heim, I. (1982). *The Semantics of Definite and Indefinite Noun Phrases*. PhD thesis, University of Massachusetts, Amherst, MA.

Heim, I. (1985). Notes on comparatives and related matters. Ms, University of Texas at Austin.

Heim, I. (1987). Where does the definiteness restriction apply? Evidence from the definiteness of variables. In E. Reuland and A. ter Meulen (eds), *The Representation of (In)definiteness*. Cambridge, MA: MIT Press.

Heim, I. (2000). Degree operators and scope. In B. Jackson and T. Matthews (eds), *Proceedings of SALT 10*, 40–64. Ithaca, NY: CLC Publications.

Heim, I. (2007). Little. In M. Gibson and J. Howell (eds), *Proceedings of SALT 16*. Ithaca, NY: CLC Publications.

Hellan, L. (1981). *Towards an Integrated Analysis of Comparatives*. Tübingen: Narr.

Hendriks, P. (1999). Review of Chris Kennedy, *Projecting the Adjective: The Syntax and Semantics of Gradability and Comparison. Glot International*, 4: 12–14.

Henkelmann, P. (2006). Constructions of the equative comparison. *Sprachtypologie und Universallenforschung*, 59: 370–98.

Heycock, C. (1995). Asymmetries in reconstruction. *Linguistic Inquiry*, 26(4): 547–70.

Higginbotham, J. (1993). Interrogatives. In K. Hale and S. Keyser (eds), *The View from Building 20: Essays in Linguistics in Honor of Sylvain Bromberger*, 195–227. Cambridge, MA: MIT Press.

Higgins, E. (1977). The varying presuppositional nature of comparatives. *Journal of Psycholinguistic Research*, 6: 203–22.

Hintikka, J. (1968). Epistemic logic and the methods of philosophical analysis. *Australasian Journal of Philosophy*, 46: 37–51.

Hirschberg, J. (1991). *A Theory of Scalar Implicature*. New York: Garland Press.

Hoeksema, J. (1983). Plurality and conjunction. In A. G. B. ter Meulen (eds), *Studies in Model-Theoretic Semantics. GRASS* vol. 1, 63–83. Dordrecht: Foris.

Horn, L. (1972). *On the Semantic Properties of the Logical Operators in English*. PhD thesis, UCLA.

Horn, L. (1984). Toward a new taxonomy for pragmatic inference: Q- and R-based implicature. In D. Shiffrin (ed.), *Meaning, Form, and Use in Context*, 11–42. Washington: Georgetown University.

Horn, L. (1989). *A Natural History of Negation*. Chicago: University of Chicago.

Horn, L. (1991a). Duplex negatio affirmat . . . the economy of double negation. *Chicago Linguistics Society*, 27: 80–106.

Horn, L. (1991b). Given as new: When redundant affirmation isn't. *Journal of Pragmatics*, 15: 305–28.

Horn, L. (1992). The said and the unsaid. In C. Barker and D. Dowty (eds), *Proceedings of SALT 2*. Ohio: Ohio State University.

Horn, L. (2008). Implicatures. In L. Horn and G. Ward (eds), *Handbook of Pragmatics*. Oxford: Blackwell.

Householder, F. (1971). *Linguistic Speculations*. Cambridge: Cambridge University Press.

Huitink, J. and Spenader, J. (2004). Cancelation resistant PCIs. In R. van der Sandt and B. Geurts (eds), *Proceedings of the ESSLLI 2004 Workshop on Implicature and Conversational Meaning*, 8–13. Nancy: University of Nijmegen.

Izvorski, R. (1995). A solution to the subcomparative paradox. In J. Camacho, L. Choueiri, and M. Watanabe (eds), *Proceedings of WCCFL 14*, 203–19. Stanford, CA: CSLI Publications.

Jackendoff, R. (1977). *X′ Syntax: A Study of Phrase Structure*. Cambridge, MA: MIT Press.

Jespersen, O. (1965). *The Philosophy of Grammar*. London: W. W. Norton & Co. Originally published London: Allen & Unwin, 1924.

Kamp, H. (1975). Two theories of adjectives. In E. Keenan (ed.), *Formal Semantics of Natural Language*, 123–55. Cambridge: Cambridge University Press.

Kamp, H. (1981). A theory of truth and semantic representation. In J. Groenendijk, T. Janssen, and M. Stokhoff (eds), *Formal Methods in Study of Language*, part 1, 277–322. Amsterdam: Mathematisch Centrum.

Karttunen, L. (1977). Syntax and semantics of questions. *Linguistics and Philosophy*, 1: 3–44.

Karttunen, L. and Peters, S. (1979). Conventional implicature. In C.-K. Oh and D. A. Dinneen (eds), *Syntax and Semantics*, vol. 11, *Presupposition*, 1–56. New York: Academic Press.

Katz, J. (1970). Interpretive semantics versus generative semantics. *Foundations of Language*, 6: 220–59.

Katz, J. (1972). *Semantic Theory*. New York: Harper & Row.

Katzir, R. (2007). Structurally-defined alternatives. *Linguistics and Philosophy*, 30: 669–90.

Kearns, K. (2007). Telic senses of deadjectival verbs. *Lingua*, 117: 26–66.

Kehler, A. (2001). *Coherence, Reference, and the Theory of Grammar*. Chicago, IL: CSLI.

Kennedy, C. (1999). *Projecting the Adjective: The Syntax and Semantics of Gradability and Comparison*. New York: Garland Press.

Kennedy, C. (2001). Polar opposition and the ontology of degrees. *Linguistics and Philosophy*, 24: 33–70.

Kennedy, C. (2007). Vagueness and grammar: The semantics of relative and absolute gradable predicates. *Linguistics and Philosophy*, 30: 1–45.

Kennedy, C. (2009). Modes of comparison. In M. Elliot, J. Kirby, O. Sawada, E. Staraki, and S. Yoon (eds), *Proceedings of the 43rd Annual Meeting of the Chicago Linguistics Society*, 141–65. Chicago, IL: CLS.

Kennedy, C. (2013). A "De-Fregean" semantics for modified and unmodified numerals. Ms, University of Chicago.

Kennedy, C. and Levin, B. (2008). Measure of change: The adjectival core of degree achievements. In L. McNally and C. Kennedy (eds), *Adjectives and Adverbs: Syntax, Semantics and Discourse*. Oxford: Oxford University Press.

Kennedy, C. and McNally, L. (2005). Scale structure, degree modification and the semantic typology of gradable predicates. *Language*, 81(2): 345–81.

Kennedy, C. and Svenonius, P. (2006). Northern Norwegian degree questions and the syntax of measurement. In M. Frascarelli (ed.), *Phases of Interpretation*, 129–57. Berlin: Mouton de Gruyter.

King, J. and Stanley, J. (2005). Semantics, pragmatics, and the role of semantic content. In Z. Szabó (ed.), *Semantics versus Pragmatics*, 111–64. Oxford: Oxford University Press.

Kiparsky, P. (1973). "Elsewhere" in phonology. In S. R. Anderson and P. Kiparsky (eds), *A Festschrift for Morris Halle*, 93–106. New York: Holt, Reinhart & Winston.

Kirchner, G. (1955). *Gradadverbien: Restrikiva und Verwandtes im heutigen Englisch*. Halle: Niemeyer.

Klein, E. (1980). A semantics for positive and comparative adjectives. *Linguistics and Philosophy*, 4: 1–45.

Klein, E. (1982). The interpretation of adjectival comparatives. *Journal of Linguistics*, 18: 113–36.

Klinedinst, N. (2007). *Plurality and possibility*. PhD thesis, UCLA.

Klooster, W. (1972). *The Structure of Underlying Measure Phrase Sentences*. Dordrecht: Reidel.

Koenig, J.-P. (1991). Scalar predicates and negation: Punctual semantics and interval interpretations. In L. Dobrin, L. Nichols, and R. Rodriguez (eds), *Proceedings of the 27th Annual Meeting of the Chicago Linguistics Society*: Parasession on Negation, 130–44. Chicago, IL: CLS.

Koontz-Garboden, A. (2011). The lexical semantics of derived statives. *Linguistics and Philosophy*, 33: 285–324.

Krasikova, S. (2009). Norm-relatedness in degree constructions. In A. Riester and T. Solstad (eds), *Proceedings of Sinn und Bedeutung 13*, 275–90. Oslo: University of Oslo.

Kratzer, A. (1999). Beyond *ouch* and *oops*: How descriptive and expressive meaning interact. Comments on David Kaplan at the Cornell Conference on Theories of Context Dependency.

Krifka, M. (1989). Nominal reference, temporal constitution and quantification in event semantics. In R. Bartsch, J. van Benthem, and P. van Emda Boas (eds), *Semantics and Contextual Expression*, 75–115. Dordrecht: Foris.

Krifka, M. (2007). Negated antonyms: Creating and filling in the gap. In U. Sauerland and P. Stateva (eds), *Presupposition and Implicature in Compositional Semantics*, 163–77. Houndmills, Basingstoke: Palgrave MacMillan.

Kubota, Y. and Matsui, A. (2010). Modes of comparison and Question under Discussion: Evidence from "contrastive comparison" in Japanese. In N. Li and D. Lutz (eds), *Proceedings of SALT 20*, 57–75. Ithaca, NY: CLC Publications.

van Kuppevelt, J. (1995). Discourse structure, topicality and questioning. *Journal of Linguistics*, 31: 109–47.

van Kuppevelt, J. (1996). Inferring from topics: Implicatures as topic-dependent inferences. *Linguistics and Philosophy*, 19: 393–443.

Larson, R. (1988). Scope and comparatives. *Linguistics and Philosophy*, 11: 1–26.

Lassiter, D. and Goodman, N. (2013). Context, scale structure, and statistics in the interpretation of positive-form adjectives. In Todd Snider (ed.), *Proceedings of SALT 23*. 587–610, Ithaca, NY: CLC Publications.

Lechner, W. (2001). Reduced and phrasal comparatives. *Natural Language and Linguistic Theory*, 19(4): 683–735.

Leech, G. (1983). *Principles of Pragmatics*. London: Longmans.

Lehrer, A. (1985). Markedness and antonymy. *Journal of Linguistics*, 21: 397–429.

Lepore, E. and Stone, M. (forthcoming). *Imagination and Convention: Distinguishing Grammar and Inference in Language*. Oxford: Oxford University Press.

Levinson, S. (1983). *Pragmatics*. Cambridge: Cambridge University Press.

Levinson, S. (2000). *Presumptive Meanings: The Theory of Generalized Conversational Implicature*. Cambridge, MA: MIT Press.

Lewis, D. (1969). *Convention*. Cambridge, MA: Harvard University Press.

Liu, C.-S. L. (2010). The positive morpheme in Chinese and the adjectival structure. *Lingua*, 120: 1010–56.

Ljung, M. (1974). Some remarks on antonymy. *Language*, 50: 74–88.

Ludlow, P. (1989). Implicit comparison classes. *Linguistics and Philosophy*, 12(4): 519–33.

Lyons, J. (1977). *Semantics*, vol. 1. Cambridge: Cambridge University Press.

Magri, G. (2011). Another argument for embedded scalar implicatures based on oddness in downward entailing environments. *Semantics and Pragmatics*, 4: 1–51.

Martinet, A. (1962). *A Functional View of Language*. Oxford: Clarendon Press.

Matsumoto, Y. (1995). The conversational condition on Horn scales. *Linguistics and Philosophy*, 18: 21–60.

Matushansky, O. (2002). More of a good thing: Russian synthetic and analytic comparatives. In J. Toman (ed.), *Proceedings of Formal Approaches to Slavic Linguistic (FASL) 10*. Ann Arbor, MI: University of Michigan Press.

Mayol, L. and Castroviejo, E. (2013). How to cancel an implicature. *Journal of Pragmatics*, 50: 84–104.

McCawley, J. (1978). Conversational implicature and the lexicon. In P. Cole (ed.), *Syntax and Semantics* vol. 9: *Pragmatics*, 245–59. New York: Academic Press.

McCawley, J. (1988). *The Syntactic Phenomena in English*. Chicago, IL: University of Chicago Press.

McConnell-Ginet, S. (1973). *Comparative Constructions in English: A Syntactic and Semantic Analysis*. PhD thesis, University of Rochester.

McCready, E. (2010). Varieties of conventional implicature. *Semantics & Pragmatics*, 3: 1–57.

McCready, E. (2012). Emotive equilibria. *Linguistics and Philosophy*, 35: 243–83.

Merin, A. and Nikolaeva, I. (2008). Exclamative as a universal speech act category: A case study in decision-theoretic semantics and typological implications. Ms, University of Konstanz and SOAS London University.

Moltmann, F. (1992). The empty element in comparatives. In A. Schafer (ed.), *Proceedings of the North East Linguistics Society (NELS 23)*, 319–33. Amherst: CLSA, University of Massachusetts.

Moltmann, F. (2009). Degree structure as trope structure: A trope-based analysis of positive and comparative adjectives. *Linguistics and Philosophy*, 32: 51–94.

Morzycki, M. (2008). Differential degrees and cross-categorial measure-phrase modification. Handout, MSU talk.

Morzycki, M. (2009). Degree modification of gradable nouns: Size adjectives and adnominal degree morphemes. *Natural Language Semantics*, 17: 175–203.

Morzycki, M. (2011). Expressive modification and the licensing of measure phrases. *Journal of Semantics*, 28: 401–11.

Morzycki, M. (2012). Adjectival extremeness: Degree modification and contextually restricted scales. *Natural Language and Linguistic Theory*, 30: 567–609.

Morzycki, M. (forthcoming). *Modifiers*. Cambridge: Cambridge University Press.

Murphy, M. L. (2006). Semantic, pragmatic and lexical aspects of the measure phrase + adjective construction. In M.-B. M. Hansen and K. Turner (eds), *Acta Linguistica Hafniensia*, 38(1): 78–100. Copenhagen: Reitzel.

Murray, S. (2010). *Evidentiality and the Structure of Speech Acts*. PhD thesis, Rutgers University.

Murray, S. (2014). Varieties of update. *Semantics and Pragmatics*, 7: 1–53.

Nakanishi, K. (2007a). *Formal Properties of Measurement Constructions*. Berlin: Mouton de Gruyter.

Nakanishi, K. (2007b). Measurement in the nominal and verbal domain. *Linguistics and Philosophy*, 30: 235–76.

Nakanishi, K. and Rullmann, H. (2009). Epistemic and concessive interpretation of *at least*. Slides for a paper presented at the meeting of the Canadian Linguistics Association, Carleton University.

Neeleman, A., van de Koot, H., and Doetjes, J. (2004). Degree expressions. *The Linguistic Review*, 21: 1–66.

Nerbonne, J. (1995). Nominalized comparatives and generalized quantifiers. *Journal of Logic, Language and Information*, 4: 273–300.

Pancheva, R. (2005). *Than* is a partitive preposition. Ms, USC.

Pancheva, R. (2006). Phrasal and clausal comparatives in Slavic. In J. Lavine, S. Franks, M. Tasseva-Kurktchieva, and H. Filip (eds), *Formal Approaches to Slavic Linguistics (FASL) 14: The Princeton Meeting*, 236–57, Ann Arbor, MI: University of Michigan Press.

Paradis, C. (2001). Adjectives and boundedness. *Cognitive Linguistics*, 12(1): 47–65.

Partee, B. (1973). Some analogies between tenses and pronouns in English. *Journal of Philosophy*, 70: 601–9.

Partee, B. (1994). Lexical semantics and compositionality. In L. Gleitman and M. Liberman (eds), *Invitation to Cognitive Science*, 311–60. Cambridge, MA: MIT Press.

Peterson, W. (2013). A scalar-based analysis of *again* ambiguities. Ms, McGill University.

Piñón, C. (2005). Adverbs of completion in an event semantics. In H. Verkuyl, H. de Swart, and A. van Hout (eds), *Perspectives on Aspect*, 149–66. Berlin: Springer-Verlag.

Pinkal, M. (1979). Semantics from different points of view. In R. Bäuerle, U. Egli, and A. von Stechow (eds), *How to Refer with Vague Descriptions*, 32–50. Berlin: Springer-Verlag.

Pinkal, M. (1995). *Logic and Lexicon*. Dordrecht: Kluwer.

Portner, P. and Zanuttini, R. (2005). The semantics of nominal exclamatives. In R. Elugardo and R. Stainton (eds), *Ellipsis and Nonsentential Speech*, 57–67. Dordrecht: Kluwer.

Potts, C. (2005). *The Logic of Conventional Implicatures*. Oxford: Oxford University Press.

Potts, C. (2007). The expressive dimension. *Theoretical Linguistics*, 33: 165–98.

Potts, C. (2012). Conventional implicature and expressive content. In C. Maienborn, K. von Heusinger, and P. Portner (eds), *Semantics: an international handbook of natural language meaning*, vol. 3, 2516–36, Berlin: Mouton de Gruyter.

Prince, A. and Smolensky, P. (1993). *Optimality Theory: Constraint Interaction in Generative Grammar*. Oxford: Blackwell, 2004.

Recanati, F. (1989). The pragmatics of what is said. *Mind and Language*, 4: 295–329.

Recanati, F. (2002). Unarticulated constitutents. *Linguistics and Philosophy*, 25: 299–345.

Rett, J. (2006). How *many* maximizes in the Balkan Sprachbund. In M. Gibson and J. Howell (eds), *Proceedings of SALT 16*, 190–207. Ithaca, NY: CLC Publications.

Rett, J. (2007). Antonymy and evaluativity. In M. Gibson and T. Friedman (eds), *Proceedings of SALT 17*, 210–27. Ithaca, NY: CLC Publications.

Rett, J. (2008). *Degree Modification in Natural Language*. PhD thesis, Rutgers University.

Rett, J. (2010). Exclamatives, MPs and NPIs. In M. Aloni, H. Bastiaanse, T. de Jager, and K. Schulz (eds), *Logic, Language, and Meaning: Proceedings of the 18th Amsterdam Colloquium*, 364–373. Berlin: Springer-Verlag.

Rett, J. (2011). Exclamatives, degrees, and speech acts. *Linguistics and Philosophy*, 34: 411–42.

Rett, J. (2012). Space, time and antonymy. Ms, UCLA.

Rett, J. (2013). Similatives and the degree argument of verbs. *Natural Language and Linguistic Theory*, 31: 1101–37.

Rett, J. (2014a). Modified numerals and measure phrase equatives. *Journal of Semantics*. Advance Access, doi: 10.1093/jos/ffu004.

Rett, J. (2014b). The polysemy of measurement. *Lingua*, 143: 242–66.

Roberts, C. (1990). *Modal subordination, Anaphora, and Distributivity*. New York: Garland Press.

Roberts, C. (1996). Information structure, plans, and implicature. In B. D. Eugenio and N. L. Green (eds), *Proceedings of the 1996 AAAI Symposium on Implicature*. Menlo Park, CA: AAAI Press.

Romero, M. (1998). *Focus and Reconstruction Effects in* Wh-*Phrases*. PhD thesis, University of Massachusetts, Amherst.

van Rooij, R. (2004). Signalling games select Horn strategies. *Linguistics and Philosophy*, 27: 493–527.

van Rooij, R. (2011). Measurement and interadjective comparisons. *Journal of Semantics*, 28: 335–58.

van Rooij, R. and Schulz, K. (2004). Exhaustive interpretation of complex sentences. *Journal of Logic, Language and Information*, 13: 491–519.

Rooth, M. (1996). Focus. In S. Lappin (ed.), *The Handbook of Contemporary Semantic Theory*, 271–98. Oxford: Blackwell.

Ross, J. (1967). *Constraints on Variables in Syntax*. PhD thesis, MIT.

Rotstein, C. and Winter, Y. (2004). Total adjectives vs. partial adjectives: Scale structure and higher-order modifiers. *Natural Language Semantics*, 12: 259–88.

Rullmann, H. (1995). *Maximality in the Semantics of Wh-Constructions*. PhD thesis, University of Massachusetts, Amherst.

Rusiecki, J. (1985). *On Adjectives and Comparison in English*. Longman Linguistics Library. London: Longman.

Russell, B. (1905). On denoting. *Mind*, 14: 479–93.

Russell, B. (2006). Against grammatical computation of scalar implicatures. *Journal of Semantics*, 23: 361–82.

Sadock, J. M. (1978). On testing for conversational implicature. In P. Cole (ed.), *Syntax and Semantics*, Vol. 9: *Pragmatics*, 281–98. New York: Academic Press.

van der Sandt, R. (1992). Presupposition projection as anaphora resolution. *Journal of Semantics*, 9: 333–77.

Sapir, E. (1944). On grading: A study in semantics. *Philosophy of Science*, 2: 93–116. Reprinted in E. Sapir, *Language*. New York: Harcourt and Brace, 1949.

Sassoon, G. (2010a). The degree functions of negative adjectives. *Natural Language Semantics*, 18: 141–81.

Sassoon, G. (2010b). Measurement theory in linguistics. *Synthese*, 174: 151–80.

Sassoon, G. (2011). Be positive! Norm-related implications and beyond. In I. Reich (ed.), *Proceedings of Sinn und Bedeutung 15*, 531–46. Saarbrücken: Saarland University Press.

Sassoon, G. (2012). The double nature of negative antonymy. In A. A. Guevara, A. Chernilovskaya, and R. Nouwen (eds), *Proceedings of Sinn und Bedeutung 16*, 543–56. Cambridge, MA: MITWPL.

Sauerland, U. (2004). Scalar implicatures in complex sentences. *Linguistics and Philosophy*, 27: 367–91.

Sawada, O. (2009). Pragmatic aspects of implicit comparison: An economy-based approach. *Journal of Pragmatics*, 41: 1079–103.

Schaden, G. (2009). Present perfects compete. *Linguistics and Philosophy*, 32: 115–41.

Schroeder, M. (2008). *Being for: Evaluating the Semantic Program of Expressivism*. Oxford: Oxford University Press.

Schwarzschild, R. (2002). The grammar of measurement. In Brendan Jackson (ed.), *Proceedings of SALT 12*, 225–45. Ithaca, NY: CLC Publications.

Schwarzschild, R. (2005). Measure phrases as modifiers of adjectives. *Recherches Linguistiques de Vincennes*, 34: 207–28.

Schwarzschild, R. (2006a). Adverbials of degree, range and amount. Presentation at the Workshop on Scalar Meaning, University of Chicago.

Schwarzschild, R. (2006b). The role of dimensions in the syntax of noun phrases. *Syntax*, 9: 67–110.

Schwarzschild, R. (2008). The semantics of the comparative and other degree constructions. *Language and Linguistic Compass*, 2(2): 308–31.

Schwarzschild, R. (2011). Stubborn distributivity, multiparticipant nouns and the count/mass distinction. In S. Lima, K. Mullin, and B. Smith (eds), *Proceedings of the North East Linguistics Society (NELS 39)*, 661–78. Amherst: CLSA, University of Massachusetts.

Schwarzschild, R. (2012). Directed scale segments. In A. Chereches (ed.), *Proceedings of SALT 22*, 65–82. Ithaca, NY: CLC Publications.

Schwarzschild, R. (2010). Comparative markers and standard markers. In M. Erlewine and Y. Sudo (eds), *Proceedings of the MIT Workshop on Comparatives*, MITWPL 69, 87–106. Cambridge, MA: MIT Press.

Schwarzschild, R. and Wilkinson, K. (2002). Quantifiers in comparatives: A semantics of degree based on intervals. *Natural Language Semantics*, 10: 1–41.

Searle, J. R. (1965). What is a speech act? In M. Black (ed.), *Philosophy in America*, 221–39. Ithaca, NY: Cornell University Press.

Sennet, A. (2011). Unarticulated constituents and propositional structure. *Mind and Language*, 26: 412–35.

Sennet, A. (2012). Context, compositionality and amity: A response to Rett. *Canadian Journal of Philosophy*, 42: 29–42.

Seuren, P. (1973). The comparative. In F. Keifer and N. Ruwet (eds), *Generative Grammar in Europe*, 528–64. Dordrecht: Reidel.

Seuren, P. (1984). The comparative revisited. *Journal of Semantics*, 3: 109–41.

Shibatani, M. (1973a). *A Linguistic Study of Causative Constructions*. PhD thesis, University of California, Berkeley.

Shibatani, M. (1973b). Semantics of Japanese causativization. *Foundations of Language*, 9: 327–73.

Shibatani, M. (1976). The grammar of causative constructions: a conspectus. In M. Shibatani (ed.), *Syntax and Semantics: The Grammar of Causative Constructions*, vol. 6, 1–42. New York: Academic Press.

Simons, M. (2010). A Gricean view on intrusive implicatures. In K. Petrus (ed.), *Meaning and Analysis: New Essays on Grice*, 138–69. Houndmills, Basingstone: Palgrave MacMillan.

Simons, M. (2014). Local pragmatics and structured contents. *Philosophical Studies*, 168: 21–33.

Simons, M., Tonhauser, J., Beaver, D., and Roberts, C. (2011). What projects and why. In N. Li and D. Lutz (eds), *Proceedings of SALT 20*, 309–27. Ithaca, NY: CLC Publications.

Skyrms, B. (2010). *Signals: Evolution, Learning, and Information*. Oxford: Oxford University Press.

Soames, S. (1982). How presuppositions are inherited: A solution to the projection problem. *Linguistic Inquiry*, 13: 483–545.

Solt, S. (2009). *The Semantics of Adjectives of Quantity*. PhD thesis, City University of New York.

Solt, S. (2010). *Much* support and more. In M. Aloni, H. Bastiaanse, T. de Jager, and K. Schulz (eds), *Logic, Language, and Meaning: Proceedings of the 18th Amsterdam Colloquium*. Berlin: Springer-Verlag.

Solt, S. (2014). Q-adjectives and the semantics of quantity. *Journal of Semantics*. Advance Access, doi: 10.1093/jos/fft018.

Spector, B. (2013). Bare numerals and scalar implicature. *Language and Linguistics Compass*, 5: 273–94.

Stalnaker (1978). Assertion. In P. Cole (ed.), *Syntax and Semantics*, vol. 9: *Pragmatics*, 315–32. New York: Academic Press.

Stanley, J. (2002). Nominal restriction. In G. Peter and G. Preyer (eds), *Logical Form and Language*, 365–88. Oxford: Oxford University Press.

Stanley, J. and Szabó, Z. (2000). On quantifier domain restriction. *Mind and Language*, 15: 219–61.

Stassen, L. (1985). *Comparison and Universal Grammar: An Essay in Universal Grammar*. Oxford: Basil Blackwell.

von Stechow, A. (1984). Comparing semantic theories of comparison. *Journal of Semantics*, 3: 1–77.

Sybesma, R. (1999). *The Mandarin VP*. Dordrecht: Kluwer.

Syrett, K., Kennedy, C., and Lidz, J. (2009). Meaning and context in children: Understanding gradable adjectives. *Journal of Semantics*, 27: 1–35.

Szabó, Z. (2001). Adjectives in context. In R. Harnish and I. Kenesei (eds), *Perspectives on Semantics, Pragmatics, and Discourse: A Festschrift for Ferenc Kiefer*. Amsterdam: John Benjamins.

Tannen, D. (1975). Communication mix and mixup, or how linguistics can ruin a marriage. In M. Noonan (ed.), *San Jose State Occasional Papers in Linguistics* vol. 1, 205–11. San Jose, CA: San Jose State University Press.

Thomason, R. (1990). Accommodation, meaning, and implicature: Interdisciplinary foundations for pragmatics. In P. Cohen, J. Morgan, and M. Pollack (eds), *Intentions in Communication*, 325–64. Cambridge, MA: MIT Press.

Toledo, A. and Sassoon, G. (2011). Absolute vs. relative adjectives: variance within vs. between individuals. In N. Ashton, A. Chereches, and D. Lutz (eds), *Proceedings of SALT 21*, 135–54. Ithaca, NY: CLC Publications.

Vendler, Z. (1957). Verbs and times. *Philosophical Review*, 56: 143–60.

Villalba, X. (2003). An exceptional exclamative sentence type in Romance. *Lingua*, 113: 713–45.

Walker, R. (1975). Conversational implicature. In S. Blackburn (ed.), *Meaning, Reference and Necessity*, 133–81. Cambridge: Cambridge University Press.

Waugh, L. (1982). Marked and unmarked: A choice between unequals. *Semiotica*, 38: 299–318.

Welker, K. (1994). *Plans in the Common Ground: Toward a Generative Account of Implicature*. PhD thesis, Ohio State University.

Winter, Y. (2005). Cross-categorial restrictions on measure phrase modification. *Linguistics and Philosophy*, 28: 233–67.

Winter, Y. (2006). Closure and telicity across categories. In M. Gibson and J. Howell (eds), *Proceedings of SALT 16*, 329–46, Ithaca, NY: CLC Publications.

Winter, Y. (2009). What neutralizes the positive? Paper presented at "Degrees under Discussion," CRISSP Colloquium, Utrecht, Brussels.

Yoon, Y. (1996). Total and partial predicates and the weak and strong interpretations. *Natural Language Semantics*, 4: 217–36.

Zamparelli, R. (2000). *Layers in the Determiner Phrase*. New York: Garland Press.

Zanuttini, R. and Portner, P. (2003). Exclamative clauses: At the syntax–semantics interface. *Language*, 79(1): 39–81.

Zipf, G. K. (1949). *Human Behavior and the Principle of Least Effort*. Cambridge, MA: Addison-Wesley.

Zwarts, J. (1997). Vectors as relative positions: A compositional semantics of modified PPs. *Journal of Semantics*, 14: 57–86.

Author index

Subject index

OXFORD STUDIES IN THEORETICAL LINGUISTICS